Management for Professionals

The Springer series “Management for Professionals” comprises high-level business and management books for executives, MBA students, and practice-oriented business researchers. The topics cover all themes relevant to businesses and the business ecosystem. The authors are experienced business professionals and renowned professors who combine scientific backgrounds, best practices, and entrepreneurial vision to provide powerful insights into achieving business excellence.

The Series is SCOPUS-indexed.

Antonio Bassi • Silvia Mari
Michela Manini • Virginie Pasquon
Editors

General Management Principles for Project Management

Effective Ways to Help Organizations Manage Business

Springer

Editors
Antonio Bassi
Project Management Association Switzerland
Lugano, Switzerland

Silvia Mari
Department of Innovative Technologies
SUPSI
Lugano, Switzerland

Michela Manini
Department of Innovative Technologies
SUPSI
Lugano, Switzerland

Virginie Pasquon
Department of Innovative Technologies
SUPSI
Lugano, Switzerland

ISSN 2192-8096 ISSN 2192-810X (electronic)
Management for Professionals
ISBN 978-3-031-98591-1 ISBN 978-3-031-98592-8 (eBook)
https://doi.org/10.1007/978-3-031-98592-8

This Springer imprint is published by the registered company Springer Nature Switzerland AG
The registered company address is: Gewerbestrasse 11, 6330 Cham, Switzerland

Introduction

Project management is not merely a set of techniques or tools but an art that intertwines strategic vision, organizational capabilities, and a profound understanding of the people involved. Today, more than ever, organizations operate in environments characterized by complexity, uncertainty, and continuous change, where the ability to manage projects effectively can make the difference between success and failure. This book aims to provide a concrete and systematic guide to addressing these challenges, founded on the principles of General Management and the international standards ISO 10006 and ISO 31000.

The ISO 10006 and ISO 31000 standards serve as fundamental references for ensuring quality and sustainability in project and risk management. These standards offer a structured approach that helps organizations develop solid processes, minimize uncertainty, and achieve their set objectives. In this book, these principles have been translated into content designed to be not only theoretically rigorous but also applicable in everyday practice.

A key element of project management, explored in depth in these pages, is communication. Communication is understood not only as the transmission of information but also as a certification of transparency and reliability. In every project, the ability to communicate clearly and effectively determines the level of trust among team members and stakeholders. Naturally, this is closely tied to the need to promote a culture of quality, where project management becomes not just an operational function but also an organizational practice capable of guiding people's behavior toward continuous improvement.

Project management cannot exist without a solid governance structure that establishes clear rules and precise responsibilities for all involved. In this context, the role of leadership is crucial: effective leadership not only defines the strategic direction of the project but also inspires and mobilizes human resources to achieve common goals. The importance of governance and leadership finds natural integration in the conscious use of historical information and lessons learned, indispensable tools for avoiding past mistakes and building solid strategies for the future.

At the same time, the centrality of people in project management is explored in depth. Competence, motivation, and team building are not merely theoretical concepts but also critical success factors that require attention and specific strategies. Actively involving people in decision-making processes not only enhances efficiency but also fosters an atmosphere of trust and collaboration. This book seeks to analyze how these elements can be integrated into a management model that addresses the needs of contemporary organizations.

Another key theme addressed is process management, which constitutes the operational core of project management. Through the adoption of approaches focused on continuous improvement, effective resource management, and risk mitigation, processes are optimized to ensure sustainable and high-quality results. This approach naturally extends to the need to make informed decisions, based on accurate data and maturity models that minimize uncertainty and maximize strategic effectiveness.

The central thread of this volume is the integration of the various aspects of project management: communication, governance, leadership, the management of people, processes, and risks. This integration is reflected not only in the structure of the book but also in its educational purpose. The text aims to provide students and professionals with a clear and coherent framework, useful for addressing the challenges of complexity and for developing cross-functional skills that combine theory with practical application.

With this approach, the book is not just a manual but a strategic guide for those aspiring to understand and manage projects effectively. Through concrete examples, theoretical reflections, and operational tools, readers will acquire an integrated perspective that will accompany them throughout their academic journey and professional practice. This volume, therefore, represents a significant contribution to the academic world and to anyone seeking to become a competent and aware leader in project management.

Project Management Association Switzerland Antonio Bassi
Lugano, Switzerland

Competing Interests The authors have no competing interests to declare that are relevant to the content of this manuscript.

Contents

About the Editors and Contributors

About the Editors

Antonio Bassi, PMP® PMP®, Degree in Electronic Engineering at Politecnico di Milano, certified Project Management Professional (PMP) by the Project Management Institute (PMI), member of the Steering Committee of the Project Management Institute—Northern Italy Chapter (PMI-NIC) 2004–2008, Project Management Lecturer at SUPSI (University of Applied Science and Arts—Switzerland), president of the Project Management Association Switzerland (APMS), member of the project team for the definition of the ISO standards ISO 21500 and ISO 21502 (project management), project/program manager, for 15 years, on innovative projects in different market sectors. For UNI is developing the national qualification norm (Italian) for the project manager. Assessor for the ISO 21500 certification. Author of numerous articles, published: Il ruolo del Project Manager, 2006, Gestire l'innovazione nelle PMI, 2007, Il valore strategico della comunicazione nel Project management, 2007, Project Manager al lavoro, 2009, Partecipare a un progetto, 2010, Maturità nei progetti—Un modello per le piccole e medie imprese, 2011, Glossario del termini di Project Management, 2014, Scoprire il Project Management, 2024, La saggezza del paradosso, 2024.

Michela Manini With over 10 years of experience in managing transformation projects using agile methodologies, she has developed deep expertise in innovation processes through both field work and serving as a digital enabler for dynamic companies.

She helps organizations navigate their digital transformation journey by implementing new agile processes founded on collaboration, communication, and adaptive leadership. Her expertise lies in fostering new skills that emerge from multidimensional systems and developing Lean processes to drive continuous organizational improvement. She holds various certifications in agile methodologies, including Scrum, Kanban, and SAFe 5.0, and has participated in Toyota Academy training sessions focusing on manufacturing process optimization (Toyota Production System).

The application of Lean principles is her primary focus in helping companies evolve into collaborative organizations that generate value through the interaction between individuals and their environment.

Beyond her role as an Agile Coach, she currently serves as a Senior Lecturer in the Lifelong Learning Department of Innovative Technology at SUPSI in Lugano, where she designs customized learning paths to facilitate cultural change and professional development.

She is also the co-founder of AgileLab Ticino, a non-profit association dedicated to promoting agile culture across Switzerland.

Silvia Mari, PMP® embarked on her academic journey with a Master's degree in Industrial Chemistry from the University of Milan, followed by a PhD in Chemistry from Universidad Autonoma de Madrid, and a postdoc research activities at San Raffaele University Hospital of Milan. She is author of 23 publications and significant collaborations in drug optimization and metabolomics, and registered expert of the European Commission.

Her transition to project management was marked by a Certificate in Advanced Studies in Management of Biotech, Medtech & Pharma Ventures from EPFL, Lausanne, subsequently by a Certificate in Advanced Studies in Project Management from SUPSI, Lugano, and finally by PMP certification by Project Management Institute. This laid the groundwork for her pivotal role in project management, orchestrating the management of projects across international boundaries.

She is currently Senior Lecturer for the Lifelong Learning department at SUPSI in Lugano. She is member of PMI and its Swiss Chapter; she is the treasurer of the local Project Management Association and member of the HR Association based in Lugano.

In her dynamic career spanning diverse fields and roles such as PMO and Business Agility in manufacturing industry, Software Platform Project Manager and Account Manager and Product Manager.

Virginie Pasquon, PMP® began her career after graduating from the Politecnico di Torino with a degree in Information Engineering.

Her career developed within major consulting firms, where she worked with global clients across various sectors, including manufacturing, telecommunications, and government institutions.

Driven by her passion for cybersecurity and business intelligence, Virginie ventured into entrepreneurship. She founded a company focused on creativity and design thinking, delivering innovative defensive cybersecurity solutions worldwide—a key milestone in her professional career.

As a senior faculty member at SUPSI's Department of Innovative Technology, Virginie shares her expertise by teaching project management in both Lifelong Learning and Master's engineering programs.

Beyond academia, Virginie was instrumental in establishing the DTI Observatories, an initiative that connects educational institutions with industry, highlighting her commitment to comprehensive learning experiences.

As a committee member of the local Project Management Association, she actively contributes to developing the Project Management Competence Center at SUPSI.

About the Contributors

Carmelo Dimauro is a senior manager with high-level experience in risk management and industrial business continuity planning. He has an extended experience in supporting the public and private stakeholders involved in the risk-based decision-making processes and emergency management planning in particular involving scenarios related to interdependent critical infrastructure systems. He has a consolidated knowledge in defining and implementing capability-based approaches to enable and foster collaborative emergency management practices in the context of public–private collaborations.

Massimo Mistretta With over 20 years of management experience, Massimo Mistretta has been at the forefront of launching and scaling numerous technology-centric products, consistently driving success across diverse industries. His extensive experience spans both the European and Californian startup ecosystems, where he has played a crucial role in guiding innovative ventures from inception to market dominance.

Specializing in Signal Processing, Video/Voice over IP Technologies, Robotic and Intelligent Process Automation, Machine Learning Systems, and Large-Scale Computing Infrastructures, his deep understanding of these fields, combined with strategic insight, has led to the successful digital transformation and innovation of several large-scale enterprises, including Fortune 500 companies.

Throughout his career, he has collaborated with leading global brands and prestigious academic institutions. Currently, he serves as CEO of Exentriq, platform provider recognized for its innovations in robotic and intelligent process automation, and holds the position of Chief Information and Security Officer at Planet Farms, a pioneer in the vertical farming industry.

Massimo is a recognized expert in modern organization management and the creator of the OASIS model for Adaptive Organizations. His contributions to the field have been widely recognized, particularly in the context of large enterprise adaptive and sustainable management practices.

Holding a degree in Computer Science from the University of London, he has co-authored the book "*Adaptive Organization*," is a keynote speaker and lectures on Adaptive and Sustainable Organization Management at the University of Applied Sciences and Arts of Southern Switzerland, where he continues to shape the next generation of leaders in organizational management.

Massimo Pirozzi MSc in Engineering, is a member of the PM World Journal Executive Team and serves on the ISIPM Board. He has authored and co-authored several books and published more than 50 articles on Project Management across five countries, receiving multiple international awards for his contributions. A Certified Professional Project Manager and Information Security Management Systems Lead Auditor, he holds credentials in Generative AI, GenAI Data Landscape for Project Managers, Prompt Engineering for Project Managers, and Sustainable Project Management. He has held executive positions in the ICT sector for many years.

Part I
Management Fundamentals

Chapter 1
Communication: Information Certification

Virginie Pasquon

1.1 Importance of Communication in Project Management

Effective communication is a pillar of successful project management. It involves the timely and appropriate generation, collection, dissemination, storage, and ultimate disposition of project information. Communication ensures that all stakeholders, including team members, clients, and suppliers, are well-informed and engaged throughout the project lifecycle.

Communication in project management refers to the exchange of information between project stakeholders. This includes verbal, written, and non-verbal communication methods. The primary goal is to ensure that all parties have a clear understanding of project objectives, progress, and any issues that may arise.

Effective communication plays a central role in the project life cycle through several key benefits. First and foremost, it ensures proper coordination by aligning and synchronizing all project activities, which leads to more organized and efficient project execution through better task management, scheduling, and resource allocation.

Communication also serves as an essential control mechanism, enabling project managers to monitor progress effectively and make timely adjustments. Through regular updates and feedback loops, they can track milestones and quickly address any deviations from the original plan. In terms of decision-making, effective communication ensures that stakeholders have access to accurate and timely information, empowering them to make well-informed decisions vital to project success.

Team motivation is another significant benefit, as clear communication of goals, expectations, and achievements helps maintain team focus and boosts morale and productivity. Additionally, open and transparent communication proves invaluable

V. Pasquon (✉)
Department of Innovative Technologies, SUPSI, Lugano, Switzerland
e-mail: virginie.pasquon@supsi.ch

A. Bassi et al. (eds.), *General Management Principles for Project Management*, Management for Professionals, https://doi.org/10.1007/978-3-031-98592-8_1

in conflict resolution, helping prevent misunderstandings from escalating and facilitating swift resolution when issues do arise.

However, when communication breaks down, projects can face serious challenges. Ineffective communication often leads to misunderstandings about project goals, roles, and responsibilities, creating confusion and errors throughout the project lifecycle. These communication gaps frequently result in delays as team members struggle to access the information they need to complete their tasks on time. Moreover, miscommunication can necessitate costly rework, driving up project expenses.

The human impact of poor communication is equally significant. Team members often experience frustration and decreased morale when communication is ineffective, which in turn affects their productivity and engagement levels. Most importantly, inadequate communication with stakeholders can lead to unmet expectations and dissatisfaction, potentially undermining the entire project's success. These negative impacts highlight the importance of establishing and maintaining effective communication channels throughout the project lifecycle.

Research has shown that projects with effective communication are more likely to succeed. Clear and consistent communication helps prevent misunderstandings, reduces conflicts, and enhances overall project efficiency. By prioritizing communication, project managers can ensure that all stakeholders are aligned and working towards common goals, ultimately leading to successful project outcomes.

1.2 Principles of Communication in Project Management

Effective communication in project management is guided by several key principles that ensure information is shared accurately, timely, and appropriately among all stakeholders. These principles help in aligning project activities, fostering collaboration, and achieving project goals. Here are the main principles:

The principle of **customer focus** underscores the importance of aligning all communication efforts with the needs and expectations of the customer. Regularly engaging with customers through surveys, interviews, and feedback sessions allows project managers to gain a deep understanding of their requirements and priorities (Kerzner, 2017). This customer-centric approach serves as the foundation for all other communication principles, ensuring that project outcomes are closely tied to customer satisfaction. Practical considerations include identifying customer needs, implementing feedback mechanisms, and using metrics like Net Promoter Score (NPS) and Customer Satisfaction Score (CSAT) to measure and improve customer satisfaction.

Leadership plays a vital role in setting the tone for effective communication within a project. Transformational leadership behaviors, such as active listening, clear articulation of ideas, and timely information sharing, have a significant impact on project success (Aga et al., 2016). By establishing clear communication protocols, fostering an environment of trust and respect, and leading by example, leaders create the conditions for open dialogue and collaboration. This involves setting communication standards, demonstrating effective communication practices, and encouraging team members to share ideas and concerns.

The **involvement of people** principle emphasizes the importance of engaging all team members and stakeholders in the communication process. Inclusive communication practices, such as ensuring all relevant parties have access to necessary information and empowering team members to take ownership of their communication responsibilities, are essential for tapping into the collective wisdom of the group. Regular updates and meetings provide opportunities for sharing progress, addressing issues, and maintaining alignment.

Communication is a process that requires consistency and efficiency. Establishing clear protocols for information sharing, including the development of a comprehensive communication plan, is crucial. Continuous assessment and refinement of these processes is necessary for optimizing communication effectiveness over the course of the project.

Finally, the **system approach** to management recognizes that communication is an integral part of the larger project management framework. Integrating communication tools and processes with project management software and maintaining a holistic view of how communication interacts with other project activities is essential for ensuring seamless coordination. By viewing communication as part of a complex ecosystem, managers can ensure that information flows freely and effectively, supporting the overall health and success of the project.

1.3 Information Certification

Effective communication is the backbone of successful project management, and it is guided by the key principles mentioned above that ensure information is shared accurately, timely, and appropriately among all stakeholders. These principles work together to align project activities, foster collaboration, and drive the entire effort to a positive closure. However, we do not have to forget information certification, which ensures information accuracy, reliability, and compliance before being communicated to stakeholders.

In order to preserve confidence, make wise judgments, and accomplish project objectives, information certification is a multi-step procedure. Ensuring the authenticity and dependability of the information supplied within a project is the first component of information certification. Verification entails comparing data to original sources, confirming computations, and making sure all information is accurate. Another crucial stage that guarantees the data is relevant and satisfies the requirements of the project and its stakeholders is validation. This may entail going over the material to make sure it is complete, pertinent, and presented in a way that the target audience can understand. Consistency is the idea that, regardless of the format or medium, the same information should be given consistently throughout all communication channels regardless of the format or medium.

Technologies like blockchain, machine learning, and artificial intelligence (AI) can greatly improve the accuracy and efficiency of information certification procedures in the current digital era. By automating validation and verification processes, these technologies lower the possibility of human error and increase overall dependability. While machine learning models can learn from historical data to predict and detect potential problems in fresh information, artificial intelligence (AI) algorithms can swiftly evaluate enormous datasets and spot anomalies or mistakes. With each piece of information being stored in a block and connected to the one before it, blockchain technology offers a transparent and safe method of information certification. This results in a chain that is both verifiable and impenetrable.

Another essential component of information certification is adherence to organizational and regulatory norms. This guarantees that all information exchanged within the project complies with all applicable laws, rules, and internal guidelines. Ensuring that the data satisfies all legal and regulatory criteria, including data protection laws, industry-specific rules, and other legal standards, is known as regulatory compliance. Information adherence to the organization's internal standards and norms, such as those pertaining to data security, confidentiality, and information sharing procedures, is guaranteed by organizational compliance.

The importance of information certification cannot be overstated. Project managers may guarantee that all stakeholders receive correct and trustworthy data by certifying information. This is crucial for decision-making and preserving trust throughout the project lifecycle. This procedure not only improves communication quality but also helps the project succeed as a whole.

Furthermore, miscommunications, delays, and expensive mistakes that could ruin a project can be avoided with the aid of efficient information certification. Stakeholders can work together more successfully, make better decisions, and react swiftly to obstacles or changes that occur throughout the project when they have access to accurate and trustworthy information. In the complicated and fast-paced corporate world of today, when projects frequently involve numerous teams, departments, and even organizations, this is fundamental.

1.4 Continuous Improvement in Communication

Continuous improvement as mentioned in the related chapter is a fundamental principle in project management that involves the systematic evaluation and enhancement also of communication practices to ensure their ongoing effectiveness and efficiency.

Once more, the implementation of feedback mechanisms is essential to ongoing development. Feedback offers important insights into the effectiveness of present methods and helps to identify areas where communication can be improved. It helps to put in place mechanisms for getting input from stakeholders and team members, such as surveys, suggestion boxes, and frequent feedback meetings. Furthermore, it is beneficial to establish an atmosphere in which interested parties are at ease offering candid and helpful criticism. Regular evaluations of communication practices should be carried out using systematic reviews of procedures, instruments, and results based on predetermined criteria to guarantee consistency and impartiality.

When it comes to improving communication methods, data and metrics are essential. Project managers can make evidence-based decisions to improve communication effectiveness by gathering and analyzing pertinent data, such as response times, communication frequency, stakeholder satisfaction, and the veracity of information presented. Decisions should be based on factual evidence rather than conjecture or gut feeling, and communication should be backed up by accurate and pertinent data.

As stated, project managers can use a variety of tactics that encourage the constant creation and enhancement of communication techniques in order to improve communication. It is necessary to give team members opportunity for training and development so they can improve their communication abilities. It's also beneficial to keep up with the most recent tools and technology for communication that can increase efficacy and efficiency. Comparing communication methods to industry norms and best practices can reveal areas for improvement and provide insightful information.

Project managers may guarantee that communication methods continue to be efficient, effective, and in line with project objectives by placing a high priority on ongoing communication improvement. This continuous process of assessment and improvement helps the project team develop a culture of excellence and contributes to the project's overall success. All parties involved must be dedicated and put in constant effort in order to communicate effectively. Project managers can provide a dynamic and responsive communication environment that adjusts to the changing needs of the project and its stakeholders by adopting the concept of continuous improvement.

1.5 Mutual Benefit Relationships with Suppliers

Successful long-term partnerships are built on a diverse approach to communication, which is necessary to develop relationships with suppliers that benefit both parties. Regular conversation is only one aspect of effective communication; another is the systematic exchange of information via a variety of platforms, including formal documentation procedures, digital platforms, and scheduled meetings. Suppliers must have easy access to channels for voicing concerns or making suggestions for improvements, as well as clear visibility into project schedules, needs, and prospective adjustments. This openness facilitates prompt problem solving and helps avoid misunderstandings. Frequent performance evaluations, strategic planning meetings, and progress updates give both sides the chance to align their objectives and candidly address any difficulties. Additionally, putting in place defined communication protocols—such as feedback systems and escalation procedures for urgent issues—helps keep the relationship consistent and dependable.

Organizations can develop more solid and robust supplier partnerships that stimulate innovation and generate long-term value for all stakeholders by cultivating an atmosphere in which both sides are at ease exchanging information and working together to find answers. This cooperative strategy frequently results in increased operational effectiveness, less risks, and the creation of strategic advantages that eventually benefit the company and its suppliers.

1.6 Governance and Competence

Effective governance and competence in communication are functional to ensure that communication practices are well-managed and that team members have the necessary skills to communicate effectively.

Establishing structures and policies to oversee communication practices ensures consistency and compliance. Practically:

- **Governance Structures**: Set up governance structures to manage communication processes. This can include communication committees, roles, and responsibilities.
- **Policies and Procedures**: Develop and implement communication policies and procedures that outline standards, protocols, and best practices. These should be regularly reviewed and updated.
- **Compliance Monitoring**: Monitor compliance with communication policies and procedures to ensure adherence. This can involve regular audits and assessments.

1.7 Stakeholder Satisfaction and Culture of Quality

Regularly engaging with stakeholders to understand their communication needs and preferences is essential for effective communication. How to do that?

- **Needs Assessment**: Conduct assessments to understand the communication needs and preferences of different stakeholders. This can involve surveys, interviews, and focus groups.
- **Tailored Communication**: Customize communication strategies to meet the specific needs of each stakeholder group. This ensures that information is relevant and accessible.
- **Regular Interaction**: Maintain regular interaction with stakeholders through meetings, updates, and feedback sessions. This helps in building strong relationships and trust.

Finally, to maintain high standards of communication quality, project managers should implement these essential practices:

- **Clear and concise messaging**: Ensure all communications are straightforward, free of jargon, and easily understood by the intended audience.
- **Quality control processes**: Verify information accuracy before distribution and maintain consistency across all communication channels.
- **Regular assessment**: Monitor communication effectiveness through feedback collection, performance metrics, and periodic reviews to drive continuous improvement.

1.8 Conclusion

Project communication represents a critical intersection between management principles and project requirements, integrating customer focus with systematic quality control processes. As projects grow in complexity, technological advancements like AI and blockchain enhance communication capabilities, yet must be balanced with maintaining meaningful interpersonal connections.

The emphasis on continuous improvement through systematic feedback and performance measurement demonstrates how communication strategies must evolve alongside project needs, particularly in global contexts. Meanwhile, the evolution of supplier relationships from transactional to strategic partnerships demands sophisticated communication competencies.

Success in project communication ultimately depends on developing a flexible framework that balances technological capabilities with human factors, formal processes with informal interactions, and standard practices with situation-specific adaptations, all while maintaining clear focus on project objectives and stakeholder needs.

References

Aga, D. A., Noorderhaven, N., & Vallejo, B. (2016). Transformational leadership and project success: The mediating role of team-building. *International Journal of Project Management, 34*(5), 806–818. https://doi.org/10.1016/j.ijproman.2016.02.012

Kerzner, H. (2017). *Project management: A systems approach to planning, scheduling, and controlling*. Wiley.

Chapter 2
Quality Culture in Project Management as Organizational Drivers

Virginie Pasquon

Organizations are under more and more pressure to provide high-quality products and services while preserving operational effectiveness in the quickly changing business environment of today. Quality in project management, as defined by ISO 10006, goes beyond simple specification compliance to include the comprehensive capacity to satisfy stakeholder expectations and promote ongoing organizational progress.

We examine how project management techniques and quality concepts can be successfully combined to improve organizational performance and produce long-term value. We'll look at how these ideas might be used in contexts other than individual projects to improve organizational capacities, encourage creativity, and create a long-lasting competitive edge.

2.1 The Evolution of Quality Management in Project-Based Organizations

The evolution of quality management in project-based organizations reflects a broader shift in management thinking from inspection-based approaches to integrated, prevention-oriented systems. This transformation has been particularly significant in how organizations view the relationship between quality and project success. Traditional approaches often treated quality as a technical function focused primarily on product conformance. However, modern organizations recognize quality as a strategic driver that influences every aspect of project and organizational performance.

V. Pasquon (✉)
Department of Innovative Technologies, SUPSI, Lugano, Switzerland
e-mail: virginie.pasquon@supsi.ch

A. Bassi et al. (eds.), *General Management Principles for Project Management*, Management for Professionals, https://doi.org/10.1007/978-3-031-98592-8_2

Modern organizations increasingly recognize that quality cannot exist in isolation. The integration of quality management principles with project management methodologies creates a powerful framework for organizational excellence. This integration:

- Enables consistent delivery of value to stakeholders
- Reduces operational inefficiencies and waste
- Promotes knowledge sharing and organizational learning
- Enhances decision-making processes
- Builds organizational resilience

2.2 Core Principles of Quality

At the core of successful project management lies a sophisticated understanding of quality principles (customer focus, leadership, engagement of people, process approach, improvement, evidence-based decision making, relationship management—ISO, 2015).That extends far beyond traditional quality control measures. These principles form an interconnected web that transforms how organizations approach project delivery and value creation. In this section explores how customer-centricity and leadership work together to create a robust foundation for quality excellence.

2.2.1 Customer-Centric Approach

Quality management begins and ends with the customer. This fundamental truth shapes every aspect of project management, from initial conception to final delivery. Modern organizations recognize that customer-centricity is not merely about meeting specifications—it's about creating meaningful value that resonates throughout the customer's experience.

This deeper understanding of customer-centricity manifests in two critical dimensions: direct engagement and value creation. Through systematic customer engagement, organizations gain invaluable insights that inform their project decisions. This involves regular stakeholder sessions where project teams actively listen to customer feedback, leveraging advanced analytics to uncover patterns and trends in customer preferences. These insights don't simply sit in reports—they actively shape project planning and execution, ensuring that deliverables consistently align with customer expectations.

The second dimension, value creation, transforms customer understanding into tangible benefits. Successful projects define clear value propositions that resonate with customer needs, aligning every project objective with specific customer success metrics. This alignment isn't static—it evolves through regular assessments of value delivery throughout the project lifecycle. As customer needs shift, project approaches adapt accordingly, ensuring sustained relevance and impact.

2.2.2 *Leadership and Strategic Quality Vision*

While customer-centricity provides the foundation, leadership acts as the catalyst that transforms quality principles into organizational reality. This transformation occurs through two interrelated mechanisms: strategic vision and cultural development.

Strategic quality vision sets the direction for the entire organization (Defeo, 2017). Effective leaders recognize that quality isn't a standalone initiative—it's an integral part of organizational strategy. They create this integration by establishing clear quality objectives that align with broader organizational goals, providing project teams with unambiguous direction while establishing measurable targets that drive concrete actions. This strategic framework becomes the bedrock for decision-making throughout the organization.

However, vision alone isn't enough. The true power of leadership in quality management lies in its ability to shape organizational culture. Leaders who excel in quality management demonstrate their commitment through consistent actions, not just words. They allocate resources strategically, actively encourage innovation, and create an environment where continuous improvement becomes second nature. This cultural transformation is reinforced through transparent communication channels and recognition systems that celebrate quality-focused behaviors.

The interplay between customer-centricity and leadership creates a self-reinforcing cycle. As leaders demonstrate their commitment to quality through strategic vision and cultural development, teams become more attuned to customer needs. This enhanced customer focus, in turn, provides leaders with richer insights to refine their strategic vision, creating a virtuous cycle of continuous improvement.

2.3 Implementing Quality Management

The implementation of quality management represents a delicate balance between structure and flexibility, where planning, control, assurance, and improvement converge into a unified approach. At its core, successful implementation begins with robust planning that establishes clear quality objectives, metrics, and standards, while simultaneously defining the roles and procedures necessary for effective quality control. This foundation supports a comprehensive quality assurance framework that emphasizes prevention over correction, utilizing standardized processes to ensure consistency across projects while maintaining the agility to adapt to specific project needs. The system becomes truly powerful when integrated with continuous improvement mechanisms that leverage data-driven insights, regular audits, and employee feedback to evolve and enhance quality practices over time. This integrated approach creates a dynamic ecosystem where quality isn't just monitored and controlled, but actively cultivated through a combination of systematic processes and human engagement, leading to sustained organizational excellence. The key lies in the system's ability to maintain rigorous standards while remaining responsive to changing project and/o organization demands, fostering an environment where quality becomes an inherent part of it rather than an imposed requirement.

2.4 Tools and Techniques

The modern quality management landscape has evolved into a sophisticated ecosystem where traditional statistical tools seamlessly integrate with technologies to create a comprehensive quality management framework. At its foundation, organizations continue to rely on proven statistical process control methods, including control charts and variance analysis, while simultaneously employing advanced quality planning tools such as Quality Function Deployment (QFD) and Failure Mode and Effects Analysis (FMEA) to anticipate and prevent quality issues before they arise. This traditional toolset has been dramatically enhanced by the integration of digital technologies, with quality management software providing real-time monitoring capabilities and automated testing systems streamlining quality control processes. The emergence of artificial intelligence and machine learning has further transformed quality management, enabling predictive analytics that can forecast potential quality issues and pattern recognition algorithms that identify subtle trends in quality data. This convergence of traditional and digital tools creates a dynamic system where quality managers can leverage both time-tested methodologies and "cutting-edge" technologies to maintain and improve quality standards, making decisions based on both historical statistical analysis and real-time data insights, ultimately leading to more proactive and effective quality management practices.

2.5 Building Organizational Capabilities Through Quality Management

The core of organizational excellence we find the ability to capture, share, and leverage knowledge effectively through quality management systems. Successful organizations recognize that quality management serves as a powerful tool for organizational learning, creating a dynamic environment where knowledge flows freely between projects and teams. This knowledge ecosystem is built upon systematic documentation of lessons learned, establishment of vibrant communities of practice, and implementation of comprehensive training programs that transform individual experiences into collective wisdom. The most effective organizations go beyond simple knowledge capture, fostering an environment where experimentation is encouraged, innovation is celebrated, and continuous learning becomes deeply embedded in the organizational culture. Through carefully designed mentoring systems and knowledge-sharing platforms, these organizations create multiple channels for knowledge transfer, ensuring that insights and best practices permeate every level of the organization. For more details, refer to the chapter "Capabilities".

The transformation of knowledge into organizational capability requires robust performance measurement and management systems that provide clear visibility into quality outcomes. Organizations must establish comprehensive metrics frameworks that balance traditional quality indicators with forward-looking measures of organizational capability development. These frameworks incorporate everything from standard quality metrics and customer satisfaction scores to more sophisticated measures of organizational learning and adaptation capacity. By linking these measurements to well-designed performance management systems, organizations create accountability for quality improvement while simultaneously fostering a culture of continuous development. This integrated approach to performance measurement and management ensures that quality initiatives don't just improve current operations but build lasting organizational capabilities that drive sustained competitive advantage.

2.6 Challenges and Success Factors

The journey toward quality is rarely straightforward, presenting organizations with a complex array of challenges that must be carefully navigated. At the forefront of these challenges lies **cultural resistance**, a formidable barrier that manifests in various forms throughout the organization. Traditional mindsets, deeply entrenched in established ways of working, often create significant inertia against quality initiatives. This resistance typically emerges not from active opposition, but from a subtle combination of skepticism, comfort with existing processes, and fear of change. Organizations frequently find that even when quality initiatives demonstrate clear benefits, maintaining momentum proves challenging as initial enthusiasm gives way to the demanding reality of sustained implementation.

The challenge of cultural transformation is further complicated by resource constraints, which create tension between quality aspirations and operational realities. Organizations must navigate the delicate balance between allocating sufficient resources for quality initiatives while maintaining efficient operations. This balancing act becomes particularly critical when building new capabilities, as the investment in training, tools, and systems must compete with immediate operational needs. The pressure to deliver short-term results often conflicts with the longer-term nature of quality improvements, creating a challenging dynamic that requires careful management and strategic thinking.

Leadership commitment emerges as a key factor in overcoming these challenges and driving successful quality implementation. As mentioned at the beginning of this chapter, effective leaders understand that their visible support and personal involvement send powerful signals throughout the organization. This commitment must extend beyond mere verbal endorsement to include tangible resource allocation and active participation in quality initiatives. Leaders who excel in this area often participate directly in quality reviews, celebrate successes, and maintain regular communication about quality priorities.

Employee engagement represents another pillar of good quality implementation. Organizations that succeed in their quality journey recognize that sustainable improvement requires more than just top-down directives; it demands the active participation and buy-in of employees at all levels. The interplay between recognition and autonomy is required in sustaining employee engagement. Well-designed recognition programs acknowledge both individual and team contributions to quality improvement, reinforcing desired behaviors and maintaining motivation. However, recognition alone is insufficient; employees must also feel they have the autonomy to make decisions and implement improvements within their sphere of influence.

Communication emerges as a thread that weaves through all aspects of quality implementation, it helps build trust, facilitates knowledge sharing, and enables rapid response to emerging quality issues. Regular feedback sessions, quality forums, and improvement workshops provide structured opportunities for dialogue, while informal channels allow for the day-to-day exchange of ideas and concerns.

The success of quality initiatives ultimately depends on an organization's ability to create a self-reinforcing cycle where leadership commitment, employee engagement, and effective communication work together to overcome cultural resistance and resource constraints. Organizations that master this delicate balance find that quality becomes embedded in their organizational DNA, driving continuous improvement and sustainable competitive advantage. This transformation doesn't happen overnight, but through persistent effort, clear vision, and unwavering commitment to quality.

2.7 Conclusion

The future of quality management is being dramatically reshaped by the convergence of multiple transformative forces, each bringing both opportunities and challenges that organizations must navigate strategically. Digital transformation stands at the forefront of this evolution, with artificial intelligence and machine learning revolutionizing how organizations approach quality management through real-time monitoring, predictive analytics, and automated quality control systems, while sustainability and social responsibility emerge as dimensions of quality that extend beyond traditional metrics to encompass environmental impact, social value, and ethical considerations. This evolution demands a fundamental rethinking of organizational capabilities and structures, pushing organizations toward more agile and adaptive frameworks that can respond rapidly to changing quality requirements while maintaining consistency and excellence. Forward-thinking organizations are already embracing this transformation by investing in digital skills development, fostering quality leadership capabilities, and building innovative governance structures that support both stability and flexibility. The integration of these elements creates a new paradigm for quality management where technical capabilities meets social responsibility, and where organizational success is measured not just in traditional quality metrics but in the broader context of sustainable value creation and social impact.

References

Defeo, J. A. (2017). *Juran's quality handbook: The complete guide to performance excellence* (7th ed.). McGraw-Hill Education.

ISO. (2015). *Quality management principles*. www.iso.org. Retrieved from https://www.iso.org/files/live/sites/isoorg/files/store/en/PUB100080.pdf

Chapter 3
Governance

Antonio Bassi

In the context of project management, governance plays a crucial role, serving as the cornerstone that supports the entire structure of a project, guiding it towards success. Governance does not merely define the distribution of decision-making power or the responsibilities of various project phases; it goes beyond, encompassing the methods by which decisions are made, communicated, and executed. It emphasizes the importance of transparency, efficiency, and consistency in every aspect of the project, ensuring that everything aligns perfectly with the broader goals and strategies of the organization.

At the core of this process lies the clear identification of roles and responsibilities, an aspect that not only simplifies decision-making but also ensures that every stakeholder is aware of their contribution to the overall success of the project. Key figures include the project manager, who handles day-to-day management, the project sponsor, who supports the project at the executive level, and the steering committee, responsible for providing strategic direction and resolving complex issues.

The decision-making process is equally fundamental, needing to be transparent, organized, and based on concrete data. This framework ensures that decisions are made promptly and in the best interest of both the project and the organization, preventing delays and misunderstandings while enabling smooth and continuous progress.

Keeping the project aligned with the organization's long-term objectives requires constant and effective communication between the project teams and upper management. This alignment is vital to ensure that the project remains relevant and synchronized with business priorities, ready to adapt to any strategic or contextual changes.

Risk management is indispensable, as identifying, assessing, and mitigating potential risks are essential to avoid unwanted surprises that could divert the project

A. Bassi (✉)
Project Management Association Switzerland, Lugano, Switzerland
e-mail: antonio.bassi@apm-switzerland.ch

A. Bassi et al. (eds.), *General Management Principles for Project Management*, Management for Professionals, https://doi.org/10.1007/978-3-031-98592-8_3

from its set goals. A systematic approach to risk management, including continuous monitoring and review, is crucial for effectively addressing any potential pitfalls.

A robust reporting and communication system is essential for keeping all stakeholders informed about project progress, emerging issues, and decisions made. This fosters a collaborative environment and maintains alignment and trust among all project participants.

It is crucial that governance in project management ensures compliance with quality standards as well as legal and ethical regulations, ensuring that the project not only achieves its objectives but does so responsibly and sustainably. This implies adhering to current laws and regulations as well as conforming to both internal and external quality standards.

In summary, governance in project management acts as a compass that guides goals and ideas towards clear and well-structured success. By establishing solid governance principles, clear decision-making processes, proactive risk management, and effective communication practices, organizations can not only ensure the achievement of set goals but also proceed consistently with the organization's vision and values.

3.1 Governance Structure

The governance structure in a project serves as the backbone through which decisions are made, communicated, and implemented, ensuring that every phase of the project is managed effectively and in line with the predefined objectives. This governance structure is not limited to merely assigning roles but also establishes a communication and decision-making system that enables the project to navigate through challenges and changes while maintaining a consistent strategic direction.

At the core of this structure are key figures such as the project manager, who holds the daily responsibility of guiding the project towards success by coordinating activities, managing resources, and ensuring compliance with the established timelines and budgets. The project manager acts as the main point of reference for the project team and stakeholders, ensuring that information flows correctly in all directions.

The project sponsor, usually a high-level figure within the organization, provides strategic support and resources, acting as a bridge between the project team and the executive level of the organization. Their approval is often necessary for key decisions and resource allocation, making their involvement crucial to the project's success.

The steering committee is another vital element of the governance structure. Comprising key members of the organization and sometimes external stakeholders, the steering committee provides strategic direction, approves significant changes to the project, and resolves high-level issues that go beyond the project manager's authority. The presence of this committee ensures that the project remains aligned with business objectives and receives the necessary support to overcome obstacles.

Beyond these primary roles, the governance structure may include various other relevant stakeholders, each with specific responsibilities and interests in the project. These can vary depending on the nature and scale of the project and may include suppliers, customers, strategic partners, and community members. Clearly defining the roles and responsibilities of each of these stakeholders is crucial to ensure that expectations are aligned and that the project proceeds smoothly.

The governance structure, therefore, acts as the project's nervous system, ensuring that decisions are made in an informed and timely manner, resources are allocated effectively, and risks are managed proactively. Through an effective governance structure, a project can navigate through uncertainties and changes while maintaining focus on its final objectives, ensuring that all stakeholders are engaged and informed throughout the process. Ultimately, a solid governance structure not only increases the project's chances of success but also strengthens strategic alignment and the value generated for the organization.

3.2 Decision-Making Processes

In the context of project governance, decision-making processes constitute a fundamental element that guides how and by whom critical decisions are made. This decision-making structure ensures that every important choice is the result of thorough and thoughtful analysis, based on accurate data and information, and is made by individuals or groups with the appropriate authority. Such an organization not only promotes transparency and accountability but also facilitates effective resolution of any disagreements or differences of opinion that may arise during the project lifecycle.

The process begins with the clear definition of who has the power to make which decisions. This can vary depending on the nature and complexity of the project, but generally includes the project manager for day-to-day operational decisions, the project sponsor for strategic decisions, and the steering committee for overall direction and high-level issues. Clearly establishing these lines of authority helps to avoid ambiguity and delays, ensuring that decisions are made efficiently.

A key element of effective decision-making processes is the availability and use of accurate information. This implies the implementation of data collection and analysis systems that provide decision-makers with a clear view of the project's status, potential risks, and opportunities. Timely access to relevant information enables informed decisions that are better aligned with the project's and the organization's objectives.

Managing disagreements or differences of opinion is another crucial component of decision-making processes within project governance. Despite the best planning, disagreements are inevitable in any complex project, arising from differences in opinions, priorities, or interpretations of data. A well-structured decision-making process includes mechanisms to address these situations, such as open and constructive discussions, mediation, and, if necessary, escalation to higher levels of authority for resolution. This ensures that disagreements do not become insurmountable obstacles but opportunities to explore alternatives and arrive at better solutions.

Finally, documentation and communication of decisions are integral parts of the decision-making processes. Documenting decisions, the reasons behind them, and the processes used to reach them helps to create a record of transparency and accountability. Additionally, effectively communicating these decisions to all interested stakeholders ensures that everyone is informed about the directions the project is taking, increasing alignment and overall support.

Decision-making processes within project governance are not just mechanisms for making choices; they are also fundamental tools for ensuring that these choices are thoughtful, informed, and aligned with the organization's broader objectives. Through a clear definition of decision-making authority, the use of accurate information, effective management of disagreements, and transparent communication, decision-making processes contribute significantly to the project's success.

3.3 Strategic Alignment

Strategic alignment in the context of project governance represents a dynamic and ongoing process that ensures harmony between the project's actions and the long-term objectives of the organization. This concept is based on the idea that, to be truly effective and generate added value, projects must not operate in isolation but rather in close synergy with the overarching vision and strategy of the host entity. Such alignment requires constant attention and adaptability, given the changing nature of both the internal and external environments in which organizations operate.

The first step in ensuring effective strategic alignment is the clear definition of the project's objectives during the planning phase. These objectives must reflect and support the organization's strategic goals, ensuring that every initiative undertaken through the project directly contributes to achieving broader milestones. Defining these objectives requires close collaboration between the project teams and the organization's upper management levels to ensure a thorough understanding and integration of business priorities.

However, strategic alignment is not a one-time act fixed at the beginning of the project; rather, it is an iterative process that requires regular review and adjustment. This is because both the internal and external contexts in which organizations operate are subject to change: new market trends, technological innovations, changes in regulations, or shifts in the organization's strategic priorities are all factors that can influence the direction and needs of a project. Consequently, it is crucial to implement monitoring and review mechanisms that allow for periodic evaluation of the project's objectives and, if necessary, adjustments to strategies to maintain alignment with broader business goals.

This process of review and adaptation requires flexibility, open communication, and, most importantly, strong leadership skills. Project leaders and sponsors must be capable of interpreting signals from both the internal and external contexts, making informed decisions, and guiding teams through the necessary changes while maintaining morale and motivation. At the same time, it is crucial to keep all stakeholders informed and engaged in the process to ensure that the changes are understood, accepted, and supported at all levels of the organization.

Ultimately, strategic alignment is a vital element that ensures not only the success of the project in terms of on-time and on-budget delivery but also its effective contribution to the organization's long-term strategic goals. Through a constant commitment to review, adaptation, and communication, organizations can navigate complex and ever-changing environments, ensuring that their projects remain relevant, agile, and aligned with their overall strategic vision.

3.4 Risk Management

Risk management is a critical component of project governance, serving as a mechanism for the prevention, monitoring, and response to uncertainties that could negatively impact the project's outcome. This systematic process is divided into several phases, each contributing to reducing the likelihood of project failure and maximizing the opportunities for success.

The first step in risk management is identification. This phase involves a careful analysis of the project environment to recognize potential risks that may arise. These risks can be of various natures, such as financial, technological, operational, legal, or market-related. Identifying risks requires a deep understanding of the project and its context, and often benefits from the input of a multidisciplinary team that can provide diverse perspectives.

Once risks are identified, they must be analyzed to understand their likelihood of occurrence and potential impact on the project. This analysis allows risks to be ranked according to their severity and priorities to be set for mitigation actions. Techniques such as qualitative and quantitative risk analysis are used to evaluate these aspects, providing decision-makers with clear information to guide subsequent phases.

The next phase is planning risk responses, which involves developing strategies to mitigate, avoid, transfer, or accept risks. The choice of strategy depends on the nature of the risk and the organization's risk appetite. For example, risks that threaten critical project objectives will require mitigation or avoidance actions, while minor risks may simply be accepted.

Implementing risk response strategies is the step that follows. This involves allocating resources and responsibilities for mitigation actions and continuously monitoring the effectiveness of these actions. During this phase, constant communication with all project stakeholders is essential to ensure they are informed of the risks and the measures taken to address them.

Monitoring and control are ongoing aspects of risk management that extend throughout the project's life cycle. This activity includes tracking identified risks, identifying new risks, and analyzing the effectiveness of response strategies. Monitoring allows for the adaptation of risk management strategies in response to changes in the project or the external environment, ensuring that risk management remains proactive and dynamic.

Risk management is an iterative and integrated process that ensures the project's resilience and flexibility in the face of uncertainties. By providing a structured framework for identifying, analyzing, planning, implementing, and monitoring risks, risk management enables project teams to anticipate and effectively address challenges, guiding the project towards success in a constantly evolving environment.

3.5 Reporting and Communication

The process of reporting and communication within project governance acts as a vital information flow, essential for keeping all stakeholders informed and engaged. This flow is not only about transmitting data and facts but also about creating an open and constructive dialogue between the project team and those with an interest in its outcome. The key to effective reporting and communication lies in its ability to adapt to the listening and comprehension needs of stakeholders, ensuring that information is not only sent but also received, interpreted, and used correctly.

Defining the requirements for reporting and communication begins with a clear understanding of the project's stakeholders: who they are, what information they need, and how frequently they require it.. This initial step ensures that status reports and communications are targeted and relevant, reducing the risk of information overload and ensuring that critical information is highlighted. For example, a software development team may need daily updates on technical progress, while a steering committee may only require weekly or monthly summaries of the project's overall status.

The frequency and format of status reports are then customized to meet these diverse needs. While weekly reports can provide continuous updates on project progress, monthly or quarterly meetings can offer opportunities for more in-depth discussions on strategy, risks, and opportunities. The format of the reports—from visual presentations to detailed documents—is chosen to facilitate stakeholders' understanding and engagement. The use of interactive dashboards and digital tools, for instance, allows for immediate visualization of project status and easy access to further details if necessary.

Communication guidelines play a fundamental role in managing expectations and proactively responding to changes and challenges. These guidelines clearly establish when and how project changes, emerging issues, or risks should be communicated. By creating an environment where open communication is encouraged and escalation paths are clearly defined, project teams can address challenges promptly, minimizing negative impacts on the project.

An effective reporting and communication strategy is rooted in its ability to be fluid and organic, adapting to the changing needs of the project and its stakeholders.

This not only ensures that critical information is shared in a timely and effective manner but also that there is mutual understanding and alignment among all parties involved. Through the creation of continuous and meaningful dialogue, project governance can navigate uncertainties and challenges while maintaining focus on the objectives and desired outcomes.

3.6 Quality Assurance

To ensure that a project meets the required quality standards, it is essential to adopt a structured approach to quality assurance, integrating policies and procedures that guide every phase from planning to execution and review. Project governance in terms of quality begins with the clear definition of quality standards, which must reflect both the specific objectives of the project and the expectations of the stakeholders. These standards should cover all crucial aspects, including time management, cost management, and the quality of the final product or service.

Once standards are defined, the implementation of periodic quality reviews becomes fundamental. These reviews are dedicated moments during which the project team assesses progress against the established standards, promptly identifying any deviations or areas for improvement. Quality reviews should be scheduled at regular intervals and integrated as an essential part of the project's lifecycle, ensuring that each phase is in compliance with the defined standards.

In parallel with periodic reviews, quality audits play a crucial role in quality assurance. Audits are independent assessments conducted to verify the project's compliance with the quality standards and established procedures. Through audits, it is possible to identify not only non-conformities but also opportunities for improvement, providing valuable feedback to the project team to guide corrective actions.

Compliance assessments are another essential tool, allowing for the objective measurement of adherence to quality standards and best practices. These assessments can be both internal and external and serve to provide a clear view of the level of quality achieved by the project, highlighting strengths and weaknesses.

For effective quality assurance, it is vital that all these practices are supported by a corporate culture that values quality and excellence. This requires a constant commitment from the project's leadership to promote high standards in team training and to encourage a proactive approach to quality management. Integrating quality assurance as a fundamental element of project governance means adopting a holistic approach that recognizes the importance of every single action and decision in contributing to the overall success of the project.

3.7 Compliance

Compliance represents the culmination of effective project governance, serving as the glue that ensures alignment with the external regulatory and ethical environment. This responsibility is not limited to mere adherence to current laws but extends to full compliance with regulations, industry-specific norms, and standards, reflecting a deep commitment to operational excellence and social responsibility.

Document management thus becomes a vital process, not only for demonstrating compliance but also for creating a transparent and traceable record of all decisions and actions taken. This aspect is crucial for supporting internal and external audits, facilitating reviews, and ensuring that every detail can be easily accessed and verified.

Similarly, contractual compliance ensures that all business relationships and partnerships are structured with clarity, fairness, and mutual respect, taking into account the legal obligations and rights of all parties involved. This not only minimizes legal risks but also promotes solid and lasting business relationships based on trust and transparency.

Equally important is ethical compliance, which represents the project's moral compass. This aspect focuses on always acting with integrity, honesty, and respect for ethical principles, regardless of external pressures or expectations of immediate gain. Ethical compliance translates into responsible business practices that not only comply with the law but also elevate the standard of behavior within the industry and the broader community.

In summary, compliance within project governance is a complex element that requires attention, dedication, and a constant commitment to transparency, fairness, and integrity. It is this commitment that not only protects the project from legal and financial risks but also builds a foundation of trust and irreproachable reputation, essential for long-term success.

Chapter 4
Historical Information and Lessons Learned in Project Management

Antonio Bassi

In the field of project management, the collection of historical information and lessons learned is a crucial practice for continuous improvement and for achieving future success, both for the specific project and for the organization as a whole. Let us deeply analyze the importance of capturing, storing, and reusing this valuable information to avoid repeating mistakes and to enhance the efficiency and effectiveness of future projects.

4.1 The Importance of Historical Information

The historical information collected from previous projects constitutes an invaluable resource for project management. These data form a rich archive of knowledge that can be consulted to guide future decisions. They do not merely describe what was done and the results obtained but also offer a detailed context on how decisions were made, which strategies were effective, and which mistakes were made. This archive thus becomes a repository of practical experience that can be used to improve the quality of decisions in subsequent projects.

Utilizing historical data allows project managers to base their planning on real scenarios rather than assumptions. This evidence-based approach significantly increases the likelihood of project success since decisions are made based on concrete evidence and results rather than theories or intuitions. For example, knowing the actual time required to complete certain activities in previous projects makes it possible to more accurately estimate future timelines, thereby reducing the risks of delays.

A. Bassi (✉)
Project Management Association Switzerland, Lugano, Switzerland
e-mail: antonio.bassi@apm-switzerland.ch

A. Bassi et al. (eds.), *General Management Principles for Project Management*, Management for Professionals, https://doi.org/10.1007/978-3-031-98592-8_4

One of the most useful aspects of historical documentation is the ability to identify patterns of errors. By analyzing past failures, teams can develop strategies to avoid them in the future. For instance, if a previous project suffered from poor communication among stakeholders, future plans can emphasize greater transparency and regular status updates to keep all stakeholders informed and engaged. Historical information can also help identify the most cost- and time-efficient techniques. Understanding which resources were effectively used in the past can guide better resource allocation in new projects, especially in resource-constrained environments where maximizing efficiency is crucial.

With accurate historical data, organizations can establish internal benchmarks for performance, costs, and deadlines. These standards help define expectations for future projects and provide a basis for evaluating progress and effectiveness. Having clear, data-based standards allows teams to aim for performance levels that are both ambitious and realistic.

Historical information is more than just an archive of old projects; it is a dynamic and vital resource that enhances project management through informed decision-making, error prevention, resource optimization, and the establishment of rigorous benchmarks. Integrating these data into the daily workflow of project teams not only increases the chances of success but also fosters an environment of continuous learning and improvement.

4.2 Forecasting and Planning

The ability to anticipate future challenges and plan precisely is one of the pillars of success in project management. By using the historical information gathered from previous projects, managers can refine their forecasting and planning techniques in specific and measurable ways.

By analyzing past projects, managers can identify recurring patterns of success or failure. This process can reveal both positive and negative trends, offering valuable insights into behaviors to replicate or avoid. For example, if multiple projects have experienced delays due to specific supply chain dependencies, managers can anticipate similar problems in future projects and plan accordingly to mitigate them.

Historical information enables managers to create and manage a database of known risks, including the impacts and mitigation strategies that have proven effective. This database can be used to make more informed risk assessments, allowing teams to prepare more robust response plans and allocate resources for risk management more efficiently.

Through the analysis of past performance, project managers have the opportunity to determine more accurately how many resources are needed for specific tasks or project phases. Historical knowledge helps identify when and where resources were underutilized or exhausted, allowing for more accurate planning and resource optimization in future projects.

Historical information provides concrete data on the actual time required to complete various types of projects or specific activities. This knowledge is important for setting realistic and achievable deadlines, reducing the risk of costly delays, and increasing the likelihood of delivering the project within the established timeframe.

The ability to adapt planning based on historical scenarios allows managers to respond better to rapid market changes. By analyzing how certain events or market conditions have affected projects in the past, teams can develop proactive strategies to adapt to similar challenges in the future.

Using historical information for forecasting and planning not only improves accuracy and efficiency but also makes the entire project management process more responsive and adaptable. This data-driven approach helps build a solid foundation for future success by maximizing project performance and minimizing risks and uncertainties.

4.3 Benchmarking and Standardization

The historical information acquired from previous projects is essential for developing reliable benchmarks and standardizing practices within an organization. These tools are fundamental for raising the overall quality of projects, reducing costs, and improving time efficiency. Let's examine in detail how benchmarking and standardization benefit from historical information.

Historical information allows for the analysis of the quality levels achieved in previous projects, identifying which practices led to the best results. Through this process, it is possible to establish quality standards that all future projects should strive to achieve or exceed. For example, if a particular approach to quality management has consistently produced superior results, it can be adopted as a benchmark for similar activities in the future.

Analyzing the actual costs of past projects helps identify areas where savings can be made without compromising quality, while establishing cost benchmarks enables organizations to avoid waste and overestimation in future planning. This process also helps identify suppliers or strategies that have led to significant savings.

Historical data on the time taken to complete various aspects of projects can serve as benchmarks for time planning. This helps set realistic and achievable deadlines based on concrete data rather than optimistic or pessimistic estimates.

Using historical information to standardize processes allows organizations to implement best practices consistently. This not only increases operational efficiency but also ensures that every project is managed using the most effective methodologies known to the organization.

With well-defined standards, it is easier to design training programs for new team members. Newcomers can be quickly brought up to the desired level of competence, ensuring that everyone understands and follows the established best practices.

Standardization does not mean stagnation. Benchmarks and standards must be regularly reviewed and updated based on new data collected from subsequent projects. This feedback loop ensures that the organization continues to improve and evolve, remaining competitive and effective in its sector.

Benchmarking and standardization fueled by historical information are crucial tools for improving project management. They enable organizations to operate with greater precision, consistency, and predictability, significantly contributing to the overall success and long-term sustainability of their projects.

4.4 Lessons Learned: Capture and Reuse

The accurate documentation of lessons learned is the fundamental element for the effective application of past experiences to future projects. This process is not limited to recording events but involves a deep understanding and critical analysis of project dynamics.

Detailed and specific documentation is essential. Beyond recording project outcomes, it is important to analyze and document decision-making processes, strategies adopted, and methodologies employed. This helps understand not only what happened but also why certain results occurred. Every lesson learned should include information on the specific context in which events occurred, such as market conditions, internal issues, and external influences that may have significantly impacted project outcomes.

The use of tools and technologies for documentation can significantly enhance the collection of lessons learned. Utilizing project management software that encourages collaborative documentation can increase the accuracy and richness of the information gathered. These tools allow team members to contribute their perceptions and observations in real-time, enriching the database with diverse perspectives. Developing and using standardized templates for documentation ensures that all essential information is systematically collected, including sections for project objectives, outcomes, encountered problems, adopted solutions, and the results of corrective actions.

Regular review and feedback are crucial. At the end of each project, debriefing sessions should be organized with the teams to discuss and document lessons learned. These sessions allow for in-depth exploration of what worked well and what needs improvement. The documentation of lessons learned should be seen as an iterative process where information is continuously updated and refined based on new experiences and feedback from team members. This dynamic approach helps keep the documentation relevant and applicable to future situations.

Making the information accessible is important. Keeping lessons learned in a central, accessible repository allows project managers and teams to easily refer to this information during the planning and execution of new projects. Promoting a corporate culture that values and actively uses lessons learned reinforces the importance of this practice. Leaders can set an example by referring to internal case studies in briefings and training sessions, encouraging everyone to actively participate in the continuous learning process.

By implementing these practices, the documentation of lessons learned becomes not only an archive of past events but a living resource that guides continuous improvement and contributes to the overall success of future projects.

4.5 Review and Analysis

The periodic review and analysis of lessons learned are fundamental processes for transforming documentation into concrete actions that improve the efficiency and effectiveness of future projects.

Conducting an in-depth analysis is important to get the most out of the lessons learned. Regularly reviewing the lessons documented from multiple projects provides a more comprehensive view that can reveal underlying trends and patterns not visible in the analysis of individual projects. This cross-project analysis helps understand broader issues that affect multiple projects and can lead to more effective global changes in project management strategies. The adoption of advanced analytical tools, such as root cause analysis or statistical analysis, can help discern the causes of successes and failures with greater precision. Additionally, applying data analytics techniques can uncover hidden correlations between variables that are not evident in a superficial review.

Expanding the scope of application of lessons learned is equally important. During the review, it is crucial to identify lessons that can be applied universally, regardless of the type of project. This helps establish best practices that can be standardized and incorporated into the organization's project management manuals. Historical information can also reveal changes in risk patterns that may not have been previously considered. Continuously updating risk models based on lessons learned ensures that mitigation plans are always current and effective.

Implementing feedback loops is another key component of the process. Encouraging continuous feedback from all project stakeholders, including team members, customers, and suppliers, can enrich the review process. This participatory approach not only increases the accuracy of lessons learned but also adherence to process updates. Organizing regular review sessions where teams can openly discuss lessons learned allows for continuous updating and collective reflection on progress and areas for improvement.

Keeping documentation dynamic is essential for long-term success. Lessons learned should not be seen as static elements. It is vital that the documentation is regularly updated to reflect new information, insights, and emerging contexts. Maintaining a dynamic and easily updatable documentation system is crucial to preserving the relevance of lessons over time. Ensuring that lessons learned are an integral part of onboarding materials for new employees and ongoing team training helps perpetuate knowledge and improve skills on an organizational basis.

Improving the review and analysis of lessons learned allows organizations not only to avoid repeating past mistakes but also to anticipate future challenges and continuously improve project management strategies. This process transforms documentation into a living asset that continues to generate added value for every new project undertaken.

4.6 Integration into Decision-Making Processes

The active integration of lessons learned into decision-making processes is a crucial step to ensure that the benefits of these past experiences are fully exploited in future projects. This approach not only improves the quality of decisions but also increases the resilience and efficiency of projects.

Protocols and standard procedures should be subject to periodic reviews to incorporate lessons learned. This helps ensure that the practices adopted are always up-to-date and effective, based on the latest knowledge. Additionally, protocols can be customized based on lessons learned, better adapting them to the specificities of certain types of projects or sectors, minimizing risks, and maximizing operational effectiveness.

Incorporating a degree of flexibility into project plans allows teams to quickly adapt based on lessons learned without the need for significant revisions. This agile approach facilitates the management of unforeseen events more effectively. Lessons learned from previous projects can provide valuable data for contingency planning, developing more robust plans that anticipate and mitigate potential problems before they occur.

Risk mitigation strategies can be continuously updated and refined using lessons learned as a knowledge base. This allows for improving risk response techniques, making the organization more resilient in the face of future challenges. Regular testing and scenario simulations based on lessons learned can help teams better prepare for crisis management, evaluating the effectiveness of risk mitigation strategies and identifying areas that need further improvement.

Ensuring that leaders and decision-makers are fully informed of lessons learned and their potential impact on strategic decisions is essential. This involvement ensures that high-level decisions are informed and guided by robust empirical analysis. Developing dashboards and analytical tools that present lessons learned in easily interpretable formats can help decision-makers quickly understand the implications of historical information and use it to guide critical decisions.

Actively integrating lessons learned into the decision-making process transforms this knowledge into concrete actions that can guide the success of future projects. This not only improves the quality of decisions made but also strengthens the culture of continuous learning and adaptation within the organization.

4.7 Knowledge Sharing and Culture

Creating a corporate culture that values and actively promotes knowledge sharing is essential for the continuous development and improvement of the organization. This aspect of project management not only increases the effectiveness of projects but also strengthens team cohesion and innovation.

Investing in knowledge management systems that facilitate access and sharing of information among employees is crucial. These platforms should allow teams to easily access lessons learned, project documents, and best practices. Utilizing modern collaboration tools, such as project management software that incorporates social functions and discussion forums, can help team members exchange ideas and solutions in real-time, increasing transparency and effective communication.

Organizing regular workshops focused on specific lessons learned from past projects is an effective way to share practical knowledge. These meetings can be led by team members who have directly managed the relevant aspects of the project, thus providing direct and practical context. Additionally, developing a continuous training program that regularly integrates new lessons learned ensures that all team members stay up-to-date on the latest techniques and practices and are trained to apply this knowledge effectively.

Implementing incentive systems to reward employees who actively contribute to knowledge sharing is another important step. This can include recognition, promotions, or other benefits that emphasize the importance of knowledge sharing. Leaders must act as active role models in knowledge sharing, demonstrating a personal commitment to learning from past experiences and sharing these lessons. This creates a multiplier effect that encourages all levels of the organization to do the same.

Regularly collecting feedback from participants on knowledge sharing platforms and workshops to assess their effectiveness and identify areas for improvement helps to continually refine knowledge sharing methods. Measuring the impact of knowledge sharing on project success provides concrete data on the effectiveness of these practices. Analyzing how the dissemination of lessons learned affects project outcomes can serve as further motivation to continue and expand knowledge sharing efforts.

Improving and integrating knowledge sharing and a culture of learning not only increases an organization's ability to manage projects more effectively but also creates a more informed, motivated, and cohesive work environment. This culture of continuous learning and active sharing of information is essential to maintaining a competitive edge and promoting ongoing innovation.

Chapter 5
General Management Principles in a Project Management Contest Adaptive Leadership

Michela Manini

5.1 Adaptive Leadership Model

Having considered the centrality of the Project Manager's role, I believe it is appropriate to contextualize it in the new way of being a leader both within a team and within the organization itself.

The new leadership model fosters every form of resource management (team, group, department… including Project management) to adopt adaptive behavior.

The origin of Adaptive leadership framework comes from Harvard University.

The new leadership model refers to two main characteristics:

- the identification of its origin in evolutionary biology
- the potential to acquire and develop new emerging skills.

We are stating that we are redesigning a leader's way of thinking and behaving.

At all organizational levels, the adaptive model supports the need for renewal which, however, often lacks shared parameters of judgment on which to base the change.

It therefore becomes necessary to support managers with objective and easily accessible tools to rethink and recreate those structures which, at various levels, regulate the exercise of leadership.

The discussed claim that leaders have a natural inclination can now be completely replaced by the possibility to train him by an educational/behavioral model; that is, the adoption of those tools necessary to interpret the life of a team and to intervene to support change where necessary.

M. Manini (✉)
Department of Innovative Technologies, SUPSI, Lugano, Switzerland
e-mail: michela.manini@supsi.ch

A. Bassi et al. (eds.), *General Management Principles for Project Management*, Management for Professionals, https://doi.org/10.1007/978-3-031-98592-8_5

As "educational" we mean a frame of constant learning based on a continuous and democratic comparison with and between different perspectives and at the same time anchored in the practice of observing the dynamics that regulate group life.

What has been expressed so far facilitates the much requested identity reconfiguration of the word "leadership" which is increasingly trending towards a facilitation of systemic change initiatives and less as a top-down action.

It can therefore be argued that in this organizational and adaptive context, even the leader (in this chapter we refer to the function of Project Manager) must consider that the approach of closeness to people can represent a sure element for the creation of a successful management model.

The current industrial revolution is dominated by a type of interdependence in which the behavior of each member of the organization or group, depends largely on his expectations regarding the intentions and behavior of others.

What are the significant challenges that the Project Manager must deal with within his function?

Certainly the first challenge is the search of ways to manage the team's internal conflict establishing a balance of well-being and satisfaction within the team.

How are these conflicts resolved especially if based on the interpretation of values that guide the team? we could say with a series of criteria from which the major one is the "authority".

Only authority is able to resolve conflicts based on the interpretation of the values that define a team. However, be careful not to confuse authority with the hierarchical principle.

The latter is in fact an efficient antidote when it comes to support routine objectives but which however encounters difficulties in achieving innovation objectives.

Authority is in fact the bearer of the relationship of trust, of the resource or of what is extremely necessary for a team/organization.

We have to pay close attention to the word "authority" as the Project Manager has now become a particular leader who has authority too.

What is meant by authority? Authority is a particular kind of relationship that one person, or a group of people, exercise to individuals.

This relationship It's basically about driving behaviors or the beliefs of others.

Authority is given up by individuals on the basis of the commitment that the leader shows towards the team; team members give authority to the Project Manager because they expect him to make his knowledge available.

The attention have to be addressed to the new adaptive leadership frame where authority plays a minor role to the advantage of a more open relationship with team members, facilitating the relationship and growth of individuals.

So a key factor we have to beware brings us back to the exercise of one's authority.

We must overcome the concept of authority to replace ourselves in a more modern and open leadership model that provides behavior closer to "coaching" by activating relational factors and declining a feeling of decision-making autonomy.

Decision-making autonomy necessarily passes through the approval of trust of the individuals and within the team.

So what can be the frame of leadership that leads to satisfying the need for trust? Here the Hungarian physicist Albert László Barabasi comes to our aid which shows how it is necessary to take into account the dynamics that impact the evolving process of the internet itself.

The most significant is that of the tendency towards clustering: the network is made up of strong ties and weak ties that intersect also and above all within a team.

The ability of a Project Manager is therefore to act as a **connector** between the member group, thus generating trust within the group.

Following to what mentioned above, we can say that Internet has enabled access to knowledge, but the ability to transform it for the growth of individuals must often be guided within the group with training in new learning models.

The latter are mainly based on the set up of collaborative networks inside and outside the team which act as catalysts of knowledge and innovative insights.

The leader authority is set up through his ability to create a team/group environment that facilitates the growth of knowledge within the individual and between team members, spreading collective well-being to support greater performance.

More: Barabasi Theory asserts that is crucial for a leader to maintain the ability to think differently.

Most breakthroughs and discoveries have not been defined by solving existing problems but by asking new questions and opening up new areas.

Thinking differently takes on a very significant meaning for the Project Manager as he takes on the responsibility of guiding people to train and acquire an "open mindset".

What behaviors has the Project Manager adopt to facilitate the creation of balanced teams, free of conflicts, and effective in achieving results?

There is not just one answer but rather a series of attributes that the Project Manager has to acquire.

The first of these is to become an "artist", becoming very close to the people in the team/s through the use, for example, of AI tools that allow him to collect the continuous sentiment of the group members. There are several tools combining Machine Learning and Emotional Intelligence to create better performing work environments that motivate people and ultimately improve performance.

But this is not enough.

Technology helps but it is necessary to know how to adopt a personal approach for each member of the group. The Project Manager must have a profound knowledge of the people who make up the team, not only in terms of skills, but also of individual aspirations and expectations.

To do this he must establish a continuous iteration in which he trains individuals to "open up" by creating a relationship of trust.

This individual well-being is necessarily spread out within the group, indirectly increasing performance capacity.

But what should we do to lead people to change a belief?

One of the most effective methods that the Project Manager can adopt is to ask questions, delving into the motivation of the belief.

Very often ideas or beliefs are based on idioms acquired through habit and not through logical understanding.

Asking questions in order to maintain this model of continuous interaction is a very challenging task as in carrying out today's activities where the attention always emerges on the project output/outcome to be achieved instead of the human relationship that is often forgotten.

What has just been specified is undoubtedly the most difficult practice for the Project Manager, but it is also the key of his success demonstrating that he is a good project leader.

Asking questions urges team members to make a cognitive effort by rethinking their beliefs and putting them (indirectly and without realizing it) into question.

Overcoming beliefs or ideas requires time and continuous dedication but leads to a transfer of trust necessary for the good climate of the group.

Let's not forget that thanks to trust, the team member establishes his own starring role which consolidates the "make sense" of being a valued part of the team.

We can therefore anticipate that the central role of the new adaptive leader is to grasp and enhance all the possible connections between people, groups, teams, institutions, visions and ideas within an organization, but also to create relationships and networks between an ever-increasing majority of "individuals" who share information, knowledge and skills.

The new leadership model that we can trace back to the Project Manager summarizes the adoption of the capacity of vision, communication, motivation, empowerment, and is able to free up unexpressed energies and resources in people, contributing to making the teams in which they operate more adaptive.

The exercise of leadership is therefore identified as a progressive and inclusive work that helps teams/groups to embrace and deal with the instability produced by the internal and external environment, through continuous adaptation.

We therefore underline that adaptive leadership becomes a function of the situation and the leader becomes an enabler of connections and disseminator of information and knowledge within the team.

In project management activities, it becomes essential for the leader to keep the members together, support the construction of knowledge communities, and must be responsible for the growth of the individuals whose development paths and projects and effective autonomy he supports.

Leader Project Manager is a process of relationships and influence.

It is a relationship that creates positive change, for oneself and for others, through motivation, sharing and co-responsibility in achieving a set goal (where clearly others do what they have to without constraints).

It is therefore a dynamic concept, which changes over time.

Asking questions in order to maintain this model of continuous interaction is a very challenging task as in carrying out today's activities where the attention always emerges on the project output/outcome to be achieved instead of the human relationship that is often forgotten.

Step back to what are the significant challenges that the Project Manager must deal within his function, we can assert that the second challenge is to find ways to avoid the risk of group-think which affects the majority of people who are part of a cohesive team/group.

Team members try to recover unanimity of thought by not considering alternatives. In group thinking, the consensus of the members is real and converges on a behavioral thought considered correct by all.

This kind of approach is convenient in the short term as it favors decision making while favoring a reduction in the exercise of critical thinking.

It is easy to understand that in the medium/long term this leads to a conformism devoid of creativity within the team.

Without creativity, therefore, the team does not innovate and does not progress.

It follows that while in the past creativity was referring only to one member of the team, today we must consider that individual creativity is no longer enough, but rather systemic creativity is needed (even within the team itself).

This means leveraging the function of the Project Manager so that he is able to evangelize the group through a cognitive effort to go beyond one's comfort zone and open up to a modern and sharing interaction.

In order to overcome the inflexibility referring to "group thinking", the recommended exercise is to reconsider the obvious through the method of "double loop learning" (agile thinking methodology) that requires a cognitive effort on the part of the Team members: "Why has it always been done in this way"? Is there a different and more current way to carry out the task?.

Project Manager has to foster the team members to rethink "why they have always acted in this way" leading them to a deep reflection on the assumptions.

This methodology leads to a group activity that forces each member to provide motivations (often linked to routines) introducing modification factors to the original root of the old behaviors…

A vital skill for exercising leadership is in fact helping those facing change to develop new confidence.

Very difficult task as it calls into question relationships, identity and tasks.

We can recap that the adaptive Leadership model helps individuals and organizations to adapt to challenging and changing environments and effectively respond to recurring problems.

This concept is especially crucial in project management.

In a project management context, adaptive leadership is the ability of a Project Manager to guide and lead his team in response to various changes, obstacles, and opportunities that arise throughout a project life cycle.

It involves not just managing tasks, but also managing people, their skills, and their reactions to change.

The Project Manager/leader has to consider three moments of behavior in his behavior:

Observe: since observation is highly subjective, the Project Manager must make the observation as objective as possible by abstracting himself from the group and distancing himself. This is an extremely difficult task and the help of a colleague may be required who helps the leader to bring an external and therefore more objective observation point. Attitudes and/or comments described without one's own interpretation must be reported.

Interpret: Most of the leader's interpretations are produced unconsciously and it normally takes little time before taking action without considering whether different interpretations exist. The adaptive leader must instead consider multiple interpretations; in this case technology comes to our aid with data driven systems that allow and propose sharing and prediction models that can facilitate a more accurate and inclusive interpretation. In very complex projects, it is recommended to set up small sharing teams.

Action: once an interpretation of a problem and once the solution has been identified, the leader can share it, supporting the team's common objective.

Adaptive leaders acknowledge that they do not have all the answers, and they are open to learning from their team.

They encourage a culture of learning and innovation, where team members feel safe to take risks, make mistakes, and learn from them.

The open minded approach helps the team to adapt quickly to changes, which is crucial in today's rapidly changing business environment.

An adaptive leader in a project management role is mainly focused both on accomplishing the project and is concerned about the impact of the project on the organization and its people too.

As a matter of fact a project is not just a set of tasks to be completed, but also a change process that affects people and systems in the whole organization.

In this way Project Managers are ready to make tough decisions and take responsibility for them.

Moreover, Project Managers as adaptive leaders play a significant role in stakeholder management.

They are aware of the interests and influences of different stakeholders and employ this understanding to lead the project through various challenges and roadblocks.

The relevant and critical activity they carry out is managing expectations and aligning the project goals with the strategic objectives of the organization.

Adaptive project leadership also involves managing the project's complexity.

Complex projects entail high uncertainty and risk, and they require a flexible and adaptive approach.

The adaptive leader recognizes the complexity and uncertainty inherent in the project employing a flexible approach to manage it.

Project Managers are not strictly devoted to the plan, quite the opposite they are ready to change the plan when necessary.

Adaptive leadership is about leading change. In a project context, this means leading the project team and other stakeholders through the change process.

In light of the above that said, Project Manager role requires excellent communication skills, as the leader needs to explain the need for change, the benefits of change, and the impact of change on different stakeholders.

Project leaders also need to listen to the concerns and fears of the stakeholders and address them effectively.

Adaptive leadership is not just about adapting to changes, but also about creating changes.

Project Manager as an adaptive leader is a change agent who initiates and drives changes in the project and the organization.

They are not afraid of challenging the status quo and are ready to take risks to achieve the project goals.

Moreover, we have to consider that technology grows much faster than the individual learning ability and resulting set action/project plans.

Technology innovation creates a gap between strategy and action that has a great impact on performance project and is difficult to resolve. Once again Project Managers are invited to address this critical issue through their competences and experiences, proving their own ability of supporting the team in bridging this gap that creates inefficiency.

In conclusion, adaptive leadership in project management is about leading the project team and other stakeholders through the complexities and uncertainties of the project, managing the change process, and creating a culture of learning and innovation.

The Project Manager as an adaptive leader plays a crucial role in the success of the project and the growth of the organization.

References

2021, McKinsey & Company, Brassey, J., De Smet, A., Kothari, A., Lavoie, J., Mugayar-Baldocchi, M., & Zelley, S. *Future proof: "Solving the adaptability paradox for the long term".*

2024, McKinsey & Company, Brassey, J., De Smet, A., Maor, D., & Rabipour, S. *Developing a resilient adoptable workforce for an uncertain future.*

2011, University of Michigan, DeRue, S. *Adaptive leadership theory: Leading and following as a complex adaptive process.*

2025, Harvard Business Review. Retrieved from https://hbr.org/topic/subject/adaptive-leadership

2009, Ingram publisher, Heifetz, R. *The practice of adaptive leadership: Tool and tactics for changing your organization and the world.*

2025, Franco Angeli, Heifetz, R., Linsky, M., & Grashow, A. *La pratica della leadership adattiva.*

2023, Harvard Business Review; Ibarra, H., Hildebrand, C. A., & Vinck, S. *The leadership odyssey.*

2024, Franco Angeli, Manini, M., Mistretta, M., & Serra, S. *L'Organizzazione adattiva.*

2025, McKinsey & Company, West, A., Kelly, G., Zucker, J., Siegel, K., Greco, L., Birshan, M., Doherty, R., & Lehmann, S. *Achieving growth: Putting leadership mindsets and behaviors into action.*

Chapter 6
Evolving Organizational Mechanics: Harmonizing Event-Driven and Process-Centric Strategies for Resilience and Sustainability

Massimo Mistretta

In today's complex and uncertain business environment, project managers face the dual challenge of maintaining flexibility while ensuring consistent progress toward project goals. Successfully balancing event-driven agility with process-centric efficiency is key to achieving resilience and sustainability in project outcomes.

By integrating the strengths of both approaches, project managers can quickly adapt to unexpected changes—such as shifting client requirements or market disruptions—while steadily improving project processes. The OASIS (Open, Autonomous, Symbiotic, Intelligent, Sustainable) model for adaptive organizations, with its emphasis on openness, autonomy, symbiosis, intelligence, and sustainability, offers project managers a robust framework to navigate these challenges.

This balanced approach not only enhances a project's adaptability and innovation potential but also ensures that project teams are aligned with long-term organizational success. Case studies like Zara's agile supply chain and GE's digital transformation demonstrate how harmonizing these strategies can lead to more effective project execution, better stakeholder engagement, and sustained competitive advantage.

In an increasingly complex and dynamic business landscape, organizations must navigate the interplay between stochastic events and deterministic processes to achieve resilience and sustainability. This chapter explores the necessity for organizations to harmonize event-driven and process-centric strategies, drawing insights from ecosystem dynamics and the OASIS model for adaptive organizations. We argue that by embracing a holistic approach that leverages the strengths of both event-driven and process-centric paradigms, organizations can enhance their agility, adaptability, and long-term success. The OASIS model provides a framework for understanding how organizations can evolve to become more resilient and

M. Mistretta (✉)
Exentriq Ltd., London, UK
e-mail: massimo@exentri.com

A. Bassi et al. (eds.), *General Management Principles for Project Management*, Management for Professionals, https://doi.org/10.1007/978-3-031-98592-8_6

sustainable in the face of uncertainty. We conclude by discussing the implications of this harmonized approach for organizational design, technology adoption, and leadership in the era of digital transformation.

6.1 Introduction

The rapid pace of technological change and the increasing complexity of global markets have compelled organizations to reevaluate their traditional approaches to management and decision-making. The mechanistic view of organizations as predictable and controllable entities is giving way to a more organic, adaptive perspective that acknowledges the inherent uncertainty and dynamism of the business environment (Jewczyn, 2010). This shift is driven by the recognition that organizations are embedded within larger ecosystems of interconnected actors, processes, and events.

To thrive in this new reality, organizations must evolve their mechanics—the underlying structures, processes, and behaviors that shape their operations and outcomes. Central to this evolution is the need to harmonize event-driven and process-centric strategies. Event-driven approaches focus on responding to discrete, isolated incidents, while process-centric strategies prioritize the design and management of end-to-end processes that create value for stakeholders (Benincasa, 2020). We argue that organizations must leverage the strengths of both approaches to achieve resilience and sustainability in the face of uncertainty.

The OASIS model provides a framework for understanding how organizations can evolve to become more adaptive and sustainable. The model emphasizes five key dimensions—openness, autonomy, symbiosis, intelligence, and sustainability, that are essential for organizations to navigate the challenges and opportunities of the digital age. By embracing these dimensions, organizations can develop the capabilities needed to sense and respond to changes in their environment, foster collaboration and innovation, and create long-term value for all stakeholders.

This article explores the importance of harmonizing event-driven and process-centric strategies, drawing on insights from ecosystem dynamics and the OASIS model. We begin by examining the limitations of traditional mechanistic approaches and the need for a new paradigm that recognizes the stochastic nature of events and the importance of deterministic processes. We then delve into the five dimensions of the OASIS model, discussing how each contributes to organizational adaptability and resilience. Finally, we present case studies and practical recommendations for organizations seeking to evolve their mechanics in the era of digital transformation.

The Interplay of Stochastic Events and Deterministic Processes: The traditional mechanistic view of organizations, rooted in Newtonian physics and Taylorism, has long dominated management theory and practice. This perspective treats organizations as machines, composed of interchangeable parts that can be optimized for efficiency and predictability. Events are seen as discrete, isolated incidents that can be anticipated and controlled through careful planning and execution. Success is measured by the organization's ability to minimize deviations from the plan and maximize short-term outcomes.

However, the mechanistic approach has several limitations that render it ill-suited for the challenges of the modern business environment. First, it assumes that events are independent and can be predicted with reasonable accuracy. In reality, events are interconnected and influenced by a complex web of factors, many of which are beyond the organization's control. Attempting to predict and control every possible scenario is not only impractical but also likely to lead to rigidity and missed opportunities.

Second, the mechanistic approach prioritizes efficiency over adaptability. By focusing on optimizing existing processes and structures, organizations may become less capable of responding to changing circumstances or pursuing new opportunities. In a rapidly evolving business landscape, the ability to adapt and respond quickly to environmental change is critical for long-term success.

Third, the mechanistic view tends to treat organizations as closed systems, ignoring the complex interactions between the organization and its environment. In reality, organizations are embedded within larger ecosystems of customers, suppliers, competitors, regulators, and other stakeholders. The actions and decisions of these actors can have significant impacts on the organization's performance and survival.

To address these limitations, organizations must recognize the interplay between stochastic events and deterministic processes. Stochastic events are those that are, unpredictable, potentially random and often the result of complex interactions between multiple factors. These events can have significant, far-reaching consequences for the organization and its ecosystem. On the other hand, deterministic processes are those that are predictable, repeatable, and driven by known cause-and-effect relationships mostly derived by a high degree of organizational structure and order.

Organizations must develop the ability to sense and respond to stochastic events while simultaneously designing and managing deterministic processes (Lengnick-Hall et al., 2019). This requires a shift from a purely event-driven or process-centric approach to a more balanced, harmonized strategy that leverages the strengths of both paradigms.

6.2 Harmonizing Event-Driven and Process-Centric Strategies

To achieve resilience and sustainability in the face of uncertainty, organizations must harmonize event-driven and process-centric strategies.

Event-driven approaches enable organizations to quickly detect and respond to unexpected changes in their environment, such as shifts in customer preferences, technological disruptions, or regulatory changes (Sunley, 2024). By empowering frontline employees to make decisions and take actions based on real-time data and insights, event-driven organizations can adapt to new circumstances and capitalize on emerging opportunities.

However, a purely event-driven approach can lead to a fragmented, reactive mode of operation that lacks coherence and long-term direction. To counter this, organizations must also embrace process-centric strategies that prioritize the design and management of end-to-end processes that create value for stakeholders.

Process-centric approaches offer organizations a powerful methodology to optimize the flow of information, materials, and resources across their ecosystem by encoding processes in real-time, one by one. This incremental approach to process management enables organizations to identify inefficiencies, reduce waste, improve quality, and enhance customer satisfaction gradually, without causing significant disruptions to their operations.

The core principle behind process-centric strategies is the idea that processes should be encoded and optimized in real-time, as they occur. Rather than attempting to map and redesign the entire value chain at once, organizations focus on individual processes, analyzing them in detail and making targeted improvements. This approach allows organizations to address the most critical issues first, while also ensuring that the changes are manageable and well-integrated into the existing system.

By encoding processes one by one, organizations can gain a deeper understanding of the specific challenges and opportunities associated with each process step. This granular level of insight enables them to identify areas where resources are being underutilized, where quality issues are occurring, or where customer needs are not being met effectively (Liker, 2004). Armed with this knowledge, organizations can then develop targeted solutions that address the root causes of these problems, rather than merely treating the symptoms.

The real-time nature of process encoding also enables organizations to be more responsive to changing conditions. As new data and insights emerge, organizations can quickly adjust their processes to optimize performance and maintain alignment with strategic goals. This agility is particularly important in today's fast-paced and unpredictable business environment, where customer preferences, market trends, and competitive landscapes can shift rapidly.

To support real-time process encoding, organizations must invest in the right tools and capabilities. This includes technologies such as collaboration and communication systems, robotic and intelligent process automation as well as process mining, which enables organizations to automatically discover, monitor, and improve processes based on recorded data traces. Organizational efforts should also include the development of cross-functional teams and collaborative platforms that enable stakeholders from different parts of the organization including external resources to contribute their expertise and insights to the process improvement effort in the most frictionless fashion.

Another key aspect of real-time process encoding is the emphasis on continuous improvement. Rather than viewing process optimization as a one-time event, organizations must cultivate a culture of ongoing learning, adaptation and incremental evolution. This requires establishing feedback loops that allow organizations to continuously monitor process performance, identify areas for improvement, and implement changes in a controlled and iterative manner.

Ultimately, the success of process-centric approaches depends on the ability of organizations to strike the right balance between structure and flexibility. While the encoding of processes provides a necessary framework for optimization, it must also allow for adaptability and innovation. By finding this balance and committing to real-time, incremental process improvement, organizations can unlock new levels of efficiency, quality, and customer value, enabling them to thrive in the long term, in an increasingly complex and dynamic business landscape.

By harmonizing event-driven and process-centric strategies, organizations can achieve a balance between agility and efficiency, adaptation and optimization. This requires a holistic, systems-thinking approach that recognizes the interdependencies between events, processes, and stakeholders. Organizations must develop the capabilities to continuously sense and interpret signals from their environment, translate these insights into process improvements, and rapidly implement changes across their networks.

Several key principles underpin a harmonized approach to event-driven and process-centric strategies:

- Continuous learning and adaptation:

- Organizations must foster a culture of continuous learning and adaptation, where employees are encouraged to experiment, take risks, and learn from failures. This requires the development of robust feedback loops that enable the organization to rapidly detect and respond to changes in its environment, as well as to incorporate new insights into its processes and strategies.
- Decentralized decision-making:
- Organizations must empower frontline employees to make decisions and take actions based on their local knowledge and expertise. This requires a shift from a command-and-control model to a more decentralized, networked structure that enables rapid information sharing and collaboration across the organization.
- Data-driven insights:
- Organizations must leverage data and analytics to gain real-time insights into their operations, customers, and ecosystem. This requires the development of advanced data collection, storage, and analysis capabilities, as well as the integration of data-driven insights into decision-making processes at all levels of the organization.
- Cross-functional collaboration:
- Organizations must foster cross-functional collaboration and break down silos between departments and teams. This requires the development of shared goals, metrics, and incentives, not necessarily monetary, that encourage employees to work together towards common objectives, as well as the use of digital platforms and tools that enable seamless communication and information sharing.
- Ecosystem perspective:

- Organizations must cultivate a new perspective over the real perimeter and boundaries of the organization by building effective partnerships with external stakeholders, such as customers, suppliers, and competitors, to co-create value, drive innovation and successfully navigate the waves of change. This requires a shift from a transactional to a collaborative mindset, where organizations view their ecosystem partners as an integral part of the organization and essential contributors to their long-term success.

6.3 The OASIS Model for Adaptive Organizations

The OASIS model provides a framework for understanding how organizations can evolve to become more adaptive and sustainable in the face of uncertainty and complexity. The model identifies five key dimensions that are essential for organizational resilience and performance: openness, autonomy, symbiosis, intelligence, and sustainability (Manini et al., 2024).

- Openness:
- Openness refers to the ability of an organization to exchange information, resources, and ideas within its environment. This requires a culture of transparency, collaboration, and trust, as well as the use of digital technologies to enable seamless communication and data sharing. Open organizations are better able to sense and respond to changes in their ecosystem, as well as to leverage external expertise and resources to drive innovation and growth by leveraging their ability to interconnect and maintain healthy exchanges and flows between entities part of the network.
- Autonomy:
- Autonomy refers to the ability of individuals and teams within an organization to make decisions and take actions independently and purposefully, based on their local knowledge and expertise. This requires a decentralized approach to decision-making, where power is distributed across the organization rather than concentrated at the top. Modern autonomous organizations are more agile and responsive, as they can quickly adapt to changing circumstances without waiting for approval from higher-ups and in many cases the end to end process is fully automated including more cognitive tasks, once the exclusive domain of humans.
- Symbiosis:
- Symbiosis refers to the mutually beneficial relationships and interactions among different types of entities within an ecosystem. In the context of organizations, this is mostly focused on fostering collaboration and synergy between humans and machines to create shared value and pursue new opportunities. Symbiotic organizations are able to leverage the collective interactions and take advantage of the beneficial patterns emerging through the interaction of both human employees and automated systems while solving complex problems.
- Intelligence:

- Intelligence refers to the ability of an organization to effectively integrate individual, collective, and artificial intelligence to acquire, process, and apply knowledge. This integration is crucial for modern organizations to make informed decisions, solve complex problems, and adapt to changing circumstances, in fact, intelligent organizations are able to harness the collective wisdom of their human employees, augmented by the computational power combined with artificial intelligence algorithms, to optimize their processes, strategies, and decision-making abilities in real-time
- Sustainability:
- Within the OASIS framework sustainability takes a broader perspective trying to go beyond carbon footprint. From an ecosystem dynamics perspective, sustainability refers to the ability of a system to maintain its long-term viability by balancing the degree of structure and order with the degree of freedom and redundancy. This requires a delicate equilibrium between efficiency and resilience, where the system retains enough organization to function effectively while maintaining sufficient flexibility to adapt to changes (Ulanowicz, 1997). Sustainable systems are able to persist and thrive by optimizing this trade-off between constraint and adaptability, contributing to the overall stability and health of the larger ecosystem in which they exist. This balance allows for both efficient resource utilization and the capacity to respond to novel disturbances or opportunities.

6.4 Case Studies and Practical Implications

To illustrate the practical application of harmonizing event-driven and process-centric strategies, we present two brief case studies.

6.4.1 Zara's Agile Supply Chain

Zara, a leading fast-fashion retailer, has successfully harmonized event-driven and process-centric strategies to achieve agility and efficiency in its supply chain. Zara's event-driven approach enables it to quickly detect and respond to changes in customer preferences and market trends (Ferdows et al., 2004). By empowering store managers to make real-time decisions about product assortment and inventory levels, Zara can rapidly adapt its offerings to meet local demand.

Under the given definition, Zara employs a process-centric approach to optimize its end-to-end supply chain, from design to production to distribution. By closely integrating its design, manufacturing, and logistics processes, Zara can quickly translate customer insights into new products and deliver them to stores governing the end to end process (Ferdows et al., 2004). This process-centric approach enables

Zara to maximize the bottom line results without aiming or implementing "maximum efficiency" logics but while retaining flexibility and improving responsiveness to changing market conditions is still able to minimize waste, reduce lead time and continuously and purposefully optimize overall operations.

Zara's success in harmonizing event-driven and process-centric strategies is rooted in its adherence to the principles outlined so far. Its culture of openness enables free flow of information and resources across the supply chain, fostering close relationships with suppliers, customers, designers, and store managers. Zara's autonomous structure allows decentralized decision-making, empowering local units to operate with purpose and adapt quickly to market changes. The company has created a symbiotic ecosystem that synergizes human creativity with machine efficiency, leveraging fast information flow to continuously learn and evolve its processes. This approach enables Zara to co-create value and drive innovation while maintaining sustainability through a careful balance of structured systems and flexible operations. By optimizing the trade-off between order and resilience.

6.4.2 General Electric's Digital Transformation

General Electric (GE), the well known multinational conglomerate, has embarked on a digital transformation journey in order to compete with new entrants and focused on strategies that had impact across its diverse business units. GE's event-driven approach leverages the Internet of Things (IoT) and advanced analytics to monitor and optimize the performance of its industrial assets in real-time (Iansiti & Lakhani, 2014). By collecting and analyzing data from sensors embedded in its products, GE can detect and predict maintenance needs, reduce downtime, and improve operational efficiency.

Simultaneously, GE has adopted a process-centric approach to streamline and standardize its business processes across its global operations. By developing, implementing and rolling out a new set of digital platforms and tools, GE has been able to break down silos between business units, improve collaboration and knowledge sharing, and drive enterprise-wide business model transformation. This process-centric approach has enabled GE to accelerate innovation by gradually shifting to new digital capabilities (Iansiti & Lakhani, 2014).

By fostering openness through "digital ubiquity" across all stakeholders, GE has created an ecosystem that enables free flow of information, leading to evolutionary digital solutions and business models. GE has developed a symbiotic relationship between human expertise and machine capabilities both mechanical and software, specifically investing in software capabilities mostly absent in previous business models (Iansiti & Lakhani, 2014). The integration of human and machine intelligence is a cornerstone of GE's digital transformation. By leveraging advanced analytics, artificial intelligence, and the collective expertise of its workforce, GE has enhanced its ability to process complex data, make informed decisions, and solve multifaceted and extremely complex problems.

6.5 Practical Insights for Organizations

These case studies presented here highlight several practical implications for organizations seeking to harmonize event-driven and process-centric strategies:

- Promote Openness and Collaborative Practices:
- Organizations should dismantle barriers and promote a culture of transparency, trust, and collaboration among both internal teams and external stakeholders. This involves adopting digital tools and platforms that facilitate open communication and easy information sharing, as well as establishing shared objectives and incentives that encourage teamwork as well as collective innovation.
- Empower Autonomous Decision-Making:
- To achieve agility and responsiveness, organizations must decentralize decision-making authority, enabling frontline employees to act based on their specific expertise and local insights. This requires clear guidelines and strategic guard-rails that align with the organization's broader objectives, along with access to real-time data and analytics to support informed and timely decisions.
- Utilize Data and Analytics Effectively:
- Organizations should prioritize investment in advanced data systems to generate actionable, real-time insights about their operations, customers, and broader ecosystem. This includes implementing strong data governance practices and ensuring that data-driven insights are seamlessly integrated into decision-making processes across all levels of the organization.
- Cultivate Symbiotic Relationships:
- It is essential for organizations to build and nurture mutually beneficial relationships with external stakeholders such as customers, suppliers, and partners. This requires shifting from a transactional approach to one that emphasizes collaboration, recognizing that long-term success is achieved through co-creating value and driving innovation together with these partners.
- Commit to Sustainability and Long-Term Effects:
- Organizations must balance efficiency with resilience to ensure long-term viability. This involves maintaining sufficient diversity and redundancy in processes and resources, rather than over-optimizing for short-term efficiency. Sustainability metrics should measure both current performance and the system's capacity to adapt to disturbances. The goal is to operate within a "window of vitality" where the organization is neither too rigid (over-connected and brittle) nor too chaotic (under-connected and ineffective). This approach recognizes that some apparent inefficiencies or redundancies may be crucial for long-term survival and adaptability in the face of unexpected challenges or changes in the environment.

6.6 Conclusion

In an increasingly complex and dynamic business environment, organizations must harmonize event-driven and process-centric strategies to achieve resilience and sustainability. By leveraging the strengths of both approaches, organizations can enhance their agility, adaptability, and long-term success in the face of uncertainty and change.

The OASIS model provides a comprehensive framework for understanding how organizations can evolve to become more adaptive and sustainable. By embracing openness, autonomy, symbiosis, intelligence, and sustainability, organizations can develop the capabilities needed to sense and respond to changes in their environment, foster collaboration and innovation, and create long-term value for all stakeholders.

As the pace of technological change continues to accelerate, the ability to harmonize event-driven and process-centric strategies will become increasingly critical for organizations seeking to thrive in the digital age. This requires a fundamental shift in mindset and culture, as well as the adoption of new technologies and practices that enable real-time sensing, learning, and adaptation.

Ultimately, the organizations that will succeed in the future are those that can effectively balance the need for agility and efficiency, short-term responsiveness and long-term value creation. By embracing the principles and practices of harmonized event-driven and process-centric strategies, organizations can position themselves for success in an increasingly complex and uncertain world.

References

Benincasa, S. (2020). *Evolutionary behavioral economics: Essays on adaptive rationality in complex environments*. Doctoral dissertation, University of Trento.

Ferdows, K., Lewis, M. A., & Machuca, J. A. D. (2004). Rapid-fire fulfillment. *Harvard Business Review, 82*(11), 104–110.

Iansiti, M., & Lakhani, K. R. (2014). Digital ubiquity: How connections, sensors, and data are revolutionizing business. *Harvard Business Review, 92*(11), 90–99.

Jewczyn, N. (2010). Assessing mechanistic and organic organizational structures: Measuring organizational uncertainty and determining an organization's proper structure. *Journal of Business Management and Entrepreneurship, 1*(6), 1–12.

Lengnick-Hall, C. A., Beck, T. E., & Lengnick-Hall, M. L. (2019). Organizational resilience: A capability-based conceptualization. *Business Research, 12*, 215–230.

Liker, J. K. (2004). *The Toyota way: 14 management principles from the world's greatest manufacturer*. McGraw-Hill.

Manini, M., Mistretta, M., & Serra, S. (2024). *Organizzazione Adattiva: L'approccio evolutivo per creare organizzazioni sostenibili*. Franco Angeli.

Sunley, M. (2024). Event-driven architecture enables a business to become more aware of everything that's happening, as it's happening. *IBM Blog*. Retrieved from https://www.ibm.com/blog/event-driven-architecture-enables-a-business-to-become-more-aware-of-everything-thats-happening-as-its-happening/

Ulanowicz, R. E. (1997). *Ecology, the ascendent perspective*. Columbia University Press.

Chapter 7
The Stakeholder Satisfaction

Massimo Pirozzi

Stakeholders, who are they? A stakeholder is a person, or a group of persons, or an organization, who has some kind of interest in, and/or may influence, or may be/perceive to be influenced by, and/or can bring a value—which could be either positive or negative—to the project, the program, the portfolio and/or the organization. Stakeholders are central in all projects and operations, because they are both the doers and the beneficiaries of each project, and while, on the one side, the stakeholder work is basic for project implementation, on the other side, the stakeholder satisfaction is directly related to the project value and, therefore, is the main project success factor. Achieving stakeholder satisfaction requires a strategic approach that includes understanding stakeholder needs and expectations, engaging in meaningful dialogue, and implementing effective practices, while, from the practical point of view, specific measures and data analysis and management are required. Despite the challenges, organizations that prioritize stakeholder satisfaction are well positioned for sustainable growth and long-term success, and, then, stakeholder satisfaction may be considered a cornerstone of organizational success and a critical driver of value creation in the modern business landscape.

7.1 Stakeholders, Who Are They?

The term "**stakeholder**" encompasses a rich and diverse array of meanings and historical contexts, reflecting a complex concept that has evolved significantly over time. Originally, in the early eighteenth century, a stakeholder was someone entrusted with the stakes of bettors, managing the interests and payments in a game or race. This initial definition centered on being a holder of interests—a theme that

M. Pirozzi (✉)
Istituto Italiano di Project Management (ISIPM), Roma, Italy

A. Bassi et al. (eds.), *General Management Principles for Project Management*, Management for Professionals, https://doi.org/10.1007/978-3-031-98592-8_7

persists in contemporary interpretations, where having a stake equates to having an interest in an outcome or entity.

The modern understanding of stakeholders, as outlined by Freeman (1984), emphasizes groups or individuals whose support is essential for an organization's existence. They are not just individuals but collective entities whose contributions are foundational to an organization's functioning and success. This concept underscores the idea that stakeholders are not merely passive entities but active participants whose interactions shape organizational behavior and outcomes.

The definition expanded further in project management literature (PMI, 1987), where stakeholders were identified as participants in projects, reflecting a broader engagement beyond organizational boundaries. Freeman (1994) expanded on this, highlighting stakeholders as participants in the joint value creation process within organizations. This emphasis on value creation underscores stakeholders' pivotal role in shaping outcomes and adding measurable value, which can be positive, neutral, or negative.

The evolution of stakeholder theory coincided with a broader shift in perspective toward organizations as complex systems embedded within society. This shift led to the development of stakeholder theory, advocating for extending the benefits of enterprise beyond shareholders to various stakeholders and promoting ethical managerial behavior. This ethical dimension underscores stakeholders' responsibilities toward organizations and societies, reflecting a broader societal context beyond mere financial interests.

The connection between "**stake**" and "**risk**" is also noteworthy. The term "at stake" implies being at risk, highlighting stakeholders' willingness to take risks to achieve their objectives. Risk, therefore, becomes an inherent aspect of stakeholder engagement across disciplines, including project management and quality management.

In summary, the concept of stakeholders encapsulates a multifaceted set of relationships and responsibilities within and beyond organizations. From its historical origins managing bets to its modern interpretation involving essential support for organizational success, stakeholders embody active participants whose interactions and contributions shape organizational objectives and outcomes. The evolution of stakeholder theory has emphasized the ethical dimension of stakeholder engagement, promoting a broader societal perspective that extends beyond financial interests. Ultimately, stakeholders represent a diverse and interconnected network of individuals and groups whose involvement is fundamental to organizational functioning and value creation.

Each organization, as well as each operation, project, program and/or portfolio—indeed, each organization is comparable to a portfolio—is characterized by a large variety and numerosity of stakeholders (Fig. 7.1), who have diverse requirements and expectations, who interact each other in different ways, and whose behavior may be (also dynamically!) positive, negative or neutral.

Since stakeholders are numerous, are different, and have different needs and expectations, their identification has necessarily to be analytical: in fact, on one hand, their centrality require a deep attention, and, on other hand, all stakeholders

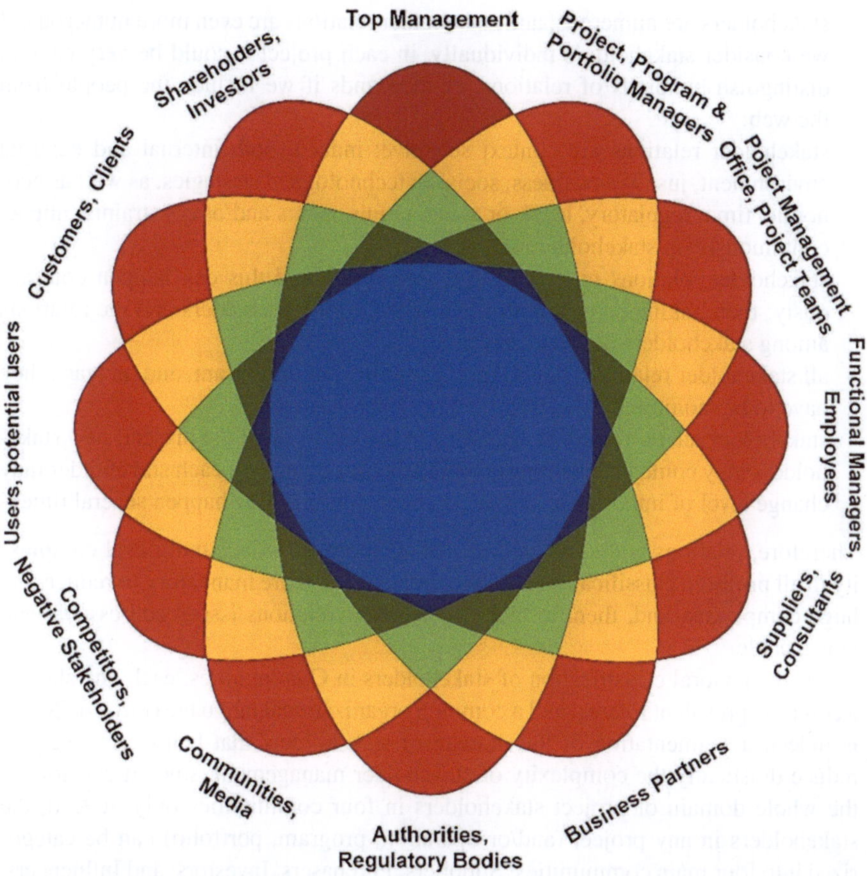

Fig. 7.1 An example of a stakeholders rose

are important for targeting project success, while, in any case, forgetting a stakeholder who could be key would be an unacceptable risk.

On the other side, project stakeholder domain is characterized by a multilevel complexity (Pirozzi, 2019):

- stakeholders are persons, or groups of persons, and we can assume that persons are the most complex systems that exist in the world;
- stakeholders are diverse, and they are diverse from different perspectives: project stakeholders, in fact, may have diverse interests and/or influence, may participate to and/or support diversely the project, they may add diverse value (either positive, or null, or negative), they may belong to diverse organizations and/or communities, and, since each organization is generally characterized also by a common business and/or social language, they may even speak or understand different organizational languages;

- stakeholders are numerous, and stakeholder relations are even more numerous: if we consider stakeholders individually, in each project it could be very easy to distinguish hundreds of relations, or thousands if we include the people from the web;
- stakeholder relations are context sensitive: indeed, both internal and external environment, just like business, social or technological strategies, as well as economic, time, regulatory, legal, or social requirements and/or constraints, impact continuously on stakeholder relations;
- stakeholder relations may influence each other, and this can happen continuously: then, taking care of both the relation with stakeholders and the relations among stakeholders becomes essential;
- all stakeholder relations, due to their centrality, are important, and, at least, they have to be monitored;
- stakeholder relations may be evolutive in the life cycle of the project: new stakeholders may come in, existing stakeholders may come out, each stakeholder may change level of importance and/or behavior, and this may happen several times.

Therefore, relations with, and among, stakeholders, introduce multilevel complexity in all projects: classification models of stakeholders are mandatory to reduce that huge complexity, and, then, to make stakeholder relations issues addressable and manageable.

The behavioral classification of stakeholders in Communities, each one sharing a common prevalent interest and a common organizational language (Pirozzi, 2017), is indeed a segmentation of the domain of stakeholders that helps effectively to reduce drastically the complexity of stakeholder management, since it categorizes the whole domain of project stakeholders in four communities only. Indeed, the stakeholders in any project (and/or operation, program, portfolio) can be categorized into four main communities: Suppliers, Purchasers, Investors, and Influencers. Each community exhibits a distinct set of interests, organizational language, and behavior related to the project.

- **Suppliers**. This community, which includes project managers, project teams, management offices, suppliers, and business partners, is primarily interested in realizing the project within optimal combinations of time, cost, and quality. Their organizational language revolves around project management discipline, and their main goal is to complete the project within predefined constraints.
- **Purchasers**. The Purchasers, typically represented by customers and end-users, prioritize the quality of the project deliverables. They are less concerned with project completion itself but rather focus on obtaining the highest possible quality from the project. Contractual obligations bind them to agreed costs and timelines. Their language is rooted in business and/or social terms, viewing the project as a means to achieve their broader business and/or social goals.
- **Investors**. Investors, encompassing sponsors, project governance, shareholders, top management, and external funders, are primarily interested in project profitability. They aim to minimize costs, fulfill income contracts, and potentially generate additional revenues over time. Quality is viewed within the context of

business prospects and financial returns. Their language is driven by business and economic considerations.

- **Influencers**. This community includes authorities (e.g., public administrations), media, local communities, lobbies, trade unions, and associations. Influencers may not be directly involved in contracting but play critical roles in shaping project outcomes. Their interests lie in participating in or influencing the project to align with broader societal or organizational goals. Influencers use a variety of languages, including media and natural language, sometimes incorporating business and economic terms as well.

In summary, stakeholders in projects and organizations encompass diverse groups with distinct interests and languages. Suppliers focus on project completion within constraints, Purchasers prioritize project quality, Investors seek profitability, and Influencers aim to participate or influence projects for broader purposes. Understanding and effectively engaging with these stakeholder communities are essential for recognizing and satisfying properly their needs and their expectations, and ultimately, to achieve both project success and alignment with broader organizational or societal goals.

7.2 The Stakeholder Perspective and the Process of Value Delivery

Due to the intrinsic relationship between stakeholder interactions and value creation across different phases of project lifecycles, the genesis and exchange of all forms of value are inherently enabled and shaped by stakeholder relationships. Definitively, effective stakeholder relations are not merely a complex management challenge but serve as the primary catalyst for value generation and exchange within project environments.

The symbiotic relationship between stakeholder relations and value dynamics can be encapsulated in three fundamental principles:

- Stakeholder relations are inherently valuable and constitute the foundational capital that underpins projects. Indeed, each contract that is signed by diverse parties represents a valuable effect of a successful relation, while the absence of robust stakeholder relations precludes the very inception of projects.
- Stakeholder relations are instrumental in generating value throughout project lifecycles. In fact, the complex interplay of material and immaterial exchanges among stakeholders drives the creation of project value.
- Stakeholder relations serve as the conduit for value exchange among diverse stakeholder communities. Effective stakeholder interactions are then pivotal for translating project value into delivered value that aligns with strategic objectives.

Project outcomes are a direct reflection of stakeholder relationships throughout project lifecycles. In fact, the symbiotic interplay among stakeholders shapes investment value, drives project value creation, and facilitates the exchange of value across stakeholder communities, and this holistic perspective underscores the centrality of stakeholder relations in realizing project objectives and delivering tangible outcomes.

In general, we may consider the process of value generation and delivery as a multiphase one, which starts with the definition of the strategy and of the relevant goals, and, then, proceeds sequentially with the evaluation and the assessment of opportunities and threats, with the development of requirements and business cases, with the prioritization of portfolios and the definition of programs and projects, with the implementation of projects, with the accomplishment of deliverables, outputs/results, and outcomes, and, finally, with the realization of benefits that, in turn, iteratively contributes to strategy definition, and so on (Pirozzi, 2021).

Going into a deeper detail, the definition of the strategy and of the goals may be realized via strategic planning and a strategic objectives definition, the evaluation and the assessment of opportunities and threats may require feasibility evaluations too, the development of requirements and business cases may include business and operational planning, the definition of scope, technical requirements, and Statement Of Work, the issue of a Request for Bid and the correspondent release of a technical/economic proposal, up to the signature of a contact (or similar) complete of its annexes, which states project definition. In project lifecycle, we will include—of course if we apply project management discipline—the verification of scope, constraints, stakeholder requirements and expectations, a structured, defined, planned and controlled approach, an effective stakeholder relationships management, up to arrive to the issue of deliverables. In the lifecycle of the product and/or the service that have been realized and/or setup by the project, deliverables will be integrated in results, performances will be measured to determine the outcomes, and these achievements will state whether original strategic goals have been met and expected benefits have been generated. Definitively, projects are operational means to achieve strategic goals via the creation and the delivery of value.

However, the process of value creation is not linear, but complex, and diverse types of value interact and integrate each other to achieve the outcomes.

Investment value, intrinsic to project initiation, evolves throughout project lifecycles, transitioning from capital investments into operational and management (O&M) investments as projects reach completion, and this evolution underscores the critical role of stakeholders in shaping and sustaining investment value over time. Similarly, project value is not solely derived from project teams' efforts but is a complex outcome influenced by diverse stakeholders interacting throughout project lifecycles. Indeed, the prevailing notion that project value is linearly derived from objective project requirements demonstrates all its limits, since only the interconnectedness of stakeholders in the value creation process may ensure the satisfaction of the diverse subjective stakeholder expectations, which is in all respect the critical success factor.

Therefore, it is convenient to emphasize the critical interplay between stakeholder expectations and project success, and we may consider a modern definition of project management that highlights its purpose: the application of knowledge, skills, tools, and techniques to meet project requirements while satisfying stakeholder expectations. However, despite the increasing recognition of stakeholders and their expectations, we should consider a persistent challenge, i.e. the dichotomy between project requirements and stakeholder expectations, which often leads to misunderstandings, affecting project success rates.

In fact, stakeholder behaviors are inherently subjective, reflecting diverse interests, while projects are often perceived as neutral and objective. This misalignment between subjective stakeholder expectations and supposedly objective project requirements lays the groundwork for potential project failures. Indeed, project requirements are not "purely" objective, because, being essentially derived from stakeholder expectations, are dynamic and subject to interpretation, leading to very common phenomena like scope creep or unmet time and budget targets.

Actually, empirical evidence of PMI's reports underscores the prevalence of project shortcomings for several years, since, on average, more than 30% of projects still fail to meet stakeholder expectations, about 50% still experience scope creep, and substantial proportions miss time and budget targets. These statistics challenge the notion that meeting project requirements alone ensures success, highlighting the pivotal role of stakeholder perspectives in project outcomes.

Basically, project success hinges on the stakeholder perspective, surpassing the traditional reliance on standalone project requirements. A project is deemed truly successful when it not only fulfills project objectives but also aligns with stakeholder expectations, emphasizing the subjective dimension of stakeholder relations in driving project success.

In the stakeholder perspective (Fig. 7.2), starting from the invested value in terms of resources, stakeholder relations both generate a value in terms of deliverables, and determine a perceived value in terms of satisfaction. Indeed, a rational domain of requirements, which is oriented to efficiency and targets project objectives, interacts with a relational domain of expectations, which is oriented to efficacy and targets project goals: each of the two domains both influences and supports the other, and a stream of project value is created to be delivered at project completion. The

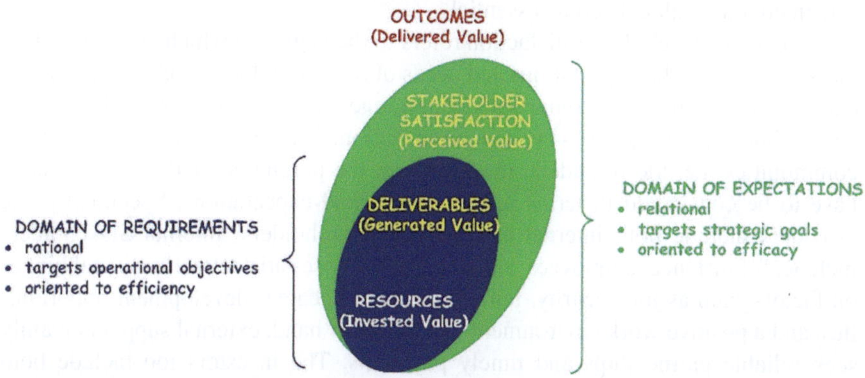

Fig. 7.2 The stakeholder perspective

perceived value acts, through and through, as a powerful "influencer" of the delivered value, because it adds "algebraically" a value—which could then be either positive or negative!—to the generated value that is contained in the deliverables.

Definitively, effective stakeholder management should target both the fulfillment of project/stakeholder requirements and the satisfaction of stakeholder expectations, which correspond to both the achievement of project operational objectives and the perception that project strategic goals will be achieved: stakeholder satisfaction, which is based on the stakeholder perceived value, instead of being "a" critical success factor, proves then to be "the" critical success factor, so transcending technical project details, so much so that project failures often trace back to unmet stakeholder expectations, then emphasizing the centrality of stakeholder satisfaction in project management.

Ultimately, stakeholder satisfaction emerges as the cornerstone of effective project management, guiding project trajectories and ensuring alignment with stakeholder objectives.

7.3 Stakeholder Satisfaction

7.3.1 The Cornerstone of Organizational Success and Value Creation

In today's interconnected business landscape, stakeholder satisfaction has emerged as a critical component for the success and sustainability of any organization. Stakeholders—ranging from employees, customers, suppliers, and investors to the broader community and environment—have, in fact, diverse interests and expectations, and understanding and addressing these interests is not just a matter of ethical responsibility, it is also a strategic imperative that can drive long-term success. Due to the multifaceted nature of stakeholder satisfaction, exploring its importance, key strategies for achieving it, its impact on organizational performance, and its crucial role in creating value, become essential.

In general, stakeholder satisfaction refers to the degree to which an organization meets or exceeds the expectations and needs of its stakeholders. Today, this concept extends beyond mere customer satisfaction, encompassing all parties that have a vested interest—a "stake"!—in the organization. Therefore, all four behavioral communities, i.e. the providers, the investors, the purchasers and the influencers, have to be considered in terms of their needs and expectations. Specifically, the providers include both internal and external stakeholders. Internal Stakeholders include, for instance, employees and managers, whose satisfaction in general hinges on factors such as job security, fair compensation, career development opportunities, and a positive work environment. On the other hand, external suppliers mainly seek reliable partnerships and timely payments. The investors too include both internal and external stakeholders, who both, usually, focus on financial returns and corporate governance. The purchasers/customers/clients/users mainly look for quality products, fair pricing, and excellent service. In the vast domain of influencers, we may concentrate on the communities, which general value corporate social responsibility and sustainability/environmental stewardship, and regulators, which are generally concerned with compliance and ethical conduct.

In general, the importance of stakeholder satisfaction cannot be overstated, since organizations that prioritize the needs and expectations of their stakeholders often enjoy several benefits, including enhanced reputation, increased loyalty, and improved financial performance. Most critically, stakeholder satisfaction is integral to the creation of value, which can manifest in multiple dimensions, including the tree dimensions of sustainability, such as financial, social, and environmental value.

A strong reputation is one of an organization's most valuable assets. Satisfied stakeholders often act as ambassadors, promoting the organization through word-of-mouth and social media. This positive publicity can attract new customers, investors, and talented employees, creating a virtuous cycle of growth and success.

In addition, stakeholder satisfaction fosters loyalty, and enhances retention. Employees who feel valued and respected are more likely to remain with the company, reducing turnover and the associated costs of recruitment and training. Similarly, customers who are satisfied with their experience are more likely to become repeat buyers and advocates for the brand.

There is also a clear link between stakeholder satisfaction and financial results, since stakeholder satisfaction is always a basic driver of the organizations' performances. In fact, organizations that meet the needs of their stakeholders often see increased sales, higher profit margins, and more stable revenue streams. Additionally, satisfied investors are more likely to provide the capital needed for expansion and innovation.

Definitively, stakeholder satisfaction is central to creating value, both in the financial sense and in broader societal terms. Value creation involves enhancing the worth or utility of the organization's offerings, which benefits all stakeholders. Referring to the three dimensions of sustainability, in terms of financial value, satisfied customers contribute to higher revenues, and loyal employees boost productivity, both of which enhance the organization's financial performance. This, in turn, attracts investors looking for stable returns. In terms of social value, when stakeholders, especially the community and employees, are satisfied, the organization contributes positively to society. This can include providing quality jobs, supporting community initiatives, and ensuring fair labor practices. Finally, in terms of environmental value, organizations that prioritize sustainability and environmental stewardship create value by reducing their ecological footprint, which satisfies environmentally conscious stakeholders and can lead to cost savings through efficiency improvements.

Achieving and maintaining high levels of stakeholder satisfaction are not evidently natural consequences of the work performed, but require a specific strategic approach that involves understanding stakeholder needs, implementing effective practices, and engaging in meaningful dialogue.

The first step in achieving stakeholder satisfaction is evidently to understand the specific needs and expectations of each stakeholder community and/or group. This can be accomplished through various means:

- **Surveys and feedback mechanisms**: regularly soliciting feedback through surveys, suggestion boxes, and other channels can provide valuable insights into stakeholder concerns and expectations.
- **Stakeholder mapping**: this involves identifying all relevant stakeholders and mapping their interests, influence, and impact on the organization. By prioritizing stakeholders based on their importance, organizations can allocate resources more effectively.
- **Market research and/or context analysis**: for external stakeholders, especially customers, market research and/or context analysis can help identify trends, preferences, and areas for improvement.

A second step in achieving and maintaining stakeholder satisfaction is implementing effective practices. In fact, to satisfy stakeholders, organizations must implement practices that align with stakeholder values and expectations, and this often requires a commitment to continuous improvement and innovation. Main issues to be carried out include:

- **Employee development and well-being**: investing in employee training, career development, and well-being initiatives can enhance job satisfaction and productivity. In today's world, the possibility of performing a hybrid work, with a "right balance" between in presence and remote work is often considered as essential, and programs that promote work-life balance, health, and wellness are also important.
- **Customer-centric approaches**: organizations should adopt a customer-centric approach, ensuring that products, infrastructures and services meet or exceed customer expectations. This can involve personalized experiences, high-quality customer service, and continuous innovation.
- **Sustainable and ethical practices**: many stakeholders, including customers and communities, value sustainability and ethical conduct. Organizations should implement practices that minimize environmental impact, promote social responsibility, and adhere to ethical standards.

A further step in achieving and maintaining stakeholder satisfaction is engaging in meaningful dialogue. Since effective communication is crucial for building strong relationships with stakeholders, organizations should engage in ongoing, two-way communication that is transparent, honest, and responsive. In this case, main issues to be carried out include:

- **Open communication channels**: establishing open lines of communication, such as town hall meetings, social media platforms, and dedicated customer service lines, allows stakeholders to voice their concerns and feel heard. In today's world, although the enormously increased connectivity, this aspect requires a

consistent effort, since people are often reluctant to be engaged due to external solicitations.
- **Transparency and Accountability**: being transparent about business practices, decisions, and performance builds trust is considered valuable by a large variety of stakeholders. In addition, organizations should also be accountable, acknowledging mistakes and taking preventive and/or corrective action when necessary.
- **Collaborative Problem-Solving**: Involving stakeholders in decision-making processes, especially when addressing issues that directly affect them, can lead to more sustainable and acceptable solutions.

From a practical point of view, stakeholder satisfaction has to be measured, and relevant data have to be analyzed and managed. Main methods for measuring stakeholder satisfaction include:

- **Surveys and Questionnaires**. Surveys are a traditional yet powerful tool to measure satisfaction. Customized surveys for different stakeholder groups can provide valuable insights into their specific expectations and perceptions of the organization. For example, employee satisfaction surveys might focus on work environment and management practices, while customer surveys could measure satisfaction with infrastructures, products and services. Longitudinal survey data can also track changes in satisfaction over time, providing a dynamic view of trends and outcomes of business strategies.
- **Interviews and Focus Groups**. Personal interactions through interviews and focus groups offer a depth of understanding that surveys cannot capture. These methods allow stakeholders to express complex thoughts and feelings that might be overlooked in structured surveys. For internal stakeholders, focus groups can uncover underlying issues in workplace culture or operational inefficiencies, while interviews with customers can reveal detailed perceptions of the product experience and service quality.
- **Observation and Behavioral Analysis**. Observational methods involve studying the actual behaviors of stakeholders, e.g., in retail settings, observing how customers interact with products or services provides insights into their real-time satisfaction and usage patterns. Similarly, employee behavior observed through performance metrics can reflect satisfaction levels and engagement with their roles.
- **Sentiment Analysis**. With the advent of digital communication, sentiment analysis has become an invaluable tool in measuring stakeholder satisfaction. By analyzing the tone and content of social media posts, reviews, and other online interactions, companies can gain a snapshot of stakeholder sentiment that is both timely and relevant. This method is particularly useful for gauging public sentiment following product launches or PR events.

Analyzing stakeholder satisfaction data is a fundamental and delicate problem, since there is always the risk of misinterpreting data. Main analysis methods include:

- **Data consolidation**: combining data from multiple sources like surveys, interviews, and online interactions provides a holistic view of stakeholder satisfaction.

Advanced data analytics can integrate these diverse data streams to uncover patterns and correlations that inform strategic decisions.
- **Trend analysis**: this involves examining data over time to identify consistent patterns or deviations in satisfaction levels. Trend analysis can help predict future changes in stakeholder attitudes and prepare the organization to address them proactively.
- **Segmentation analysis**: data segmentation involves dividing stakeholders into subgroups based on shared characteristics or responses. This targeted analysis helps in crafting customized strategies that cater to the specific needs of different groups, enhancing overall satisfaction.
- **Impact Analysis**: determining the impact of specific actions on satisfaction levels is crucial for strategic planning. Using statistical tools to analyze causality and effect sizes helps in prioritizing the actions that have the most significant impact on improving stakeholder satisfaction.

Once measures and analysis have been made, good practices in stakeholder satisfaction management include:

- **Continuous feedback loop**: implementing a continuous feedback mechanism ensures that the organization remains in tune with stakeholder needs. This can involve regular surveys, community forums, and open channels of communication that encourage ongoing dialogue with stakeholders.
- **Strategic integration of feedback**: incorporating stakeholder feedback into the strategic planning process ensures that business decisions are aligned with stakeholder expectations. This integration helps in adapting business practices to better meet stakeholder needs and builds a stronger alignment between the organization's objectives and stakeholder interests.
- **Transparency and communication**: effective communication and transparency about business operations and decisions build trust and satisfaction. Clear communication about changes and policies helps mitigate concerns and fosters a positive relationship with all stakeholders.
- **Customized strategies**: developing tailored strategies for different stakeholder groups acknowledges their unique needs and expectations. Customized programs for enhancing satisfaction could include targeted marketing campaigns for customers, tailored training programs for employees, and personalized communication strategies for investors.

Of course, achieving stakeholder satisfaction is not without its challenges. Organizations must navigate conflicting interests, resource constraints, and dynamic environments. However, by adopting a proactive and flexible approach, these challenges can be effectively managed by balancing conflicting interests, managing resource constraints, and adapting to dynamic environments.

Indeed, stakeholders often have conflicting interests. For example, investors may prioritize short-term financial returns, while employees may seek job security and benefits. Balancing these interests requires a nuanced approach:

- **Stakeholder prioritization**: organizations should prioritize stakeholders based on their influence and impact on the business. While all stakeholders are important, some may require more immediate attention.
- **Negotiation and compromise**: finding common ground through negotiation and compromise can help reconcile conflicting interests. This involves understanding the underlying concerns and working towards mutually beneficial solutions.
- **Long-term perspective**: Adopting a long-term perspective can help balance short-term pressures with sustainable growth. For instance, investing in employee development may reduce short-term profits but lead to long-term productivity gains.

In addition, resource constraints, such as limited budgets and personnel, can hinder efforts to achieve stakeholder satisfaction. Effective resource management is then essential via:

- **Prioritization and Focus**: focusing on high-impact initiatives that address the most critical stakeholder needs can maximize the use of limited resources.
- **Leveraging Technology**: technology can enhance efficiency and effectiveness in engaging stakeholders. For example, digital platforms can facilitate communication, feedback collection, and data analysis.
- **Partnerships and Collaborations**: collaborating with other organizations, industry groups, and communities can pool resources and expertise to address common challenges.

Ultimately, the business environment is constantly evolving, driven by technological advancements, regulatory changes, and shifting market dynamics. Organizations must be adaptable to maintain stakeholder satisfaction, via:

- **Continuous monitoring**: regularly monitoring the external environment and stakeholder sentiments can help organizations stay ahead of changes and respond proactively.
- **Agility and Flexibility**: cultivating an agile organizational culture that embraces change and innovation can enhance responsiveness to emerging stakeholder needs.
- **Scenario planning**: developing contingency plans for various scenarios can prepare organizations for potential disruptions and ensure continuity in stakeholder engagement.

The impact of stakeholder satisfaction on organizational performance is profound and multifaceted. Satisfied stakeholders contribute to a positive organizational culture, enhanced reputation, and sustainable growth. Importantly, they also drive the creation of value across financial, social, and environmental dimensions. In fact, a culture that values and prioritizes stakeholder satisfaction fosters a positive work environment, employees are more engaged, motivated, and committed to the organization's goals, and this, in turn, enhances productivity and innovation. In addition, organizations that consistently meet stakeholder expectations build a strong reputation, and a positive reputation attracts new customers, investors, and partners, creating a competitive advantage in the market. Moreover, since a sustainable growth is achieved when organizations balance economic performance with social and environmental responsibility, satisfied stakeholders are more likely to support and contribute to the organization's long-term success. Ultimately, since stakeholder satisfaction is intrinsically linked to value creation, when stakeholders are satisfied, they contribute to the diverse forms of organization's.

In conclusion, stakeholder satisfaction is a cornerstone of organizational success and a critical driver of value creation in the modern business landscape. By understanding and addressing the diverse needs and expectations of stakeholders, organizations can build strong, lasting relationships that drive reputation, loyalty, and financial performance. Achieving stakeholder satisfaction requires a strategic approach that includes understanding stakeholder needs, engaging in meaningful dialogue, and implementing effective practices, while, from the practical point of view, it requires specific measures and data analysis and management. Despite the challenges, organizations that prioritize stakeholder satisfaction are well positioned for sustainable growth and long-term success. As the business environment continues to evolve, the ability to adapt and respond to stakeholder needs and expectations will remain a critical determinant of organizational success and value creation.

References

Freeman, R. E. (1984). *Strategic management: A stakeholder approach* (Pitman series in Business and Public Policy). Harpercollins.

Freeman, R. E. (1994). The politics of stakeholder theory: Some future directions. *Business Ethics Quarterly, 4*(4), 409–421.

Pirozzi, M. (2017, June). The stakeholder perspective. *PM World Journal VI*(VI). Featured Paper.

Pirozzi, M. (2019). *The stakeholder perspective: Relationship management to enhance project value and success*. CRC Press, Taylor & Francis Group.

Pirozzi, M. (2021, February). The perceived value: A powerful influencer of project success. *PM World Journal X*(II). Featured Paper.

Project Management Institute. (1987). *Project Management Body of Knowledge (PMBOK), Project Management Institute*. Republished electronically in 2018 by Max Wideman.

Chapter 8
Strategy Definition

Michela Manini

8.1 Strategic Impact

The world of business is constantly evolving, demanding organizations to adapt and innovate to maintain their competitive edge. In this rapidly changing landscape, the role of strategic management and the importance of project management become increasingly important. It is relevant to observe the interconnection between the two, highlighting the essential part project management plays in the successful implementation of business strategies.

Strategic management is a critical system that guides businesses in setting goals, executing plans, and achieving objectives. It is the driving force behind any successful organization as it provides a clear sense of direction, outlines measurable goals, and is a guide to understanding the dynamics of the business environment.

Project management, on the other hand, is the application of processes, methods, skills, knowledge, and experience to achieve specific project objectives according to the project acceptance criteria within agreed parameters. It is a critical discipline that imparts the required competencies to plan, schedule, monitor, control, and close a project.

The role of a Project Manager is pivotal in connecting strategic management to the actual execution of strategies. They are the bridge between the strategy and the team members who do the work. They translate the strategic goals into actionable plans and ensure that each team member understands their role in achieving these objectives.

Project Managers also play a crucial part in maintaining an open line of communication between the executives and the team members. They serve as a liaison,

M. Manini (✉)
Department of Innovative Technologies, SUPSI, Lugano, Switzerland
e-mail: michela.manini@supsi.ch

A. Bassi et al. (eds.), *General Management Principles for Project Management*, Management for Professionals, https://doi.org/10.1007/978-3-031-98592-8_8

ensuring that the project aligns with the organization's strategic goals and that the team's progress and challenges are communicated back to the top management.

So the Project Manager's role is not just to manage the project but to align it with the company's strategic objectives, thereby ensuring that the project contributes to the company's overall success. We will further delve into the specifics of this role, providing a comprehensive understanding of the importance of project management in strategic implementation.

8.2 Project management: A Strategic Way for Organizational Success

The role of a Project Manager extends beyond the limits of overseeing projects. The Project Manager stands as the linchpin between the strategy and the execution, serving as the catalyst for strategic implementation.

As a Project Manager, understanding the organization's strategic objectives is paramount. This understanding shapes the direction of the project, aligning it with the overall business goals.

A crucial part of strategic implementation is feedback gathering.

Feedback serves as the lifeblood of continuous improvement. It provides insights into the strengths, weaknesses, opportunities, and threats within the organization. A Project Manager, therefore, operates as a feedback aggregator, collecting and synthesizing information from all corners of the organization.

The Project Manager's role in feedback gathering extends to conducting regular meetings with team members, key stakeholders, and senior management. These meetings provide a platform for open communication, where ideas, concerns, and suggestions are freely expressed.

The insights gleaned from feedback are invaluable in strategic implementation. They inform the decision-making process, guiding the development, and refinement of strategies. Additionally, they highlight potential pitfalls and bottlenecks in the project lifecycle, enabling proactive management.

Feedback also plays a vital role in fostering a culture of continuous learning and improvement within the organization. By openly discussing successes and failures, the organization can learn from past experiences and improve future performance.

The role of a Project Manager in strategic implementation is multifaceted.

Through effective feedback gathering and utilization, a Project Manager can significantly contribute to the successful realization of the organization's strategic objectives.

8.3 The Horizontal Position of Project Manager: Leveraging Benefits

The modern strategic view supports the change of the traditional vertical hierarchy toward an horizontal one. The role of a Project Manager, often considered as a vertical position within the company hierarchy, is experiencing a shift towards a more horizontal structure.

In this horizontal structure, the Project Manager operates fostering a democratic environment. This approach can contribute to a more agile and resilient organization.

One of the primary benefits of an horizontal structure is the increase in communication efficiency.

The Project Manager operating in a direct line of communication, allowing for faster decision-making and problem-solving.

It removes the need for information to pass through several layers of management before reaching the necessary individuals.

Furthermore, an horizontal structure promotes a sense of ownership and responsibility among team members. Everyone in the team feels involved and invested in the project's success. The Project Manager, in this case, acts more as a facilitator or coach, guiding the team towards an open collaborative network.

This structure also fosters innovation and creativity. With a non-hierarchical structure, team members are encouraged to share their ideas and solutions, leading to more innovative and effective strategies.

The horizontal positioning of a Project Manager also aligns with the growing trends of remote work and digital communication tools. It allows for a more flexible and adaptable team structure, capable of responding to changes quickly.

In conclusion, the horizontal position of a Project Manager can bring numerous benefits to an organization. By fostering effective communication, promoting a sense of ownership, encouraging innovation, and adapting to modern work trends, this approach can significantly contribute to the successful implementation of company strategies. However, it's crucial to remember that this approach may not suit every organization and must be adapted based on the company's culture and specific needs.

Project Manager has a unique role within an organization. Unlike traditional roles that adhere to a vertical hierarchy, a Project Manager operates on an horizontal plane, interacting and coordinating with multiple departments and teams simultaneously.

The Project Manager's role is not limited to a single team or department; rather, it cuts across the entire organization. They are the bridge that connects various verticals, ensuring smooth communication, aligning objectives, and synchronizing efforts towards a common goal.

This horizontal placement comes with its own set of challenges and opportunities. On the one hand, Project Manager does not have formal authority over team members. This could potentially lead to conflicts, resistance, and lack of accountability. On the other hand, being in this unique position allows the Project Manager to have a broader perspective, an holistic view of the project, and the organization as a whole.

Project Manager can effectively navigate this horizontal plane, build strong relationships with team members and stakeholders, foster an environment of collaboration and mutual respect, and ultimately drive the organization towards its strategic goals.

Chapter 9
The Systemic Approach in Project Management

Antonio Bassi

The systemic approach goes beyond traditional project management by offering a more holistic and integrated perspective that considers the project not just as a series of activities or objectives to achieve but as a complex system of interdependent components.

9.1 Fundamentals of the Systemic Approach

The systemic approach in project management is based on understanding a project as a system—a set of interdependent parts working together to achieve common goals. This vision integrates people, processes, technologies, and resources into a cohesive unit, emphasizing the importance of interaction and collaboration among these elements for the success of the project.

Defining a system in this context recognizes that every project component does not act in isolation but is part of a broader network of relationships and interactions. This implies that every decision, action, or change in one part of the system can have repercussions on other parts.

The principles guiding the systemic approach in project management are numerous, but among the most relevant are holistic thinking, interconnection, and adaptability. Holistic thinking focuses on viewing the entire project rather than isolated parts. This approach allows for a better understanding of how the various project components influence each other and how they can work together to achieve the set goals.

Interconnection, another fundamental principle, involves understanding how every decision or action in one part of the project influences other parts. This

A. Bassi (✉)
Project Management Association Switzerland, Lugano, Switzerland
e-mail: antonio.bassi@apm-switzerland.ch

A. Bassi et al. (eds.), *General Management Principles for Project Management*, Management for Professionals, https://doi.org/10.1007/978-3-031-98592-8_9

principle emphasizes the importance of considering the impact of actions on the entire project rather than limiting oneself to isolated evaluations.

Lastly, adaptability refers to the project's ability to adapt effectively to internal and external changes. In an ever-changing environment, the ability to adapt plans, processes, and strategies is crucial to keeping the project aligned with objectives and responsive to new challenges.

In summary, the fundamentals of the systemic approach in project management combine a holistic view of the project with an emphasis on interconnections and adaptability. These principles guide project managers in creating and managing projects that are not only efficient and effective but also capable of successfully navigating the complexities and uncertainties of the modern context.

9.2 The Systemic Approach in Project Management

The systemic approach to project management is a methodology that considers a project as a system composed of various interdependent and interacting elements. This approach emphasizes the importance of understanding how the different components of the project—resources, processes, people, and environment—work together to influence the overall outcome. It allows project managers to better understand the broader context in which the project operates, improving the ability to make informed decisions and adapt to an evolving environment.

9.2.1 Holistic Thinking in Project Management

Holistic thinking in project management represents a fundamental paradigm that transforms how projects are conceived, planned, and managed. This approach emphasizes the importance of perceiving the project not as a simple aggregation of independent parts but as a complex and interconnected system where every element—from human resources to processes, materials, and technologies—plays a crucial role and is influenced by the whole.

Incorporating holistic thinking into project management means embracing a global vision that takes into account every aspect of the project, evaluating potential interactions and interdependencies. This perspective allows anticipating how decisions in one area can create cascading effects in others, influencing critical aspects such as timing, costs, and the quality of the final result. It invites moving beyond the perspective of single optimization in favor of a strategy that aims for the overall benefit of the project, sometimes accepting necessary compromises to achieve the best possible systemic result.

Adopting holistic thinking facilitates project managers in making strategic decisions by considering the overall impact of their choices rather than merely solving isolated problems. The integration of continuous feedback and monitoring mechanisms allows for constant verification of how effectively each component contributes to the general objectives, promoting effective holistic project management.

The enhancement of interrelationships and interdependencies among the various project components not only prevents challenges arising from a narrow view but also paves the way for innovative solutions that consider the entire system. This approach, therefore, not only helps to navigate more securely through project complexities but also guides projects toward success with a broader and more integrated vision, ensuring that every decision made is informative, thoughtful, and, above all, in harmony with the common goal.

Holistic thinking in project management is revealed not only as a working methodology but also as a managerial philosophy that emphasizes connection, balance, and integration among all parts of a project. This invites project managers to consider the project as a living organism where the health and effectiveness of each part contribute to the well-being and success of the entire system.

9.2.2 Interdependence of Components in Project Management

The interdependence of components in project management represents a fundamental principle that illuminates the complexity and interwoven reality of modern projects. This concept emphasizes the importance of recognizing that no element of a project operates in isolation; rather, every decision, resource, or activity is intrinsically connected within a complex system where actions in one area can have significant repercussions in others.

Understanding the network of connections and interdependencies within a project thus becomes crucial for effective management. This holistic view helps navigate complexity by recognizing how sequences of activities, resource allocations, and strategic decisions are interconnected, requiring careful consideration of their potential mutual influences. The dynamic management of these interdependencies, therefore, requires planning that takes into account the entire project system, embracing flexibility, and promoting open and collaborative communication within the team to ensure coordinated and conscious action.

When facing the ripple effects generated by changes in one part of the project, there arises the need for a reactive and adaptable approach that allows for prompt responses and adjustments to plans accordingly. This response flexibility, together with constant monitoring, ensures that the project can evolve without these variations compromising the overall objectives. Through careful observation of internal dynamics, project managers can anticipate the need for adaptation, maintaining alignment with the project's vision and goals.

In this context, the project manager plays a key role in weaving together the various parts of the project into a harmonious whole, ensuring that each element contributes effectively toward the final objectives. The holistic and careful management of interdependencies not only optimizes the efficiency and effectiveness of the project management process but also creates a cohesive work environment where collaboration and communication are fundamental pillars.

Successfully addressing the interdependence of components in project management, therefore, requires a balance between a global vision and attention to detail, between strategic planning and the ability to adapt. This approach not only facilitates navigation through project complexities but also lays the foundation for lasting success, demonstrating how a deep understanding of interdependence dynamics can turn challenges into opportunities, guiding the project toward achieving objectives with synergy that reflects the true essence of project management.

9.2.3 Feedback and Adaptability in Project Management

In the dynamic field of project management, the importance of embracing the principles of "Feedback and Adaptability" cannot be underestimated. In an environment constantly subject to uncertainties and changes, the ability to systematically gather feedback and respond with agility and flexibility becomes essential to guiding projects toward success. This approach emphasizes a continuous cycle of communication and adaptation, which is fundamental to effectively addressing challenges and seizing opportunities that arise along the way.

Feedback acts as a compass for the project manager and their team, providing the necessary directions to navigate the project. By collecting both internal and external feedback, it is possible to obtain a clear and current view of the project's progress. The information collected from team members offers an internal perspective on the effectiveness of the methodologies adopted and potential areas for improvement, while external feedback from clients and stakeholders ensures that the project remains aligned with their expectations and needs. This set of data plays a crucial role in promptly identifying issues that need attention and implementing necessary corrections.

However, collecting feedback is only one side of the coin; the other side is represented by the ability to dynamically adapt to this information. Adaptability in project management manifests in the flexibility to adjust plans, strategies, and work processes in response to new discoveries or changes in the project environment. This elasticity allows the project team to promptly face emerging challenges and take advantage of previously unexpected opportunities, ensuring that changes are smoothly integrated and that all stakeholders are involved and informed.

The implementation of iterative cycles of review and feedback constitutes the core of this process, promoting an environment of continuous improvement and organizational learning. Through regular performance reviews and comparisons between achieved results and set objectives, the project team can refine its practices and strategies, ensuring a constant evolution toward excellence in project management.

Integrating feedback and adaptability into the fabric of project management thus creates a dynamic and resilient work environment capable of navigating complexities and uncertainties successfully. This not only significantly enhances the chances of achieving the set project objectives but also enriches the overall experience of teams and stakeholders, laying the foundations for long-term growth and success.

In summary, adopting an approach based on feedback and adaptability transforms how projects are managed, emphasizing the importance of open communication and strategic flexibility. This mindset not only facilitates overcoming challenges but also catalyzes innovation and continuous improvement within project teams, demonstrating that the ability to constantly adapt and learn is at the heart of success in project management.

9.2.4 Balance and Homeostasis in Project Management

In the world of project management, the pursuit of harmonious balance and the ability to maintain dynamic stability emerge as fundamental principles for effective project management. These concepts underscore the need to carefully balance the different parts of the project, ensuring that each receives the necessary attention without being overburdened or neglected, while also retaining the ability to agilely adapt to both internal and external changes.

Effective balancing in project management involves the careful management of all project components. This includes the balanced allocation of human and material resources, strategic planning that anticipates the needs of each project phase, and a distribution of workload that prevents overburdening while simultaneously promoting optimal productivity. The goal is to create an environment where each element of the project contributes proportionally to achieving overall objectives, ensuring that the project progresses smoothly and productively.

Dynamic stability, on the other hand, reflects a project's ability to remain flexible and responsive to changes. This requires constant monitoring of the project's internal and external context and the preparation of contingency plans to address unforeseen scenarios. A proactive approach to change management, supported by open and transparent communication within the team and with stakeholders, enables the project to adapt quickly, minimizing the negative impacts of changes and maintaining focus on the main objectives.

The synergy between balancing the various parts of the project and dynamic stability creates the conditions for resilient and adaptable project management. By carefully monitoring the project's evolution and adjusting strategies, project managers can successfully navigate complexities and uncertainties, ensuring that the project not only responds effectively to challenges but also takes advantage of emerging opportunities.

In conclusion, the concept of "Balance and Homeostasis" in project management emphasizes the importance of management that is both balanced and flexible. Through careful resource management, strategic planning, and the ability to adapt to changes, project managers can ensure that their projects proceed toward success in a coordinated and productive manner. This approach not only enhances the project's efficiency and effectiveness but also creates a more sustainable and responsive work environment where collaboration and innovation are encouraged, laying the groundwork for long-term success in a continually evolving project context.

9.2.5 Systems Thinking and Problem Solving

Systems thinking and problem-solving are fundamental pillars in the landscape of project management, offering an approach that harmonizes analysis and creativity to address challenges innovatively and effectively. This methodology goes beyond simply identifying solutions to isolated problems, aiming instead to identify strategies that benefit the entire project system. The goal is to ensure that each solution contributes positively to the whole, maintaining a balance that reflects the project's overall needs and promotes long-term success.

An approach that combines analytical and creative thinking proves essential in navigating project challenges. Analytical thinking allows breaking down problems into manageable components, carefully examining them to identify root causes and evaluate possible solutions in a logical and structured manner. At the same time, creative thinking opens the door to innovative solutions, inviting exploration of new possibilities and consideration of unconventional approaches that may offer unexpected advantages.

This synergy between analysis and creativity facilitates the adoption of integrated solutions that consider the entire project system. Instead of merely responding to immediate needs, the impact of each solution on the entire project is evaluated, aiming to prevent new problems from arising and maximizing overall benefits. This requires a deep understanding of the project's dynamics and its interdependencies, as well as the ability to think holistically to find solutions that are sustainable and consistent with overall objectives.

In addition to solving specific problems, a systemic and integrated approach to project management significantly contributes to the project's long-term success. By encouraging project managers to look beyond immediate issues, this method allows for the identification of opportunities for improvement and innovation that emerge from understanding the project's interrelationships and internal dynamics. In this way, the adopted solutions not only address current challenges but also enrich the project by promoting efficiency, adaptability, and growth.

Systems thinking and problem-solving in project management emphasize the importance of a balanced and holistic approach that values both analysis and creativity. By seeking integrated solutions and considering the overall impact on the project, project managers can guide their teams through complexity and challenges, ensuring that every decision made not only solves specific problems but also constructively contributes to the whole, laying the groundwork for the project's long-term success.

9.2.6 Holistic Approach to Risk Management

The holistic approach to risk management in project management stands out for its ability to look beyond traditional risk management focused on isolated aspects to embrace a comprehensive vision that considers the entire project as an integrated system. This advanced methodology requires identifying, analyzing, and managing risks not only as isolated entities but as parts of an interconnected network that influence and are influenced by the entire project.

Implementing risk management at the system level means adopting a broader perspective where risks are not considered individually but in the context of their mutual interactions within the project. This approach allows understanding how risks in a specific area can have repercussions on other parts of the project, highlighting the need for mitigation strategies that consider the overall impact of risks on the entire system.

Identifying and analyzing risks holistically enables the development of more effective and comprehensive risk management plans that take into account possible synergies between risks and opportunities emerging from proactive risk management. This type of management increases the project's resilience, allowing it to successfully navigate uncertainty by ensuring informed decisions oriented toward the benefit of the entire project.

Adopting a holistic approach to risk management requires going beyond the identification and mitigation of obvious risks by inviting an integrated and comprehensive view of the project. This involves considering not only immediately recognizable risks but also those potentially less obvious that may emerge from the project's complex internal dynamics. Using specific tools and methodologies that allow a comprehensive assessment of risks is essential to effectively addressing this challenge.

Proactive risk management strategies are essential in this context as they allow anticipating and planning for potential problems before they manifest. This includes developing detailed contingency plans and conducting simulations to assess the impact of potential risks on the project. Adopting a proactive approach not only reduces the risk of negative impacts on the project but also contributes to creating a more controlled and predictable project environment.

Ultimately, a holistic approach to risk management in project management transforms how risks are perceived and managed, shifting from a fragmented view to an integrated understanding of the project as a complex system. This not only improves risk management but also enriches overall project management, providing project managers with the tools to navigate uncertainty with greater confidence and guide their projects toward success in an increasingly complex and interconnected environment.

9.2.7 Learning Cycles and Continuous Improvement

The adoption of learning cycles and continuous improvement represents a fundamental pillar in the systemic approach to project management, emphasizing the importance of leveraging experiences and feedback to continuously evolve management practices. This iterative process, involving planning, execution, review, and adaptation, serves to continuously optimize the project, ensuring that each phase contributes to overall improvement.

In the systemic context, learning is seen as an incessant process enriched by direct experiences and feedback collected both internally and externally. Each project thus becomes an invaluable source of learning, offering teams the opportunity to refine their skills and gain a deeper understanding of project dynamics. This cycle of learning and improvement not only allows effectively addressing current challenges but also anticipates and mitigates potential future problems, enhancing management capacity and team resilience in the face of new developments.

The application of an iterative approach to project improvement emphasizes the importance of continuously evaluating progress and adapting strategies based on new information that emerges. This helps keep the project aligned with set objectives and allows for prompt responses to both internal and external changes, ensuring flexible and responsive management.

The constant interaction between the project team, stakeholders, and the external environment through the collection and analysis of feedback enables the identification of opportunities for improvement and innovation. This process of continuous feedback and strategic adaptation not only improves the project's efficiency and effectiveness but also stimulates the evolution of professional skills and enriches the organization as a whole.

By incorporating learning cycles and continuous improvement, project managers and their teams can take advantage of accumulated experience to tackle future challenges with greater preparation and confidence. This holistic approach not only strengthens the project's immediate performance but also lays the foundation for sustainable growth and long-term success by promoting a corporate culture that values innovation, adaptability, and continuous learning.

9.3 Application in Project Management

9.3.1 Integrated Management of Parts

The adoption of a systemic approach in project management radically transforms how projects are conceived, managed, and completed. This methodology centers around the vision of the project as a unified system where every component—from human resources to technology, from finances to materials—is interconnected and plays a vital role in overall success. The project manager becomes the catalyst for this holistic vision, ensuring that all parts of the project are effectively and functionally coordinated.

Managing resources under the umbrella of a systemic approach becomes an exercise in balance and integration. Each resource, with its specificities, must be optimally utilized, avoiding both waste and shortage. This balance requires a deep intuition of the project's dynamics and the ability to predict how various resources interact with each other and with different project phases, ensuring that allocations harmoniously support the project's overall progress.

Similarly, time planning takes on a new dimension in a systemic context. It is not just about outlining deadlines but understanding the causal relationships and dependencies between different activities. This understanding helps ensure that the project advances consistently and coherently, respecting established priorities and adapting when necessary to emerging needs.

Risk management takes on a broader perspective. Recognizing that risks in one area can influence the entire system, the project manager engages in an in-depth analysis and planning that considers potential interactions. Mitigation strategies are developed with the aim of minimizing the overall impact on projects, requiring careful monitoring and strategic adaptability to navigate uncertainty.

Finally, attention to the quality of the final product is intrinsic to the systemic approach. This focus on quality permeates every project phase, from conception to delivery, requiring a constant commitment from the entire team. The integration of high-quality standards ensures that the final product not only meets but exceeds stakeholder expectations, reflecting the effectiveness of the systemic approach as a whole.

The systemic approach to project management requires a holistic and integrated vision that goes beyond the mere sum of its parts. The project manager, acting as a conductor of this complex symphony, ensures that every decision contributes to the overall harmony and success of the project. This approach not only maximizes the likelihood of achieving set goals but also promotes a dynamic and cohesive work environment where decisions are well-considered and oriented toward the well-being of the overall project system.

9.3.2 Communication and Collaboration

This method emphasizes the vision of the project as a cohesive whole where every element—from team members to stakeholders—plays a crucial role in determining the effectiveness and overall success of the project. Consequently, the indispensable need for open communication and close collaboration emerges to ensure alignment and collective awareness of the impact of individual actions on the entire project system.

Open communication represents the pillar upon which effective project management is built, acting as a catalyst for the free flow of information at all levels of the project. This flow of communication ensures that every team member is constantly updated on goals, changes, progress, and any emerging issues. Promoting an environment where transparency reigns supreme encourages everyone to share ideas, doubts, and proposals, thereby creating fertile ground for the timely identification of problems and the exploration of new opportunities for improvement.

Similarly, effective collaboration becomes a means by which the various skills and visions within the team and among external stakeholders harmoniously merge toward achieving project goals. This collective commitment, extending from the planning phase to the project's completion, allows for the appreciation of the various skills and know-how within the group, enriching the project and amplifying its chances of success.

Highlighting a systemic approach makes it essential to recognize how every decision and every action taken affects the entire project system. In this context, communication and collaboration play a central role in promoting a positive impact, facilitating careful management of interdependencies, and offering effective solutions to problems that arise. Maintaining a high level of alignment and awareness among all stakeholders helps significantly reduce the risk of misunderstandings and conflicts, simplifying the path toward achieving set goals.

In summary, the importance of open communication and close collaboration emerges as fundamental within the systemic approach to project management. These practices not only enhance efficiency and effectiveness in conducting projects but are also crucial in forging an inclusive work culture centered on shared success. It is through constant dialogue and targeted collaboration that it can be ensured that every action taken constructively contributes to the well-being of the entire project system, guiding the project toward success with a unified and coherent vision.

9.3.3 Monitoring and Feedback

Within the framework of the systemic approach to project management, the implementation of monitoring and feedback mechanisms plays a crucial role. This essential component allows project managers and their teams to accurately assess the effectiveness of the strategies implemented while ensuring the possibility of intervening with timely and targeted changes. This continuous process of evaluation and adjustment is fundamental to navigating the dynamic evolution of a project, ensuring that the actions taken are always aligned with the set objectives and adaptable to new challenges that may emerge.

Constant monitoring of the project provides a clear view of the progress, highlighting areas of success and those needing intervention. Through the use of key performance indicators (KPIs), progress reports, and project management tools, the project manager can collect valuable data on the project's trajectory. These data, analyzed regularly, serve as a basis for informed decisions, allowing for early detection of any deviations from the original plan and enabling corrective action to be taken accordingly.

At the same time, feedback gathered both within the project team and from external stakeholders plays a fundamental role in deepening the understanding of project dynamics. Feedback offers direct insights into the perceptions, experiences, and expectations of those involved, providing an invaluable source of information for continuous improvement. Whether formal feedback is collected through review meetings and surveys or informal feedback arises from daily interactions, every opinion helps shape the adopted project management approach.

The effective integration of monitoring and feedback into the project lifecycle allows for a proactive approach to problem-solving and strategy optimization. This not only enhances the agility and resilience of the project in the face of changes but also increases its capacity to generate value for the organization and stakeholders. Moreover, it fosters a work environment focused on learning and growth, where every team member feels valued and involved in contributing to the project's success.

The application of solid monitoring and feedback practices in project management is indispensable for ensuring that the project remains on a positive trajectory toward achieving its goals. These mechanisms not only provide the necessary information to guide timely and targeted decisions but also promote a culture of transparency, accountability, and continuous improvement—key elements for success in an increasingly complex and dynamic project environment.

9.4 Advantages of the Systemic Approach

The systemic approach to project management provides an integrated and holistic vision that considers each component as part of an interconnected system. This method emphasizes integrated management of resources, balancing various elements, and managing interdependencies to optimize project success. Open communication and close collaboration are essential to align teams and stakeholders, facilitating informed decision-making and effective risk management. Additionally, continuous monitoring and constant feedback allow for proactive strategy adjustments, enhancing project effectiveness and fostering a work environment focused on learning and continuous improvement.

9.4.1 Better Understanding of the Project

Adopting a systemic approach in project management radically transforms project management, offering a deep understanding of its dynamics. This methodology allows one to visualize the project not as a series of isolated tasks but as an integrated system where every component—from human resources to technologies—interacts and contributes to achieving overall goals. Such a holistic approach opens the way to a series of significant benefits that enhance overall effectiveness in conducting projects.

The holistic vision that characterizes the systemic approach provides project managers and their teams with a complete perspective on the project. This vision allows for a clear identification of how the various parts of the project interact with each other, revealing the interdependencies that may exist between different phases and resources. Such cross-sectional understanding is fundamental to anticipating potential bottlenecks and optimizing the use of available resources, ensuring that the project progresses smoothly and efficiently.

The ability to identify and understand interdependencies within the project is one of the most valuable aspects of the systemic approach. This awareness allows for anticipating how changes in one area may affect other parts of the project, enabling project managers to plan preventive actions and act promptly to address any emerging challenges.

A holistic understanding of the project also facilitates strategic and informed decision-making. With a comprehensive view of the project's dynamics, project managers can more accurately assess the impact of their choices, ensuring that every decision contributes positively to the project's overall goals and the well-being of the entire system.

Furthermore, the systemic approach significantly improves risk management. By identifying how specific risks may affect the entire project, it is possible to develop mitigation strategies that consider the complex interactions between various components, increasing the project's resilience in the face of uncertainties.

Another significant advantage is the increased adaptability of the project. Being aware of the intricate internal dynamics, teams are better equipped to respond quickly to both internal and external changes, ensuring that the project remains aligned with expectations and set objectives.

The optimization of resources is the final piece of the puzzle that completes the benefits of the systemic approach. A clear vision of the project's needs and priorities allows for a more targeted and efficient allocation of resources, reducing waste and maximizing the team's effectiveness.

In conclusion, adopting a systemic approach in project management not only improves project management capabilities through more accurate planning, informed decision-making, and effective risk management but also creates a flexible and responsive work environment deeply oriented toward collective success and achieving overall objectives.

9.4.2 Greater Efficiency

Adopting a systemic approach in the field of project management profoundly transforms how projects are perceived and managed, leading to a significant increase in the efficiency and effectiveness of operations. This methodology, focused on analyzing the interactions between the various components of the project, allows project managers and their teams to make well-thought-out choices that are strategically valid and oriented toward minimizing waste and optimizing processes.

Through the lens of the systemic approach, the project is viewed as a living organism where each part is essential to the well-being of the whole and where operational synergies are valued. This holistic perspective facilitates the identification of strengths and areas needing improvement, avoiding overlaps and duplications in efforts. Consequently, every action taken is targeted and effectively contributes to the overall progress of the project.

The core of efficiency in the systemic approach lies in the ability to harmonize resource utilization with the actual needs of the project. This way of operating requires a thoughtful distribution of personnel, time, and capital based on an accurate assessment of project needs, resulting in a significant reduction in waste and an increase in operational efficiency.

The adoption of strategic decisions illuminated by a comprehensive view of the project represents another key aspect of this approach. Decisions become the result of in-depth reflection on their systemic impact, ensuring that each choice not only addresses immediate issues but also strengthens the project's resilience and long-term success.

Furthermore, the systemic approach is distinguished by its ability to identify and eliminate waste, optimizing the ratio between resources used and results obtained. By anticipating interactions between activities and analyzing their possible consequences, a culture of value is promoted, where only actions that truly contribute to the project are pursued.

Finally, the effectiveness of this approach is manifested in the simplification of workflow. Fully understanding the interdependencies and priorities of the project allows for outlining optimal operational routes, accelerating the completion of critical phases, and improving the project's overall agility.

The systemic approach to project management not only enhances the efficiency and quality of the work performed but also establishes a work culture that is conscious and sustainability-oriented. Leveraging informed decisions, strategic resource utilization, and a constant quest for optimization, this methodology not only ensures the timely success of projects but also lays the foundation for a dynamic, reactive, and inherently improvement-focused work environment.

9.4.3 Problem Prevention and Resolution

The use of the systemic approach in project management proves to be an effective strategy that radically transforms how projects are conducted, offering significant advantages in preventing and resolving problems. This methodology, which centers on the analysis of interdependencies among the various components of the project, enables project managers and their teams to anticipate obstacles and criticalities, thus ensuring a smoother and trouble-free workflow.

The ability to foresee challenges before they manifest translates into more reliable project management that is less prone to unforeseen events. With a holistic view of the project, teams gain greater ability to identify early warning signs related to potential problems, allowing for strategic planning that takes into account the complex internal dynamics of the project. This facilitates the adoption of preventive measures and targeted mitigation strategies that can be proactively implemented to prevent such issues from negatively impacting project progress.

One of the keys to the success of the systemic approach is its ability to transform problem management from reactive to proactive. Instead of merely responding to setbacks as they arise, teams are equipped with the necessary tools to develop effective solutions in advance, thereby reducing the time and costs associated with their management. This not only prevents the occurrence of certain problems but also ensures that when problems do arise, there are already action plans in place to address them efficiently.

In addition to preventing and quickly resolving problems, the systemic approach helps minimize the impact of any criticalities on the project as a whole. Timely identification and intervention on specific issues prevent them from turning into major obstacles, especially in large-scale or highly complex projects where the consequences of an unmanaged problem can be particularly severe. As a result, the project can proceed according to the established plans, meeting the goals and deadlines set.

Finally, the effectiveness of the systemic approach is also reflected in the decision-making processes within the project team. Equipped with a deep understanding of potential challenges and their related solutions, project managers and their teams can make quick and well-informed decisions. This awareness helps create an agile and adaptable work environment where decisions are made with confidence based on a comprehensive understanding of the project.

Adopting a systemic approach in project management not only optimizes project management, making it more efficient and resilient in the face of challenges, but also promotes a corporate culture focused on proactivity, collaboration, and operational excellence. This philosophy not only elevates the quality and effectiveness of the work performed but also lays the foundation for the sustainable success of projects in an increasingly complex and ever-changing environment.

9.5 Challenges of the Systemic Approach

9.5.1 Complexity

The introduction of a systemic approach in project management opens the door to significantly enriched project management, providing teams with a broader perspective and advanced tools to tackle challenges. However, this method brings with it inherent complexity that requires not only a deep understanding of project dynamics but also a high level of competence in the field of project management. The ability to skillfully navigate the multiple interdependencies and variables of the project becomes a fundamental requirement for success.

Managing complexity emerges as the main challenge of this approach, given that every project is configured as a set of interconnected components whose interactions can be unpredictable. This network of connections exponentially increases the project's complexity, requiring project managers to have a higher level of understanding and management skills, capable of appreciating the project's holistic nature and effectively coordinating its various parts.

Addressing this complexity requires advanced skills not only in traditional project management but also in analytical and critical thinking skills, as well as a deep knowledge of the principles governing complex systems. These skills are essential for facilitating collaboration and coordination among the different components of the project, ensuring that decisions made at the local level align with the overall objectives.

The effectiveness of a systemic approach also relies on the use of specific tools and methodologies designed to map and manage interdependencies within the project. The introduction of advanced project management software, system modeling techniques, and risk analysis methodologies can present a challenge for teams unaccustomed to such tools, requiring a period of adaptation and training.

One of the most delicate challenges in applying a systemic approach is finding the right balance between the project's global vision and attention to detail. This balance is crucial to ensure both effective management of individual tasks and alignment with the holistic vision, especially in large-scale or highly complex projects where managing the details can easily overwhelm the overall vision.

Finally, the introduction of a systemic approach can raise issues related to organizational change management. The need for a cultural and operational shift to fully adopt this methodology may encounter resistance, requiring significant effort to overcome and promote effective adoption of the systemic approach within the organization.

Despite the challenges, the systemic approach remains a highly powerful strategy in project management, offering a greater understanding of project dynamics and more effective control over its variables. Overcoming the difficulties associated with this approach can lead to significant improvements in project management, establishing a solid foundation for long-term success and an organizational culture focused on efficiency, innovation, and resilience.

9.5.2 Cultural Change

The introduction of a systemic approach in the field of project management brings with it challenging but also significant opportunities for growth and development, both for projects and for the organization as a whole. This methodology, centered on integration and understanding the relationships among the different components of a project, requires specific skills and a holistic vision to be implemented successfully.

Complexity represents one of the main challenges associated with adopting this approach. Managing a project as a complex system, with all its interconnected parts, requires not only a deep knowledge of project management techniques but also the ability to analyze and synthesize information from different areas of the project. For project managers, this means developing new strategies that allow them to tackle and break down complexity into more manageable elements while maintaining a global vision that ensures consistency and effectiveness of the project as a whole.

Another significant obstacle is the need for a cultural change within organizations. Implementing a systemic approach may require a radical review of existing business processes and organizational mindset, pushing toward greater emphasis on integration, collaboration, and openness to change. This transformation may encounter resistance as it involves moving away from established practices and experimenting with new ways of working. To overcome this challenge, it is essential that leadership shows a clear commitment to change, supported by transparent communication and training initiatives that help organization members understand and embrace the benefits derived from the systemic approach.

Managing interdependencies among the different parts of the project is another area of challenge. The ability to effectively coordinate interdependent components requires careful planning and the ability to anticipate how decisions in one area may affect other parts of the system. This involves adopting advanced negotiation skills, conflict resolution capabilities, and accurate strategic planning to prevent and manage potential misalignments or problems.

Successfully facing these challenges requires a collective commitment and collaboration from all levels of the organization. The key to overcoming the obstacles associated with the systemic approach lies in continuous skills development and training, as well as promoting an organizational culture that values innovation, adaptability, and teamwork. This shared commitment not only facilitates the adoption of the systemic approach but also strengthens the organization's ability to cope and thrive in complex and dynamic contexts.

In conclusion, while the systemic approach to project management presents considerable challenges, addressing them with determination and targeted strategies offers the possibility of achieving significant improvements in project management. This approach not only enhances the efficiency and effectiveness of projects but also stimulates organizational growth, preparing the organization to successfully manage projects in an increasingly complex and rapidly evolving environment.

9.5.3 Managing Interdependencies

Within the framework of the systemic approach applied to project management, managing interdependencies emerges as a crucial task full of challenges but fundamental to project success. This aspect of the work requires project managers and their teams not only to possess strong analytical skills and attention to detail but also top-notch communication skills. The close connection between the various parts of the project means that any decision, change, or delay can trigger cascading effects throughout the system, requiring a high level of coordination and vigilance to prevent or manage these repercussions.

Interdependencies within a project manifest in various forms, ranging from logistical and temporal connections to technical and resource-related ones. The task of deciphering these connections, understanding both their individual dynamics and how they interact, can prove particularly challenging. The challenges arise not only in recognizing these relationships but also in navigating their often unpredictable and multidimensional nature. Therefore, project managers are called upon to have a deep understanding of the project in all its facets to guide the team through this intricate web of connections.

Effectively addressing the challenges posed by interdependencies requires developing and implementing strategies based on careful planning, constant monitoring, and transparent communication. These elements allow anticipating potential areas of conflict or slowdown and acting promptly when situations arise that could negatively impact the project. The key lies in keeping all stakeholders fully informed and involved, ensuring they are aware of the existing dependencies and the possible consequences of their decisions and actions.

Collaboration and communication among team members and stakeholders become, therefore, critical aspects, although they can be hindered by linguistic differences, diverse priorities, and divergent expectations. Creating an environment where communication flows freely and effectively is crucial to synchronize efforts and direct them toward achieving common goals.

At the same time, successfully addressing interdependencies requires significant flexibility from project managers, who must be ready to adapt strategies and plans in response to new information or changes in the project environment. This adaptability not only facilitates navigating the complexities associated with interdependencies but also contributes to establishing a resilient project culture ready to respond dynamically to emerging challenges.

Navigating the challenges related to managing interdependencies in a systemic project management context requires a sophisticated set of skills that range from technical analysis to strategy to interpersonal communication. Overcoming these challenges not only optimizes efficiency and effectiveness in project execution but also strengthens the overall capacity of the organization to carry out ambitious initiatives in an increasingly connected and dynamic environment.

9.6 Advantages and Challenges

The systemic approach to project management introduces significant complexity, requiring advanced skills and a deep understanding of project dynamics to manage the interdependencies of interconnected components effectively. It also necessitates cultural change within organizations, emphasizing integration, collaboration, and adaptability. Managing interdependencies is a key challenge, demanding careful planning, constant communication, and flexibility to navigate the cascading effects of decisions. By addressing these challenges with strategic focus and commitment, organizations can enhance project efficiency and resilience, ultimately fostering growth in a dynamic and complex environment.

9.6.1 Advantages

Adopting a systemic approach in project management profoundly transforms project management by offering an integrated and coherent vision that goes beyond the mere sum of its parts. This method leads to better coordination among various activities, ensuring that work on one element can facilitate or even accelerate work on another. This harmonious interaction reduces duplication of efforts and optimizes the use of resources, ensuring that they are employed efficiently and at the right time.

One of the most appreciated qualities of this approach is its ability to provide the project with greater flexibility in the face of challenges. A deep understanding of interdependencies between parts allows managers to anticipate problems and adjust plans quickly, making the project more resilient to unforeseen events. This agility is especially valuable in dynamic environments where conditions can change rapidly, requiring modifications to objectives or work methods.

Moreover, the systemic vision significantly enriches the understanding of the internal and external dynamics that influence the project. It allows for predicting how changes in one component can affect the entire system, facilitating more informed risk management and more effective strategic decisions. This level of awareness enables the identification of unexpected synergies and the best exploitation of opportunities that arise during project development.

Overall, the systemic approach not only improves efficiency and effectiveness in project delivery but also promotes a more collaborative and adaptive work environment. By facilitating communication and cooperation among team members and stakeholders, it allows navigating complexity more confidently and successfully completing projects. This methodology, therefore, not only provides immediate benefits to project management but also contributes to the long-term growth of the organization, preparing it to successfully face the challenges of an increasingly complex and interconnected landscape.

9.6.2 Challenges

The implementation of a systemic approach in project management, despite the numerous benefits it offers in terms of integration, flexibility, and understanding of project dynamics, also involves significant challenges. These difficulties arise mainly during the transition to a more holistic vision of project management and require attention and dedication to be overcome.

One of the main challenges in adopting this approach is the need to change the organizational mindset. Traditionally, organizations may be used to operating according to compartmentalized schemes where different sectors or departments work relatively isolated from each other. Moving to a systemic approach implies promoting a culture of collaboration and information sharing, which may require considerable effort from the organization members to adapt. This paradigm shift necessitates commitment at all levels—from leadership to individual teams—and may take time to be fully integrated into daily practices.

Another significant challenge is managing the complex interdependencies that characterize a systemic approach. In a project viewed as an integrated system, decisions made in one part can have direct or indirect effects on other parts of the system. This requires a much more sophisticated capacity for analysis and planning than what is needed in a more fragmented management context. Project managers must develop a deep understanding of the project's dynamics and be capable of anticipating the potential consequences of their choices, a task that can prove particularly complex given the often unpredictable nature of such interactions.

Overcoming these challenges requires a structured approach. It is crucial to promote open and transparent communication within the organization to help team members understand the benefits of a systemic approach and adopt the new practices required. At the same time, training and skills development play a crucial role in preparing project managers and their teams to navigate the complexity of interdependencies. Finally, leveraging advanced project management tools that facilitate the visualization and management of relationships between different parts of the project can be useful.

Despite the challenges, the systemic approach continues to offer transformative potential for project management. By proactively addressing the difficulties related to organizational change and the complexity of interdependencies, organizations can leverage the advantages of more integrated and holistic project management, leading to more effective outcomes and continuous improvement of project management practices.

Part II
People Management

Chapter 10
Core Competencies Management

Virginie Pasquon

The development of competencies stands as a pillar of organizational success in today's complex business environment. Part of these competencies serve as the foundation that enable successful project completion and organizational advancement. The systematic development and validation of project management competencies has become increasingly critical as organizations face growing complexity in their projects and heightened stakeholder expectations. This comprehensive approach to competency development ensures that organizations can consistently deliver superior results while fostering a culture of excellence that aligns with strategic objectives.

10.1 Why Defining Competence Standards?

The establishment of comprehensive competency standards represents a critical first step in developing project management excellence. These standards must encompass the full spectrum of skills, knowledge, and qualities necessary for successful project execution.

Organizations must approach this process through a collaborative effort that involves multiple stakeholders, including executive leadership, departmental heads, subject matter experts, and frontline managers. This inclusive approach ensures that the resulting standards reflect diverse perspectives and address the multifaceted requirements of modern project management.

The development of competency standards requires careful consideration of both technical and interpersonal capabilities. Technical competencies encompass

V. Pasquon (✉)
Department of Innovative Technologies, SUPSI, Lugano, Switzerland
e-mail: virginie.pasquon@supsi.ch

A. Bassi et al. (eds.), *General Management Principles for Project Management*,
Management for Professionals, https://doi.org/10.1007/978-3-031-98592-8_10

strategic planning, organizational development, and risk assessment, while interpersonal competencies include communication, team management, and conflict resolution (Dias et al., 2014). Additionally, industry-specific expertise plays an important role in establishing standards that reflect the unique challenges and requirements of particular sectors or fields.

These standards serve multiple purposes within the organization. They provide clear guidelines for career development and performance evaluation, enabling individuals to assess their current capabilities and identify areas for improvement. Furthermore, they inform recruitment strategies by helping organizations identify candidates whose skills and characteristics align with project management requirements. This alignment between competency standards and talent acquisition ensures greater team cohesion and improved project outcomes.

10.2 Investing in Training and Development

Recognizing that competence is always changing and improving, organizations understand the importance of investing in ongoing training and development programs. These initiatives act as stimulants for developing talent, improving abilities, and promoting a culture of education and development in the project management community.

Organizations that adopt the concept of continuous improvement recognize that project management is always changing due to new technologies, evolving methodologies, and shifting dynamics within the organization.

Therefore, it is essential to invest in continuous training and development not just as a strategic decision but as a foundational requirement to keep up with industry trends and stay competitive.

This includes technical skills in project planning, scheduling, and risk management as well as soft skills like communication, collaboration, and adaptability. Additionally, companies acknowledge the significance of adding leadership development initiatives to their training schedules.

Successful project management depends not just on technical skills but also on the capacity to motivate, inspire, and lead teams towards common objectives.

Leadership training programs provide project managers with the necessary tools, perspectives, and insights to effectively handle intricate organizational dynamics and lead confidently with resilience.

Training and development programs address a variety of topics that reflect the complexities of project management. These programs, for example, can provide a comprehensive way to boost skills and advance professionally by teaching students how to use project management software and increasing their negotiation and conflict resolution abilities. Furthermore, firms use a number of delivery techniques to ensure accessibility and flexibility in their training and development programs. This could include traditional classroom training sessions, online courses, workshops, seminars, and peer-to-peer learning platforms. Organizations can increase engagement and participation in training activities by catering to different learning preferences and schedules.

Using a **learning management system** (LMS) that provides various multimedia options such as videos, podcasts, interactive modules, and written materials enables employees to select the format that aligns with their learning preferences and availability. This adaptability allows for a variety of preferences to be met and enables participants to interact with the training material in a way that is meaningful to them.

Providing asynchronous learning options allows employees to access training materials when it suits them best, helping them manage both their professional growth and personal responsibilities. Organizations enable individuals to interact with training materials independently by offering recorded webinars, self-paced modules, and online resources, encouraging a feeling of independence and control in their learning process.

Creating training materials and platforms that are able to be viewed on mobile devices allows employees to easily access learning resources on their smartphones or tablets, no matter where they are. This method is designed for people who like to access information while on the move or during free time, ensuring that learning is easily available and seamlessly incorporated into their everyday schedules.

Providing customized learning paths based on personal preferences, skills, and career goals allows employees to customize their training to match their specific objectives and interests.

Virtual collaboration and peer learning can be enhanced by utilizing discussion forums, group projects, and online communities to encourage participants to take part in collaborative learning, exchange ideas, and benefit from the expertise of the group. Organizations promote an atmosphere suitable for sharing knowledge, working together, and ongoing improvement by encouraging a feeling of community and camaraderie among learners.

10.3 Encouraging Professional Certification

Professional certifications such as Project Management Professional (PMP) IPMA or PRINCE2 are valuable assets for enhancing project management competence (IPMA, 2023; Kuster et al., 2023). These certifications are widely recognized within the industry and serve as standardized benchmarks for assessing the proficiency and expertise of project managers and team members.

Encouraging project managers and team members to pursue professional certifications not only validates their skill sets but also highlights the organization's commitment. By obtaining certifications such as PMP, IPMA or PRINCE2, individuals demonstrate their dedication to mastering established methodologies, best practices, and ethical standards in project management.

To attain professional certification, candidates must undergo rigorous examination of core project management principles, methodologies, and frameworks. They must demonstrate proficiency in areas such as project initiation, planning, execution, monitoring, and closure, as well as exhibit mastery of relevant tools and techniques essential for effective project delivery.

Apart from validating individual competence related to PM, professional certifications offer several tangible benefits to both individuals and organizations. For project managers and team members, certification provides a recognized credential that enhances credibility and marketability in the job market. Certified professionals are often sought after by employers seeking assurance of competency and proficiency in project management roles.

Moreover, professional certification fosters a culture of **continuous learning** and professional development within the organization. Encouraging employees to pursue certification reflects a commitment to investing in their growth and career advancement, thereby enhancing employee engagement, retention, and morale.

From an organizational standpoint, a workforce comprised of certified project management professionals instills confidence among stakeholders and clients. Certification serves as tangible evidence of the organization's adherence to industry standards and commitment to delivering high-quality projects on time and within budget.

Furthermore, organizations that prioritize professional certification benefit from enhanced project management capabilities, improved project outcomes, and increased competitiveness in the marketplace. Certified professionals bring a wealth of knowledge, skills, and expertise to the table, enabling organizations to tackle complex projects with confidence and efficiency.

10.4 Fostering a Learning Culture

Organizations must recognize the pivotal role of continuous learning in driving innovation, adaptability, and performance excellence. Cultivating a learning culture helps create an environment where knowledge sharing, collaboration, and skill enhancement are not only encouraged but actively nurtured and celebrated.

In the past, companies depended on the expertise of their staff members. If companies lacked the necessary expertise internally, they would bring in someone who possessed that knowledge. However, depending on the expertise of certain individuals will no longer suffice to remain successful in the future because of obstacles like the *War for Talent* (Chambers et al., 1998), the mass resignation, and increasing skill gaps and shortages. Organizations must prioritize the strategic advancement of employees. Equally important is the need for them to cultivate a culture of learning that enables the organization to strategically enhance skills, retain staff, and enhance employee satisfaction.

Developing a culture of learning takes time and involves organization-wide changes: organizations must proactively invest in initiatives that empower professionals to expand their knowledge base, develop new skills, and stay ahead of emerging trends and best practices in the field.

Central to cultivating a learning culture is the promotion of peer-to-peer learning opportunities. By harnessing the collective wisdom and experience of project management professionals within the organization, teams can leverage diverse perspectives, insights, and lessons learned to tackle challenges, foster innovation, and drive continuous improvement.

Organizations can facilitate peer-to-peer learning through various mechanisms, including:

- Structured mentorship programs
- Cross-functional collaboration platforms
- Communities of practice

These platforms serve as incubators for idea exchange, problem-solving, and collaborative learning, fostering a sense of camaraderie and collective ownership among project management professionals.

In addition to peer-to-peer learning, organizations should organize workshops, seminars, and training sessions designed to address emerging trends, industry best practices, and evolving methodologies in project management. These forums provide opportunities for skill development, knowledge acquisition, and professional growth, empowering individuals to enhance their competencies and excel in their roles.

Furthermore, providing access to a rich array of learning resources is essential for promoting continuous learning and skill enhancement. This may include online courses, e-learning modules, industry publications, webinars, and conferences tailored to the specific needs and interests of project management professionals.

By democratizing access to learning resources, organizations empower individuals to take ownership of their professional development journey and pursue areas of interest and specialization.

Cultivating a learning culture requires leadership commitment, organizational support, and a mindset that prioritizes learning as a strategic imperative. Leaders are pivotal in championing a culture of curiosity, experimentation, and continuous improvement, *leading by example* (Schrage, 2024) and fostering an environment where learning is embraced as a core value.

10.5 Promoting Cross-Functional Collaboration

Competence transcends technical proficiency to encompass collaboration and communication skills that are vital for navigating complex projects successfully. Encouraging cross-functional collaboration is essential for unlocking the full potential of project teams, as it enables them to harness diverse perspectives and expertise from various domains, fostering innovation and enhancing problem-solving capabilities.

At its core, cross-functional collaboration involves breaking down silos and fostering synergies across different departments, disciplines, and levels of expertise within the organization. By bringing together individuals with diverse backgrounds, skill sets, and perspectives, cross-functional teams are better equipped to tackle multifaceted challenges and capitalize on emerging opportunities.

Encouraging cross-functional collaboration requires a deliberate effort to create an environment that values openness, respect, and inclusivity. Project managers play a main role in facilitating collaboration by fostering a culture of trust, transparency, and shared ownership among team members.

One of the key benefits of cross-functional collaboration is the ability to leverage the collective intelligence and expertise of team members to generate innovative solutions to complex problems. By combining insights from diverse disciplines and perspectives, project teams can gain fresh insights, challenge conventional thinking, and explore new avenues for achieving project objectives.

Moreover, cross-functional collaboration promotes knowledge sharing and transfer across different parts of the organization, enabling individuals to learn from one another and broaden their skill sets. By creating opportunities for interdisciplinary interactions and exchanges, organizations can foster a culture of continuous learning and professional development among project team members.

Effective cross-functional collaboration also enhances communication and coordination within project teams, mitigating the risk of misunderstandings, conflicts, and delays. By establishing clear channels of communication and promoting open dialogue, project managers can ensure that all stakeholders are aligned with project goals and priorities, fostering a sense of shared purpose and commitment.

10.6 Mentorship and Coaching Programs

Mentorship and coaching programs should be strategic for talent development in organizations. These initiatives create structured pathways for knowledge transfer and professional growth. In project management, pairing experienced project managers with emerging talent can build meaningful relationships.

The dynamic between mentors and mentees extends beyond simple knowledge sharing to encompass broader professional development objectives: experienced project managers serving as mentors bring invaluable practical wisdom to these relationships, offering insights that can only be gained through years of hands-on experience. They guide mentees through the complexities of project environments, helping them develop critical thinking skills and navigate challenging situations. This guidance proves particularly valuable when mentees face novel challenges or need to make difficult decisions in their project work.

The coaching aspect of these programs adds a structured dimension to professional development, focusing on specific skill enhancement and performance improvement. While mentorship often addresses broader career development and navigation of organizational dynamics, coaching targets particular competencies and measurable outcomes. This dual approach ensures comprehensive professional development that addresses both immediate performance needs and long-term career objectives.

Beyond individual development, these programs serve essential organizational functions by creating robust succession pipelines and ensuring knowledge retention. They help organizations maintain continuity in project management practices while fostering innovation through the fresh perspectives brought by emerging talent. This combination of experience transfer and new thinking creates a dynamic learning environment that strengthens the organization's project management capabilities.

The success of these programs depends on careful matching of mentors with mentees, clear objective setting, and regular evaluation of progress. Organizations must provide adequate support and resources while ensuring that both mentors and mentees understand their roles and responsibilities in the development process. When properly implemented, these programs create lasting value by developing capable project leaders while maintaining organizational knowledge and expertise.

10.7 Performance Evaluation and Feedback

Performance evaluations are driving both individual growth and organizational success. These processes provide structured frameworks for assessing competencies, tracking progress, and fostering continuous improvement in dynamic organization environments.

Effective performance evaluation requires establishing clear, objective metrics aligned with project goals.

For example, a software development project manager might be evaluated on:

- Sprint velocity improvements (e.g., 20% increase in story points delivered)
- Team retention rates above 85%
- Client satisfaction scores exceeding 4.5/5

These metrics should encompass both quantitative and qualitative aspects of performance, enabling comprehensive assessment of project managers and team members. Regular evaluation cycles ensure timely identification of strengths and development areas, allowing for proactive intervention and support. Constructive feedback complements formal evaluations through specific, actionable insights.

Example Rather than stating "communication needs improvement," effective feedback identifies particular scenarios: "During the stakeholder meeting on Project X, providing a written summary of technical changes would have enhanced clarity for non-technical participants."

When delivered promptly and supportively, feedback helps individuals understand their performance impact and areas for improvement. This ongoing dialogue creates opportunities for reflection and adjustment, enabling continuous professional development and enhanced project outcomes.

The implementation of transparent performance metrics fosters accountability and collaboration within project teams. When team members clearly understand how their contributions align with project objectives, they become more invested in collective success. This transparency also facilitates informed decision-making and strategic planning at organizational levels.

Through systematic evaluation and feedback processes, organizations create environments conducive to continuous learning and excellence in project management practice. Project managers and team members to continuously learn, adapt, and excel in the pursuit of project success.

10.8 Technological Advancements

Management is undergoing a profound transformation, driven by technological advancements that are revolutionizing also how projects are planned, executed, and monitored (Nieto-Rodriguez, 2023). Embracing these innovations, including project management software and collaboration tools, helps organizations achieve efficiency, effectiveness, and adaptability in project execution. Traditional methods, which relied heavily on manual processes and in-person meetings, are being replaced by digital tools that enhance collaboration, streamline workflows, and enable data-driven decision-making.

Digital transformation in project management involves integrating tools like automation, cloud-based platforms, AI, machine learning, and data analytics throughout the project lifecycle. This shift allows for better communication among distributed teams, real-time updates, and more efficient task management. Tools such as Slack, Microsoft Teams, Asana, and Trello are highlighted for their roles in facilitating seamless collaboration and progress tracking.

These tools break down barriers to collaboration, fostering a culture of transparency, inclusivity, and teamwork within project teams. By providing platforms for virtual meetings, brainstorming sessions, and document collaboration, these tools empower professionals to overcome logistical challenges and leverage the **collective intelligence** of the team.

Access to these technologies is not only about equipping project management professionals with the tools they need to thrive in a rapidly evolving landscape but also about fostering a culture of innovation and adaptability within the organization.

10.9 Celebrating Success and Learning from Failure

Celebrating project successes is more than just a gesture of acknowledgment; it's a powerful tool for reinforcing a culture of achievement and excellence within an organization (Project Management Institute, 2017). When teams come together to celebrate the completion of a project or the achievement of significant milestones, it serves as a collective recognition of their hard work, dedication, and collaboration. This celebration not only boosts morale but also strengthens team cohesion and fosters a sense of pride and accomplishment among team members.

Moreover, celebrating success provides an opportunity for organizations to showcase and highlight best practices, innovative approaches, and exemplary performance that contributed to the project's successful outcome. By publicly recognizing and rewarding outstanding contributions, organizations reinforce behaviors that align with their values and strategic objectives, inspiring individuals to strive for excellence in future endeavors.

Equally important is the practice of **embracing failure as a learning opportunity** within the organization. In today's dynamic and rapidly evolving business landscape, failure is an inevitable aspect of innovation and growth. Instead of viewing failure as a setback or a source of blame, organizations should embrace it as a valuable opportunity for reflection, adaptation, and improvement.

Encouraging a culture where failure is openly acknowledged and discussed helps destigmatize mistakes and fosters psychological safety within teams.

When individuals feel comfortable taking risks and experimenting with new ideas, they are more likely to innovate and push the boundaries of what is possible. Embracing failure as a learning opportunity encourages resilience and perseverance, instilling a growth mindset within the organization.

Furthermore, learning from failure enables organizations to identify root causes, analyze patterns, and implement corrective actions to prevent similar mistakes from occurring in the future.

Organizations foster a culture of innovation and continuous improvement, as discussed in the related chapter, by recognizing accomplishments and learning from mistakes. This promotes long-term success and sustainable growth.

Recognizing and celebrating achievements inspires individuals to strive for excellence and reinforces behaviors that contribute to high performance and organizational success. Similarly, embracing failure as a natural part of the learning process fosters resilience, adaptability, and a growth mindset, positioning organizations for success in the face of uncertainty and change.

10.10 Adapting to Industry Trends and Best Practices

Maintaining relevance and adaptability requires keeping up with industry changes and best practices. Project planning, execution, and delivery are altered by new technologies, approaches, and tactics as industries change. Organizations may foster innovation and prosper in a competitive environment by adopting these trends and best practices. Additionally, it gives businesses the ability to foresee and proactively react to shifts in consumer preferences, market dynamics, and technology developments. Organizations can make well-informed decisions and strategic investments by keeping an eye on trends and benchmarking against peers to obtain insights into opportunities, challenges, and competitive pressures. It became obvious that establishing a culture of innovation and ongoing development is essential: promoting experimentation, creativity, and risk-taking enables businesses to question the status quo, increase process efficiency, and provide solutions that go above and beyond for clients.

10.11 Conclusions

Enhancing skills, especially in project management, is more than just a technical training program; it's a strategic necessity that calls for the careful coordination of several organizational components (Thomas & Mengel, 2008). Unwavering dedication to fostering an atmosphere that encourages learning, teamwork, and creativity is necessary for success in this undertaking. Organizations can only develop the skills necessary to produce outstanding project outcomes and preserve competitive advantage in a business environment that is becoming more and more complicated by taking such a comprehensive approach.

References

Chambers, E. G., Foulon, M., Handfield-Jones, H., Hankin, S., & Michaels, E. (1998). The war for talent. *The McKinsey Quarterly, 3*, 44–57.

Dias, M., Tereso, A., Braga, A. C., & Fernandes, A. G. (2014). The key project managers' competences for different types of projects. In Á. Rocha, A. Correia, F. Tan, & K. Stroetmann (Eds.), *New perspectives in information systems and technologies, volume 1. Advances in intelligent systems and computing* (Vol. 275). Springer. https://doi.org/10.1007/978-3-319-05951-8_34

IPMA International Project Management Association. (2023). *ICB4—IPMA individual competence baseline*. Retrieved from https://ipma.world/ipma-standards-development-programme/icb4

Kuster, J., Bachmann, C., Hubmann, M., Lippmann, R., & Schneider, P. (2023). Reference list for the Individual Competence Baseline (ICB) from IPMA (International Project Management Association). In *Project management handbook. Management for professionals*. Springer. https://doi.org/10.1007/978-3-662-66211-3_6

Nieto-Rodriguez, A. (2023). *Digital transformation in project management*. Project Management Institute. Retrieved from https://antonionietorodriguez.com/digital-transformation-in-project-management/

Project Management Institute. (2017). Celebrate good times: We asked the project management community: How do you celebrate project success? *PM Network, 31*(6), 20–21.

Schrage, M. (2024). Like it or not, you are always leading by example. *Harvard Business Review*. Retrieved January 13, 2025, from https://hbr.org/2016/10/like-it-or-not-you-are-always-leading-by-example

Thomas, J., & Mengel, T. (2008). Preparing project managers to deal with complexity—Advanced project management education. *International Journal of Project Management, 26*(3), 304–315. https://doi.org/10.1016/j.ijproman.2008.01.001

Chapter 11
Creating and Managing a Project Team

Silvia Mari and Monica Mannelli

The human being is biologically programmed to respond to two very basic and primordial needs: the need to survive and the need to be loved, to be accepted into a group of peers, to live in society.

Every action that we undertake is subconsciously led by an attempt to respond to and fulfil these two needs: be with others and simultaneously distinguish ourselves from others, in a quest for domination. Today, this duality that traces back to our animal ancestors, shows all of its contradictions and complexity when we find ourselves working in a team.

In its "The Hedgehog effect: Building high performance teams" Manfred Kets de Vries explains this paradox very effectively by borrowing an old tale from Arthur Schopenhauer, included in a series of essays called Parerga und Paralipomena, in which he narrates the dilemma hedgehog face during winter. The hedgehogs during the wintertime move closer to each other in an attempt to protect themselves from the cold, but by doing so they hurt each other with their spines. Hence, they move away to feel more comfortable. However, the cold draws them closer again, leading to the same situation of discomfort in a continuous ballet of back and forth that stops only once they are able to find the right distance from each other that allows them to benefit from the warmth of the group, without hurting each other with the proximity.

This simultaneous need for intimacy and distance, for acceptance and supremacy is one of the fundamental reasons why people often find it hard to work successfully in a team.

S. Mari (✉)
Department of Innovative Technologies, SUPSI, Lugano, Switzerland
e-mail: silvia.mari@supsi.ch

M. Mannelli
Lombardi SA, Bellinzona-Giubiasco, Switzerland
e-mail: monica.mannelli@lombardi.group

A. Bassi et al. (eds.), *General Management Principles for Project Management*, Management for Professionals, https://doi.org/10.1007/978-3-031-98592-8_11

11.1 The Human Factor

When building up a team to serve a given scope, project managers often tend to focus on works to be done, deadlines to be respected and budget not to be exceeded. This is because the success of a project is typically measured by its capability to obtain a given output within a given time and with given resources. This very classical approach, however, risks to put the human factor on the side, forgetting that any project in the end is initiated, developed, and used by human beings. If a project is a mix of integrated efforts of different disciplines to produce a sole outcome, then a project team must be a mix of people with different backgrounds and expertise, but with complimentary skills and a common goal. Hence it is evident how team building is an essential project managers' skill.

Trying to build up a team only concentrating on rational goals, structures, and constraint, can lead to forget that human beings are far from being rational creatures. Each and every person brings his own backpack of experience, perspective, needs and personal skills with them and while the technical aspects of a project are easily monitored and measured, the barriers that can be arise from different outlooks, role conflicts and poor communication are more difficult to detect and to act upon.

Keeping the Hedgehog Paradox in mind an effective project manager or leader should be able to mitigate the effects of this irrationality by creating a safe environment for everyone to perform, strive and fail without the fear of getting hurt from the group dynamics.

11.2 How to Build Up a Team that Is Effective and Performing?

Let's assume that we have the privilege of setting up our own brand-new team from scratch to serve a given scope of work, and let's assume, for the sake of reasoning that we have readily available an abundance of potential project team members with various degrees of competences and skills in the field of the project scope of work. Most Project Manager—this is especially true in an existing organization where people already know each other before coming together as a project team—would have the natural tendency to include in its team the very best performer of every specific work area related to the project scope, wrongly believing that this might be the key to project success.

By drawing a simple parallelism with team sports we can very easy imagine why this approach is doomed to fail. In sports team, as well as in project teams there are two basic concepts that the coach in the first case and the project manager in the second case needs to have present. To turn a group of people into an effective team first of all there has to be a common goal to which people commit to, but most importantly there have to be clearly defined roles and responsibilities people feel accountable for. As in a soccer game having a team of 11 attackers running after the ball to score and completely forgetting to defend their own area would never serve the final goal of winning the match, the same situation can be found in a project team. Assigning roles and responsibilities is a fundamental task of a Project Manager and understanding the granularity of the actions needed to reach the expected output is a basic pre-condition to set up a team that serves the goal.

Luckily enough an effective Project Manager would have in its personal toolbox a powerful help to support him in this task: the Work Breakdown Structure (WBS). By breaking down the project into smaller parts, a WBS clarifies what needs to be done and helps communicate this to all stakeholders and at the same time clearly defined tasks can be easily assigned to team members, ensuring accountability and ownership.

Let's go back to the assumption of a Project Manager having the freedom to choose from a potential infinite catalogue its team members. We well know that in real life this would rarely be the case. Most of the time, especially when a project is run in an existing and stable organization, setting up a project team is the result of fine negotiations and sometimes hard fights between line and project managers over a set of scarce resources.

Hence, once a project starts, the Project Manager (PM) would have built up its own new project team, based on readily available resources and project goals. With the support of the WBS he or she would have assigned the right person to the right task to fulfil the common goal of producing the expected outcome. The most dangerous mistake that can be done is to think that half or most of the work has been already done. And this is because—as B.W. Tuckman's Team Dynamics Model explains in detail—teams are far from being fix, steady organizations. They instead are living entities, that evolve through time and space and typically go through various stages of maturity and performance during their life cycle.

In its Team Dynamics Model, B.W. Tuckman identified four typical stages of life of a group or a team. An effective Project Manager must be aware of these stages and of the actions that he or she do to navigate the team across each phase with success, leading it to the next one (Fig. 11.1).

- **Forming Phase: Approach and Orientation**

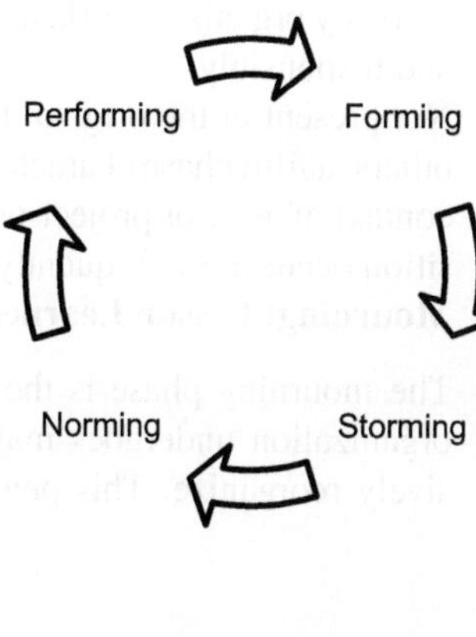

Fig. 11.1 B.W. Tuckman's team dynamics model

- In the initial "Forming" phase, the team finds itself in a state of courtesy and cautious approach. Team members are seeking security and reveal little about themselves, not yet seeing themselves as a cohesive unit. This phase is characterized by uncertainty and the desire to establish a secure foundation. During this phase, supporting mutual knowledge is fundamental. The manager plays a crucial role, guiding the team and making the team's objectives transparent, communicating them repeatedly to ensure everyone is aligned. Creating an environment where each member feels safe and encouraged to participate is essential for the long-term success of the project.
- **Storming Phase: Confrontation of Interests and Frustration**
- The "Storming" phase is characterized by the confrontation of interests and frustration. At this stage, the "I" wants to stand out from the "we", latent conflicts emerge, and team members show a desire to stand out, vying for informal leadership. This phase sees self-orientation and the formation of cliques. To help the team overcome this phase, it is important to highlight common goals and accept diverse opinions and attitudes, making them transparent. Identifying and managing conflicts is crucial, promoting an environment where divergences can be openly discussed and constructively resolved.
- **Norming Phase: Role Definition and Development of Interaction Modes**
- During the "Norming" phase, the team develops and institutionalizes group standards, interaction modes, and other rules of the game. This is a period where roles are defined, and norms are established to guide team behaviour. In this phase, it is useful to initiate the development of shared guidelines, both formal and informal, to ensure everyone has a common understanding of expectations and acceptable behaviours. Strengthening the sense of belonging is fundamental, as is assigning specific tasks and responsibilities to team members, increasing their accountability and commitment to the project.
- **Performing Phase: Cooperation and Work Capacity**
- The "Performing" phase is characterized by a work orientation, openness among team members, solidarity, performance orientation, and goal-directed behaviour of the team. In this phase, the team operates efficiently and collaboratively, with the manager intervening minimally, as the team tends to self-regulate. However, it is important not to rush to this phase without adequately resolving previous conflicts. To support the team in this phase, it is useful to create spaces for autonomously organized work, allowing members to manage their tasks independently and responsibly.
- Not present in the original model developed by Tuckman but added later on by others, a fifth phase characterizes the typical life cycle of a team, especially in the context of agile or project-oriented organizations where changes in team composition occur more frequently than in stable organizations: the mourning phase.
- **Mourning: Lesson Learned and Goodbye**
- The mourning phase is the moment when the project comes to an end, or an organization undergoes major change that leads the team to dissolve or massively reorganize. This phase is characterized by the dissolution of the group

structure, as the tasks and objectives of the team have been completed or completely changed.

- It involves reflection on the achievements and the processes, as well as on the emotional responses to the disbanding of the team relationships project outcomes.

The Project Manager in this phase should ensure an adequate support to the members of the team by paying to this phase transition as much attention as to the other phases by providing opportunities for feedback, celebration, and acknowledgment of the team's work and individual contributions.

Keeping in mind as a Project Manager that all project teams systematically go through these different phases and having present what role the leadership plays in navigating people and the team through it, can help accelerate the transition from the most difficult phases into the performing one. Her are some practical tips for PMs to be applied in the forming, storming and norming phases to proactively lead this process and not be overwhelmed by it.

1. **Demonstrate respect and consideration for all employees as valued members of the team**. Are employees encouraged by example and admonition to respect each other? Do they know enough about each other's job to appreciate the contributions others are making? Does a general atmosphere of consideration exist?
2. **Identify individual job responsibilities and performance standards and see that they are known**. Are individual discussions held to ensure that each employee knows their job's standards and responsibilities? Does each team member understand how their portion of the project is important to overall project success?
3. **Work to secure good communications with employees as individuals and as a team**. Do team members feel their inputs and suggestions are valued? Do they receive regular feedback on how they are doing? Is advance warning of changes conveyed whenever possible, along with reasons why changes are necessary? Are regular ex-change meetings held? Are team members included in decision-making?
4. **Establish individual and group goals, preferably in coordination with those concerned**. Are individual goals established for each team member? Is consideration given to each individual's opportunities for professional development? Are group goals established and communicated to the team? Is a goal established that encourages growth in team development factors—team planning, conflict resolution, and problem solving?
5. **Reward teamwork and team-building efforts**. Who issues rewards? Project managers? Functional managers? Are rewards mostly based on factors surrounding the job environment—pay, bonuses, and working conditions—or are they based on factors having to do with the job itself, such as accomplishment, recognition, responsibility, and growth? Does management know the difference between rewarding an individual as a member of a team and rewarding an individual as an individual? Are individuals singled out and rewarded for their

performance on the project team? Do team members have input into what and how rewards are given and to whom?

6. **Practice and encourage loyalty to the team**. Does the project manager de-fend team members against unfair criticism? Is there a climate of trust on the project team? Is effective leadership practiced by project managers?

11.3 Creating Global High-Performing Innovation Teams

The explosion of new knowledge in technical fields leads inexorably to greater specialization. Fields spawn subfields. More generally, highly specialized professionals thus find themselves needing to collaborate to carry out integrative development projects.

In parallel, shorter product life cycles are dramatically reducing the lead time for getting new products to market. A structured approach in which managers plan each aspect of a large development project, allowing different tasks to be accomplished separately by specialists in carefully structured phases, is prohibitively time-consuming. Instead, simultaneous work on related tasks must be coordinated and negotiated as part of a dynamic collaborative journey.

In short, in today's organizations, the design, development, and production of new products is a fast-pace interdisciplinary endeavour—calling for teams rather than highly structured functional organizations to get the job done (Edmondson & Nembhard, 2009).

Products with shorter product lifecycles (Kessler & Chakrabarti, 1996), especially in high-tech industries, shorten the lead time for development. Moreover, increasing competition due to globalization further contributes to the speed at which companies must develop innovative new products to compete in ever more diverse markets (Denison et al., 1996). These increasing pace of technological change and market competition demand teams that can quickly adapt, collaborate virtually, and deliver innovative solutions efficiently, overcoming traditional barriers of distance and organizational silos.

Recent research by Johnsson (2023) emphasizes the need for a systematic approach to developing global high-performing innovation teams (gHITs).

For a group to become a team and start performing may take about 4–6 months, and only a few teams become high-performing due to internal conflicts (Wheelan, 2009). As cognitive proximity affects knowledge sharing (Hung et al., 2021), virtual teams often suffer from lack of physical interaction, technophobia, and processes to align common work processes and cultures (Ebrahim et al., 2009). Even though research clearly shows that the team leader should understand the processes of group formation (West et al., 2004; Hallgren, 2009; Adkins, 2010), there have been problems related to group dynamics that have led to struggles with innovation; namely, the wasting of valuable time and energy. One reason for such a struggle might be that there is no time to properly create these kinds of teams (Edmondson & Nembhard, 2009). Still, when reviewing structured ways of creating innovation teams, there is a lack of focus as to how to prevent the problems that arise in the development of the group. Additionally, to meet the ever-increasing pace of new product launches, global innovation teams should preferably avoid the 'storming' phase to become high-performing as fast as possible, as it otherwise risks consuming valuable resources.

Johnsson's research proposes a model, process, and guidelines for creating such teams, addressing the challenges of global collaboration and the need for rapid innovation.

- **The importance of team composition**: When forming gHITs, consider diversity in skills, culture, and perspectives. This diversity contributes to enhanced creativity and problem-solving capabilities.
- **Leadership and management support**: Ensuring top management commitment and appropriate leadership styles are crucial for the success of global innovation teams.
- **Communication and technology**: Effective use of communication technology is essential for overcoming geographical barriers and facilitating collaboration among team members.
- **Group development process**: Understanding and managing the stages of group development (forming, storming, norming, performing) is critical for accelerating team performance.
- **Organizational context**: The broader organizational environment plays a significant role in supporting and enabling gHITs to function effectively.

11.4 Motivation and Team Engagement

Motivation refers to the driving force or reason behind a person's actions, behaviour, or attitude. It is what inspires and encourages individuals to achieve their goals and objectives. Motivation can be distinguished into intrinsic or extrinsic. Intrinsic motivation comes from within a person, such as personal satisfaction or enjoyment, while extrinsic motivation comes from external factors, such as rewards or recognition.

If the motivation is the internal drive that fuels an individual's desire to act (e.g. it's the "why" behind their actions), the engagement is the emotional connection and commitment an individual feels towards their work, team, and organization (e.g. it's about how they feel about their work environment).

Motivation focuses on individual goals, while engagement focuses on organizational goals. Motivation drives individuals to act; while engagement fosters a deeper connection and commitment to the organization (Mari & Pirozzi, 2024).

According to the ADP Research Institute (Hayes & Buckingham, 2020) engagement is defined as the emotional state of mind that causes people to do their best work, sustainably.

11.4.1 But How Can We Measure "Engagement"?

Common standards (e.g. PMBOK Guide 7th Ed.) clarify that degree of stakeholder satisfaction mainly relies in work performance data and in having a conversation with stakeholders to gauge their satisfaction with the project deliverables and the overall management of the project. Project and iteration reviews, product reviews, stage gates, and other methods are ways to obtain periodic feedback.

However, assessing perceived values while having conversations could be very subjective. The influence of stakeholders on the project's outcomes is so important that it is mandatory to rely on a better structured and systematic approach, where engagement could be continuously measured and monitored. So, beside work performance data, surveys or questionnaires can be used to assess the degree of satisfaction (Mari & Pirozzi, 2024).

An example of such structured surveys come from a very long-established data-analytics services such as Gallup Inc. Gallup actually relies on an employee engagement database of more than 35 million respondents, it is active in such filed for more than 80 years. According to its Q$^{12®}$ Survey, in 2015 Adkins reported that almost 70% of US workers are not engaged at work, that means that a huge majority of the workforce is not involved in, enthusiastic about, and committed to their work. That means that the vast majority of employees are disengaged and don't seem to view their work as meaningful.

11.4.2 Why Are We Globally so much Disengaged?

In Professor Daniel M. Cable's research, answer is provided from a neuroscience perspective. He introduced the concept of seeking system, which is the part of our brain that is activated from our aspirations, what we desire and what we want. The response of such seeking system is comparable of a dopamine system activation (Cable, 2018).

Let's go back in late 1800s. During the America's Industrial Revolution, Henry Ford introduced the concept of assembly line in order to scale up and reduce cost of production. It happens that scaling up production means that managers need a way to control the behaviours of employee. The definition of management itself is "controlling things or people". In other words, our species invented bureaucracy and management practices so that thousands of people could be controlled through measurement and monitoring. As a general consequence, organisations deactivated employees' seeking system and activate their fear systems, which narrows their perception and encourages their submission. However, according to Prof. Cable's theory, we need to understand that employees' lack of engagement isn't really a motivational problem. It's a biological one. Or better said, a neurobiological one.

Our evolutionary tendency to disengage from tedious activities isn't a bug in our mental make-up. It's a feature. It's our body's way of telling us that we were designed to do better things. To keep exploring and learning. Part of our brain urges us to learn new things and find new ways to use our unique skills, instead of performing monotonous generic tasks.

Unlike the short-term motivation of extrinsic rewards such as financial bonuses, an activated seeking system has long term impacts on our motivation (VandeWalle et al., 1999). This is because we are motivated to do a lot of things based on hope and aspiration that are not described by backward-looking rewards.

11.4.3 How Can We Improve Team Engagement?

Professor Bonnie Nardi in her anthropological study on World of Warcraft (Nardi, 2010) identify three triggers that could activate human seeking system:

- possibility of expression of our own unique skills as part of a team
- possibility to explore new things
- possibility to find a sense of purpose

In that sense, curiosity is the key for change. When everyone on a team is curious, they are more likely to move away from their comfort zone and old habits and work together in new ways. A necessary skill for team and project leaders is the use of play and experimentation to activate employees' seeking system so to adapt and thrive in a changing environment.

Over the last two decades organizations have found new ways to boost curiosity and capitalize creativity by working on technology that employees understand better than leaders. Many organizations developed programs that give people free time to experiment with their own project and interest. Some examples of such programs are the "Bootleg time" of 3M, the "Creative Capital" of Dealogic, the "Ship It" of Atlassian or the Google's "20%" (Arndt, 2006; D'Onfro, 2015). Despite there are relevant differences among each organization program, we could identify two elements that all these programs have in common: they are capable to give people ownership of the vision; and most importantly, they give people safe space to try, experiment and fail.

Blanchard and Bowles introduced the four keys acronym P.U.C.K., that perfectly describe modern team leading values:

- **Provide** a clear sense of purpose with values and goals, reinforce it with a team charter or a covenant that gave team members a reason to trade self for selflessness.
- **Unleashing** and developing skills, continuously building individual skills that in turn bolster collective skill.
- **Creating** team power.
- **Keeping** the accent on the positive (positive reinforcement).

Citing Ken Blanchard and Sheldon Bowles: "*A team is a wonderful thing, ...It allows us to achieve things far beyond our own ability, while at the same time it keeps us humble*" (Blanchard & Bowles, 2000).

Bibliography

Adkins, L. (2010). *Coaching agile teams: A companion for scrum masters, agile coaches, and project managers in transition*. Addison-Wesley Professional. isbn-13:978-0321637703.

Adkins, A. (2015). *Majority of U.S. employees not engaged despite gains in 2014, Gallup*. Gallup. Retrieved from https://news.gallup.com/poll/181289/majority-employees-not-engaged-despite-gains-2014.aspx

Arndt, M. (2006, May 10). 3M's seven pillars of innovation. *Business Week*. Retrieved from https://www.bloomberg.com/news/articles/2006-05-09/3ms-seven-pillars-of-innovation

Blanchard, K., & Bowles, S. (2000). *High five! The magic of working together*. William Morrow. isbn-13: 978-0688170363.

Cable, D. M. (2018). *Alive at work: The neuroscience of helping your people love what they do*. Harvard Business Review Press. isbn-13:978-1633694255.

D'Onfro, J. (2015, April). The truth about Google's famous '20% time' policy. *Business Insider*. Retrieved from https://www.businessinsider.com/google-20-percent-time-policy-2015-4

Denison, D. R., Hart, S. L., & Kahn, J. A. (1996). From chimneys to cross-functional teams: Developing and validating a diagnostic model. *Academy of Management Journal, 39*(4), 1005–1024.

Ebrahim, N. A., Ahmed, S., & Taha, Z. (2009). Innovation and R&D activities in virtual team. *European Journal of Scientific Research, 34*(3), 297–307. Retrieved from http://ssrn.com/abstract=1501442; http://www.eurojournals.com/ejsr.htm

Edmondson, A. C., & Nembhard, I. M. (2009). Product development and learning in project teams: The challenges are the benefits. *Journal of Product Innovation Management, 26*, 123–138. https://doi.org/10.1111/j.1540-5885.2009.00341.x

Hallgren, E. W. (2009). How to use an innovation audit as a learning tool: A case study of enhancing high-involvement innovation. *Creativity and Innovation Management, 18*(1), 45–58.

Hayes, M., & Buckingham, M. (2020). *The definitive series: Employee engagement full research report*. Retrieved from https://www.adpresearch.com/assets/the-definitive-series-employee-engagement/

Hung, S. W., Cheng, M. J., Hou, C. E., & Chen, N. R. (2021). Inclusion in global virtual teams: Exploring non-spatial proximity and knowledge sharing on innovation. *Journal of Business Research, 128*, 599–610. https://doi.org/10.1016/j.jbusres.2020.11.022

Johnsson, M. (2023). Creating global high-performing innovation teams—Insights and guidelines. *Journal of Innovation Management, 11*(2), 71–117. https://doi.org/10.24840/2183-0606_011.002_0004

Kessler, E. H., & Chakrabarti, A. K. (1996). Innovation speed: A conceptual model of context, antecedents, and outcomes. *Academy of Management Review, 21*(4), 1143–1191.

Kets de Vries, M. F. R. (2005). *The hedgehog effect: The secrets of building high performance teams*. Wiley. isbn: 978-1-119-20826-6.

Mari, S., & Pirozzi, M. (2024, January). Managing stakeholder engagement: A critical success factor. *PM World Journal, XIII*(I), 1–15. issn:2330-4480.

Nardi, B. A. (2010). *My life as a night elf priest: An anthropological account of world of warcraft (Technologies of the imagination: New media in everyday life)*. University of Michigan Press. isbn-13:978-0472050987.

Tuckman, B. W. (1965). Developmental sequence in small groups. *Psychological Bulletin, 63*(6), 384–399. https://doi.org/10.1037/h0022100

VandeWalle, D., Brown, S. P., Cron, W. L., & Slocum, J. W. (1999). The influence of goal orientation and self-regulation tactics on sales performance: A longitudinal field test. *Journal of Applied Psychology, 84*, 249–259. https://doi.org/10.1037/0021-9010.84.2.249

West, M. A., Hirst, G., Richter, A., & Shipton, H. (2004). Twelve steps to heaven: Successfully managing change through developing innovative teams. *European Journal of Work and Organizational Psychology, 13*(2), 269–299. https://doi.org/10.1080/13594320444000092

Wheelan, S. A. (2009). Group size, group development, and group productivity. *Small Group Research, 40*(2), 247–262. https://doi.org/10.1177/1046496408328703

Part III
Process Management

Chapter 12
Continuous Improvement in Project Management

Virginie Pasquon

The Continuous Improvement (CI) idea, based on the Japanese management philosophy of Kaizen, represents a paradigm change in our understanding of operational excellence and project management. This methodology arose from the convergence of classical management theory with Japanese industrial methods, particularly among management theorists such as W. Edwards Deming and Toyota employees. In project management, the term CI has evolved into much more than a collection of tools and processes; it now refers to a holistic management philosophy that dictates how businesses originate and complete projects.

Continuous improvement is based on the premise that every process, no matter how well planned or effective it is today, has room for improvement. As a result, this conceptual underpinning contrasts sharply with more traditional methods to project management, which emphasize following established procedures and employing relatively inflexible methodology.

Instead, CI takes a more dynamic approach, viewing project processes as living systems that can be constantly adjusted and optimized through systematic observation, analysis, and improvement.

The use of continuous improvement in diverse management contexts requires a complex synthesis of numerous fundamental management principles.

First, it applies systems thinking (Russell L. Ackoff) by identifying the interconnection of project processes and overall organizational performance.

Second, it accepts the concept of organizational learning, which states that knowledge gathered from each project iteration may be applied to improve future performance.

Third, it employs quality management principles, emphasizing process control and outcome monitoring, to get superior results.

V. Pasquon (✉)
Department of Innovative Technologies, SUPSI, Lugano, Switzerland
e-mail: virginie.pasquon@supsi.ch

A. Bassi et al. (eds.), *General Management Principles for Project Management*,
Management for Professionals, https://doi.org/10.1007/978-3-031-98592-8_12

In practice, continuous improvement in project management reveals itself in numerous essential areas. The **process dimension** focuses on removing inefficiencies, minimizing unpredictability, and optimizing workflows. The **people dimension** focuses on employee engagement, skill development, and cultivating a problem-solving mindset. The **organizational dimension** focuses on the structural and cultural elements required to enable continuous improvement, such as leadership commitment, resource allocation, and performance measurement methods.

Continuous improvement in project management has the transforming capacity to create a **learning organization**, as management theorists define it. This atmosphere encourages innovation and adaptation as natural results of project activity, rather than as standalone activities. Project teams that employ a CI framework improve their capacities for identifying problems, determining root causes, and developing solutions. This increased analytical power enables businesses to handle both urgent project obstacles and systemic concerns that impact their long-term performance.

Furthermore, constant improvement in project management acts as a link between strategic goals and day-to-day implementation.

By incorporating feedback loops that connect project outcomes with organizational learning, CI enables organizations to refine their project management approaches while simultaneously building institutional knowledge and capability. This dual focus on immediate performance improvement and long-term capability development distinguishes CI from more traditional project management methodologies.

Integrating continuous improvement principles into project management also helps address a fundamental challenge in modern organizational theory: **the balance between efficiency and adaptability**. While traditional project management approaches often emphasize standardization and control, CI introduces flexibility and responsiveness without sacrificing operational discipline. This balance becomes increasingly important as organizations face growing complexity and uncertainty in their project environments.

This understanding of continuous improvement as both a philosophical framework and practical methodology sets the stage for a deeper exploration of its implementation in project management contexts.

12.1 Benefits of Continuous Improvement

Implementing a CI approach within projects enables organizations to achieve the following significant advantages:

- **Operational effectiveness**: recognizing and removing inefficiencies and waste in PM procedures. Organizations have the ability to enhance resource management and speed up delivery times.

- **Quality**: By evaluating and refining, mistakes and flaws can be recognized and corrected, leading to enhanced overall quality of outputs and increased customer satisfaction.
- **Decreased negative risks**: Ongoing Enhancement enables organizations to anticipate and address possible threats and risks related to projects, lowering the chances of project failures and setbacks.
- **Customer satisfaction**: Improving project management techniques allows organizations to meet customer needs and expectations more efficiently, thereby boosting their reputation and building customer trust.
- **Adaptability**: Adopting a Continuous Improvement approach enables organizations to be more agile and reactive to market changes and new challenges, promoting their development and achievement in the long run.

12.2 Continuous Improvement Culture

A culture of Continuous Improvement serves as the basis for an organization's enduring success. This culture encourages a proactive mindset towards change and innovation, essential for adapting and thriving in the constantly changing business environment. Fostering a Continuous Improvement Culture involves more than just urging employees to propose enhancements and embrace new concepts. It also entails offering them the essential support, resources, and acknowledgment to execute these enhancements successfully. Ultimately, it's not only about generating great ideas but also about implementing them perfectly.

12.3 Continuous Improvement Processes in Project Management

To enable Continuous Improvement in project management, it is essential to implement organized processes and particular methodologies. Critical procedures involve performing a thorough analysis of previous projects to extract lessons learned, pinpointing opportunities for enhancement in project management processes with stakeholder engagement, and implementing recognized best practices that have been successful in comparable projects.

12.4 Continuous Improvement Techniques and Approaches

In the pursuit of Continuous Improvement, project management utilizes various tools and techniques to evaluate, analyze, and refine project processes and performance. These tools provide an organized method and reliable data to guide choices and improve procedures. Here are some of the most frequently used tools and techniques:

- **PDCA (Plan-Do-Check-Act)**: A systematic approach to problem-solving and continuous improvement that consists of four iterative steps. In the Planning phase, objectives and processes are established. The Do phase involves implementing the plan on a small scale. The Check phase measures and analyzes the results, while the Act phase implements improvements based on the findings. This cycle continues iteratively, fostering ongoing enhancement of processes and outcomes.
- **KAIZEN**: A Japanese philosophy emphasizing continuous, incremental improvements involving all employees from top management to front-line workers. This approach focuses on making small, ongoing changes that collectively result in significant improvements over time. It promotes a culture of continuous learning, waste elimination, and standardization of best practices.
- **Lean thinking**: A methodology focused on maximizing customer value while minimizing waste. It emphasizes creating more value with fewer resources by identifying and eliminating activities that don't add value to the final product or service. This approach includes principles such as value stream mapping, flow optimization, and pull systems to enhance efficiency and effectiveness.
- **TQM (Total Quality Management)**: A comprehensive management approach that focuses on long-term success through customer satisfaction. It involves all members of an organization in improving processes, products, services, and the culture in which they work. TQM emphasizes measurement, systematic management, strategic planning, and continuous improvement of all organizational processes.
- **Retrospective meetings**: A traditional method for assessing project outcomes and recognizing opportunities for enhancement. In these gatherings, team members evaluate previous actions, emphasizing both achievements and obstacles. By examining these elements, we can identify what was effective and what wasn't, allowing us to make adjustments that enhance future processes.
- **SWOT analysis**: This method helps recognize the project's strengths, weaknesses, opportunities, and threats, delivering a perspective of the project's environment. By examining these elements, we can identify the aspects of the project that require enhancement and formulate approaches to tackle them.
- **Root cause analysis**: An essential method for identifying the fundamental reasons behind issues or mistakes in the project. By examining the symptoms and their effects on the project, we can ascertain the underlying cause and create focused solutions to tackle it. This method is especially beneficial when addressing complicated issues that necessitate an organized strategy.

- **Benchmarking**: Entails evaluating the effectiveness, methods, and tactics of a project compared to those of successful companies or programs in the sector. This task assists in pinpointing areas that need enhancement and in implementing industry-leading practices.
- **Process mapping**: This method entails generating a visual diagram of the project's workflow, pinpointing essential steps, and examining their interconnections. This approach enables us to identify inefficiencies, bottlenecks, and opportunities for improvement, helping us to optimize processes and boost overall performance.

12.5 The Role of Post-Project Reviews

Recognizing the significance of performing detailed Post-Project Reviews (PPRs) is an essential element of the Continuous Improvement strategy. PPRs act as a vital tool for assessing the effectiveness of finished projects, pinpointing improvement opportunities, and executing corrective measures to boost project delivery and performance. Utilizing the insights obtained from PPRs, we can enhance our project management processes, improve resource allocation, and promote long-term growth and success.

12.6 Feedback Mechanisms

Feedback mechanisms are vital instruments for assessing project performance, obtaining insights from different stakeholders, and perpetually enhancing project management practices. Below are several typical feedback systems employed:

- **Surveys and Questionnaires**: Sent to team members, clients, suppliers, and different stakeholders to gather structured feedback on project effectiveness, client contentment, and potential improvement areas.
- **Interviews and Focus Groups**: Conducted to collect detailed feedback from key stakeholders, enabling extensive discussions and a full understanding of different perspectives.
- **Feedback Meetings**: Regularly held with the project team and stakeholders to assess project advancement, identify challenges, and collaboratively create solutions.
- **360-Degree Assessments**: Include assessing the project team's performance through feedback from peers, managers, partners, and clients to gain understanding of the team's abilities and strengths.
- **Anonymous Feedback**: Offers stakeholders a chance to give feedback without revealing their identity, encouraging openness and genuine input.

12.7 Implementation of Identified Improvements

The execution of enhancements recognized through Continuous Improvement is an important phase in the project management cycle. This process entails not just pinpointing areas for enhancement but also executing effective actions and preventive measures to reach concrete and lasting outcomes. Here are several important aspects to think about while executing:

- **Comprehensive planning**: Prior to beginning the implementation, it's needed to meticulously outline the required steps. This involves establishing specific goals, identifying necessary resources, and outlining the timeline and stages for implementation.
- **Project team and stakeholders participation**: Engaging the project team and valuable stakeholders in the execution process. Effective communication of goals, delegation of distinct roles and responsibilities, and fostering teamwork are essential measures for successful execution.
- **Steady implementation**: While carrying out corrective and preventive measures, it's needed to ensure uniformity and clarity in the strategy utilized are needed. Following set guidelines, honoring deadlines, and actively overseeing advancements are crucial components for guaranteeing improvements' success.
- **Flexibility and adaptability**: While a comprehensive plan is mandatory, unforeseen challenges and difficulties can occur during execution. Flexibility and adaptability, being prepared to adjust strategies, and proactively tackling problems are essential for overcoming these obstacles.
- **Open communication**: Keeping an open and clear communication channel is essential to guarantee that all stakeholders are updated on implementation activities, advancements, and any directional shifts.
- **Ongoing assessment and oversight**: Following implementation, the next step is to assess and oversee the impacts of the enhancements made consistently. Assessing outcomes relative to established goals, contrasting them with the original circumstances, and implementing required modifications or improvements are essential actions to guarantee that the advancements are sustainable over time.

12.8 Progress Monitoring and Evaluation

Monitoring and evaluating progress are not merely control activities but also chances to adjust and enhance strategies based on the outcomes obtained and the changing requirements of the project. This is how it can be accomplished:

- **Root cause analysis**: When progress does not meet expectations, it is essential to determine the fundamental reasons. This could include analyzing strategies, pinpointing new chances for enhancement, and addressing any discrepancies.

- **Adjustment of goals**: Following the evaluation of progress and newly obtained information, it may be essential to adjust project goals. This guarantees that the team concentrates on the intended outcomes and prioritizes as needed.
- **Revising corrective actions**: When monitoring indicates that corrective and preventive measures are not working, it is crucial to make prompt modifications. This might entail implementing new strategies, altering current procedures, or redistributing resources.
- **Adjusting to changing demands**: Project needs can develop, necessitating prompt and proactive modifications to strategies and procedures. Being adaptable and responsive to these changes is essential for ensuring project success.

12.9 Challenges and Opportunities

Integrating continuous improvement (CI) in project management creates a complicated environment full of obstacles and possibilities. This duality defines the essence of enhancement endeavors, where every challenge frequently hides possible paths for organizational development and creativity. Grasping this complex connection between challenges and opportunities is vital for professionals executing effective CI initiatives.

The resistance to change represents one of the toughest challenges in executing ongoing improvement efforts. This opposition appears as personal hesitance to let go of known habits, organizational stagnation, and ingrained cultural standards. Numerous people have concerns regarding job stability or changes in their roles, whereas others remain doubtful about the advantages of new practices. To successfully address this resistance, organizations need to introduce thorough educational programs that clarify both the reasons behind and the processes of CI.

This entails creating training programs that showcase measurable advantages via case studies and success narratives. A practical change management framework is mandatory for overcoming resistance. Organizations need to implement organized procedures that recognize and enable change leaders in various departments while establishing efficient feedback systems to tackle issues and modify strategies when necessary.

Clear communication regarding changes and their effects, along with frequent sharing of success stories, fosters trust and comprehension across the organization. The trap of superficiality poses another major obstacle in CI execution. Numerous organizations unintentionally concentrate on superficial enhancements that do not tackle the fundamental issues of challenges.

This method usually leads to short-term solutions that need constant attention, resulting in wasted resources and an inability to attain enduring enhancements.

To address this challenge, organizations need to create detailed root cause analysis frameworks that utilize effective problem-solving techniques. This consists of forming cross-functional teams focused on in-depth problem examination and establishing systems for monitoring and analyzing frequent issues.

The necessity of balancing innovation and enhancement arises as an essential factor. Organizations often find it challenging to balance gradual enhancements with significant innovations. This imbalance commonly results in a heightened emphasis on optimization, compromising innovation, which leads to lost chances for transformative change and diminished competitive edge.

The answer is to create what management experts refer to as an ambidextrous organizational structure, which features distinct yet linked paths for ongoing improvement and innovation efforts. This method enables organizations to seek both gradual enhancements and groundbreaking innovations at the same time.

Maintaining interest in CI initiatives poses another considerable difficulty. Organizations frequently struggle to sustain long-term dedication because of initiative fatigue, conflicting priorities, and insufficient visible advancement.

Tackling this challenge necessitates creating thorough engagement frameworks that include recognition systems and career advancement opportunities linked to CI expertise. Organizations should prioritize making progress evident and impactful by utilizing effective visualization methods and conducting regular review meetings that acknowledge successes and sustain enthusiasm.

The struggle between adaptability and organization presents continuous difficulties in CI execution. Organizations must manage the fine line between keeping structured processes and ensuring flexibility to adapt to change.

Inflexible procedures can hinder adaptability to shifts in the market, whereas overly demanding documentation needs might lead to bureaucratic delays. The answer is in creating adaptable frameworks that offer organization while preserving flexibility. This involves developing scalable enhancement procedures and setting up consistent review systems that enable modifications in response to evolving circumstances (Ashkenas, 2014).

12.10 Emerging Opportunities

The digital transformation age offers unmatched possibilities for improving CI applications. Sophisticated data analytics capabilities enhance decision-making processes, whereas automation tools can simplify regular improvement procedures. The ability to monitor and adjust in real-time, along with AI-driven prediction and optimization tools, opens new avenues for more successful enhancement efforts.

Contemporary workplace culture has progressed to foster a supportive environment for CI adoption. There is a growing focus on ongoing learning and a higher willingness to embrace change and innovation. Organizations today prioritize sustainability and long-term strategies more, as improved collaboration tools and methods enable more effective execution of enhancement initiatives.

Present market trends also create new prospects for applying CI. The rising focus on agility and adaptability corresponds effectively with CI principles, and the greater importance given to innovation fosters backing for enhancement efforts. The growing significance of sustainable practices and the increased emphasis on customer experience offer further incentives for organizations to undertake extensive improvement initiatives.

12.11 Integration Plan: Connecting Ongoing Enhancement and Creativity

Organizations must develop integration strategies to avoid a false distinction between continuous improvement and disruptive innovation. This involves creating dual operating systems that support traditional CI procedures for operational excellence while also establishing parallel innovation paths for revolutionary ideas. Organizations should develop means for exchanging ideas amongst various systems, ensuring that discoveries from each area contribute to and improve the others.

Developing adaptable skills is critical to this coherent strategy. Organizations must develop adaptive improvement techniques that can accommodate both incremental changes and dramatic advancements. This entails designing hybrid methods that combine diverse procedures and establishing constant evaluation mechanisms to ensure effectiveness.

12.12 Conclusion

The future of continuous improvement lies in creating integrated systems that effectively balance structure with flexibility while combining incremental improvements with innovative thinking. Successful organizations will maintain a long-term focus while delivering short-term results, adapting to changing conditions while preserving core principles. By understanding and actively addressing these challenges while seizing emerging opportunities, organizations can develop robust continuous improvement programs that drive both operational excellence and innovation. The key to success lies not in choosing between competing approaches but in masterfully navigating this complex landscape, turning challenges into opportunities for growth and transformation.

References

Ashkenas, R. (2014, July 23). It's time to rethink continuous improvement. *Harvard Business Review*. Retrieved from https://hbr.org/2012/05/its-time-to-rethink-continuous

Chapter 13
Innovative Process Approach

Michela Manini

The goal of process innovation is to drive improvements, optimize operations, reduce costs, increase productivity, and deliver better outcomes.

Process innovation can occur in various areas within an organization but mainly in operative ones.

In this chapter we will delve into the impact of Innovative approach within a project management.

Before addressing what is meant by an innovative process approach, it is necessary to underline the difference between project and process, which is often confused and used incorrectly.

It must be declared that projects relate to new and never previously carried out actions, while processes refer to actions that take place repeatedly.

From this first selection it emerges that the project refers to the creation of full new contents/services/products or the implementation of a change while the process has the aim of creating value by repeatedly carrying out an action.

The advantage highlights how projects are aimed at creating change while processes are organized to resist change by establishing a repeating workflow.

From a financial point of view, the project has a well-defined beginning and end to a defined scope and resources, while the process sustains a repetition that is not always constant and equal and therefore not easy to estimate even if planned in advance.

If we consider both activities from the "innovation" side, we are immediately led back to an inevitable symbiosis: the project serves the process and vice versa.

It is in fact possible to learn from the result of a process by giving life to a new project enabling to start a process of continuous improvement at the end of a project.

M. Manini (✉)
Department of Innovative Technologies, SUPSI, Lugano, Switzerland
e-mail: michela.manini@supsi.ch

A. Bassi et al. (eds.), *General Management Principles for Project Management*, Management for Professionals, https://doi.org/10.1007/978-3-031-98592-8_13

Project and process both play an important role in achieving organizational objectives and therefore it is necessary to be able to exploit them correctly.

Processes are ongoing procedures that help achieve business objectives, while projects are methods for modifying processes, launching new products or services, or making changes.

In the world of project management, the relationship and interaction between a project and a process are symbiotic too.

They cannot exist independently of each other and the success of one relies on the effective implementation of the other.

Projects are endeavors designed to achieve planned objectives, which could be defined in terms of outputs, outcomes or benefits.

If the project objectives are achieved within deadline, cost and quality constraints, so it is usually deemed to be a success.

On the other hand, processes represent a series of actions or steps taken in order to achieve a particular result.

They are defined sequences transforming inputs into outputs and through a recurring wave.

In the field of project management, processes provide the framework and guidelines for managing and controlling projects. They ensure that there is a systematic and consistent approach to project execution, thus reducing uncertainties and increasing the likelihood of success.

It is very important to consider the symbiotic relationship between project and process aids in risk management, quality control, and overall project success.

Step back to what we meant as a "good approach in project management activities", we can state to first analyze and understand the phases of the approach that Project Manager can take in consideration for a better plan.

In project management, choosing the correct approach is crucial to reach good results.

Adopting a different or a specific development of the project, this could make the difference.

The choice of the approach depending on the nature of the project, as is the complexity and the sense of uncertainty.

It is relevant to recap the standard and mostly employed approaches:

- ***The incremental one*** that is referring to phases or blocks unpacked representing a set of functionalities that is progressively delivered and activated.

This kind of approach has its roots from the open methodologies and operations as each functional part is autonomous supporting a quick result within limited time, and lead by implementing the project in sections.

The incremental approach allows you to offer value from the early phases, enable a path to a continuous improvement management.

- ***The iterative one***, is based on repeated development cycles where each iteration provides a refinement of the deliverable, which is reviewed and refined at each cycle.

It is used when the project requires continuous improvements and optimizations (it roots from agile methodologies—see Scrum), and is required a reduction risk by correcting errors gradually. Product has to be advanced one part at a time and it is necessary to therefore integrate it.

This approach allows you to continuously test the product in early phases, in order to minimizing errors at the end of the project.

- ***The adaptive one***, based on the ability to respond quickly to changes.

Instead of trying to predict everything in advance, it constantly adapts to new information and emerging needs.

Its main features are short development cycles, continuous feedback from stakeholders, adaptation of the work plan according to changing priorities.

It is ideal for projects with high uncertainty, where requirements are subject to frequent changes or where it is difficult to fully define the deliverable from the start.

– ***The predictive one***, is based on detailed and complete planning at the beginning of the project.

Everything that will be accomplished is defined, from start to finish, and the plan is followed precisely.

This method is particularly employed when the requirements are clear and stable, (nowadays is quite impossible to find a so called situation…) and there is a particular need for prediction and control.

For this reason the "predictive approach" (unfortunately still very popular today) has to be considered as the main cause of multiple errors and failures.

We can underline as "non linear behaviors" are phenomena in which the effects are not proportional to the causes. This means that small changes in initial conditions can lead to drastically different results, making it very difficult to make accurate predictions. This is known as the butterfly effect.

Referring to "operation activities", non linear behaviors can emerge in various ways.

For example, a small change in customer demand can lead to large fluctuations in sales.

Likewise, small changes in the manufacturing process can have a significant impact on the quality of the final product.

These non linear behaviors make operations planning a challenge. Companies must be able to quickly adapt to these variations, which are often unpredictable. This requires agile operations management, with flexible processes and the ability to respond quickly to changes (adaptive approach).

Moreover, companies can use tools such as data analytics and advanced forecasting to better manage these non linear behaviors. These tools can help identify patterns and trends, making it easier to predict possible future scenarios and plan accordingly.

The adaptive approach involves remaining flexible and ready to change strategy based on changing environmental. This does not mean that there is no planning or structure, but rather that those plans and structures are fluid and changeable.

The initial plan is just the starting point and can be adjusted as new information rises up or changes occur.

Adaptive organizations are those that are able to change their direction or strategy in response to a change in their environment (see Agile culture).

Meanwhile flows must be able to adapt to ensure that the right information gets to the right people.

This may include changes in the market, technology, competition or regulations.

These organizations have structures and processes that are flexible and agile, allowing them to respond quickly and effectively to changes.

To support these organizations, the adaptive approach emphasizes process flexibility.

This means that processes are not fixed or stiff, but can be modified or adapted as needed.

This may include adapting processes to respond to changes in priorities, new opportunities or emerging challenges.

People and information flows must also be flexible in an adaptive approach.

People must be ready to change roles or responsibilities based on the needs of the organization (specially within a team of project management). Information at the right time.

Lastly, the organization itself must be flexible.

This means that the structure and culture of the organization must be such that it supports and encourages adaptability.

This can include fostering a culture of learning and innovation, creating flexible organizational structures and promoting collaboration and open communication.

The adaptive approach refers to a way of managing projects and organizations that places particular emphasis on flexibility and the ability to adapt to changes.

As above described, this methodology is particularly effective in dynamic and uncertain contexts, where conditions can change rapidly and unpredictably.

The Project Manager therefore also has the function of dispenser for the transfer of this approach within and out the team and with all stakeholders involved or impacted by the activities.

In particular, this approach requires that project plans are not strict and steady, but flexible and dynamic, ready to be modified based on new needs that emerge during the execution of the project.

Having say that, the Project Manager has a key role in facilitating communication between team members and promoting a climate of collaboration and continuous learning.

The adaptive approach also involves enhancing the skills and knowledge of all team members, fostering the sharing of information and testing of new solutions.

This fact promotes innovation leading team members to come up with creative ideas and solutions to solve problems that arise during project execution.

Finally, the adaptive approach encourages the use of digital tools and techniques to support project management, such as project management software, which allows you to monitor the progress of the project in real time and operating promptly in case of need.

Last but not least, the adaptive approach is a powerful tool for managing projects in an effective and innovative way, promoting the creation of value and adaptability to new market challenges.

Generally for simple projects we can apply the method PDCA: Plan, Do, Check and Adjust, leading to improve project outcomes.

Introducing a successful model to manage simple activities through PCDA: Plan, Do, Check and Act.

A PDCA cycle based on the scientific method of proposing a change in a process, is implementing the change, measuring the results, and taking appropriate action.

It is known as the Deming Cycle or Deming Wheel after W. Edwards Deming, who introduced the concept in Japan in the 1950s.

PDCA cycle is a four-stage model providing a framework for developing, testing and implementing changes leading to quality improvement.

- **Plan**: Determine goals for a process and needed changes to achieve them.
- **Do**: Implement the changes.
- **Check**: Evaluate the results in terms of performance.
- **Act**: Standardize and stabilize the change or begin the cycle again, depending on the results.

13.1 New Role of Project Manager in A.I. Process Approach

It is necessary to underline that within corporate entities, the main function of governance, management and execution of organizational changes is attributed to project management.

So Project Manager has a widespread responsibility of maintaining a constant balance between the demand for innovation and the creation of value too.

The role of the Project Manager in an A.I. process approach is multifaceted.

Project Managers are responsible for overseeing the implementation and use of A.I. technologies, ensuring that they align with the project's goals and objectives.

This includes determining which A.I. technologies are most appropriate, managing the integration of these technologies into existing processes, and monitoring their performance.

How A.I. can be integrated into project management and how Project Managers can utilize these tools to enhance their operations?

One of the most significant benefits of A.I. in project management is its ability to automate routine tasks. Project Managers often spend the majority of their time on administrative tasks such as scheduling meetings, sending reminders, updating project status, etc.

A.I. powered project management tools automating these routine tasks, freeing up the Project Manager's time so they can focus on more strategic aspects of the project.

For instance, an A.I. tool can be programmed to send out automated updates to the team, keeping everyone on the same page without the Project Manager having to manually update each team member. Similarly, A.I. can also assist with scheduling by analyzing team members calendars and suggesting optimal meeting times.

A.I. can also play a crucial role in risk management. With its ability to analyze vast amounts of data and identify patterns, A.I. can predict potential risks before they become an issue.

This can be priceless for Project Managers, as it allows them to mitigate risks proactively rather than reactively.

Moreover, A.I. can also improve decision-making. It can provide Project Managers with data-driven insights, helping them make informed decisions.

For example, A.I. can analyze past project data to predict how certain decisions might impact the project's timeline, budget, or quality.

This can help Project Managers make better decisions that are aligned with the project's objectives.

The role of the Project Manager, therefore, evolves with the integration of A.I.

They become more of a strategic leader, leading team and making informed decisions based on data-driven insights provided by A.I.

Project Managers also need to adapt to this new technology, learning how to leverage A.I. tools effectively to enhance their project management processes.

In conclusion we can state that project management in the organizational field lives in a duality value.

On one hand, project management derives from the reception and declination of the company strategy, but on the other hand it continuously feeds it through the improvement activities carried out over and over in each project.

From this double value, it can be highlighted that the centrality of the Project Manager function generates continuous enrichment in horizontal skills (empowering skills) generated by the exchange of information and relationships.

References

2008, Mursia, Bozzi, G., Branduardi, C., Cappelli, F., Moro, W., & Valagussa, M. *Dal Progetto al processo.*

2022, University of Stellenbosch Dep Industrial Engineering, Du Preez, N. D., & Louv, L. *A framework for managing the innovation process.*

2025, McKinsey, Jeffery, B., Weddle, B., Brassey, J., & Thanker, S., *Thriving workplaces: How employers can improve productivity and change lives.*

2021, Little, Brown & Company, Kissinger, H., Schmidt, E., & Huttenlocher, D. *The age of AI.*

2019, Columbia Business School Publishing, Krippendorff, K. *Driving innovation from within.*

2017, Guerini Next, Liker, J. K., & Hoseus, M. *Toyota culture.*

Chapter 14
Resource Management Process

Silvia Mari

Resource management is the process of estimating what resources will be needed to complete a project, acquiring them, making a schedule for their allocation and monitoring their utilization during the execution of a project, program or portfolio of projects. Project resources can be simply defined as anything needed to execute project tasks (e.g. raw materials, human resources, machinery and equipment, financial resources, time, information and data).

Managing resources is a key and relevant aspect for any type of organization, and the same ISO 9001:2015 includes the Clause 7.1 specifically for "Managing Resources." This clause outlines the requirements for organizations to determine and provide the necessary resources to establish, implement, maintain, and continually improve their Quality Management System (QMS).

Clause 7.1 covers key aspects of the process of managing resources, including people (by ensuring the competence, awareness, and adequate number of personnel); infrastructure (the physical and technological structures necessary for operations, such as buildings, equipment, and IT systems); environment for the operation of processes (by creating a suitable work environment that supports the effective functioning of processes); monitoring and measuring resources (to ensure their ongoing suitability and effectiveness) and organizational knowledge (the need to maintain and utilize organizational knowledge to improve the QMS itself).

Usually, the project manager or project management office (PMO) oversees the resource management process, but some organizations have a dedicated resource manager who specializes in this area. A resource manager is responsible for leading the process of defining resource requirements, estimating costs, procuring resources and ensuring they're properly allocated and utilized. One of its key responsibilities

S. Mari (✉)
Department of Innovative Technologies, SUPSI, Lugano, Switzerland
e-mail: silvia.mari@supsi.ch

A. Bassi et al. (eds.), *General Management Principles for Project Management*, Management for Professionals, https://doi.org/10.1007/978-3-031-98592-8_14

is to develop a resource management plan to guide the resource planning efforts of the organization.

Resource management is even more important for project portfolio management than it is for managing individual projects. Any organization, in fact, needs to ensure they allocate resources strategically to manage multiple projects simultaneously. For example, they can minimize costs by using the same resources across projects.

By adhering to the principles of ISO 9001:2015, organizations can effectively manage their resources, leading to improved efficiency, reduced costs, and enhanced overall performance.

Resource management is a critical aspect of project management that involves planning, allocating, and managing resources to ensure that project objectives are met efficiently and effectively. Effective resource management involves forecasting, allocating, monitoring, and adjusting resources to ensure efficient use.

The resource management process can be divided into two key functions: resource planning and resource management.

Resource planning is the ongoing process of creating strategic resource plans to meet demand. Demand refers to work requests or demands from the organization. Resources can be viewed as supply, and supply must equal or outweigh demand as projects come online to be delivered. The steps involved in resource planning include:

- Identifying Demand: understanding the work requests or demands from the organization.
- Assessing Supply: evaluating the available resources to meet the demand.
- Capacity Planning: identifying the needed capacity for operational efforts (ongoing endeavors) before considering discretionary efforts (opportunity exploration).
- Resource Acquisition Plans: identifying shortages and gaps in resources and developing plans to bridge these gaps.

Resource management works jointly with resource planning to evaluate, create a disposition of, and implement changes to resource forecasts, resource reservations, and resource commitments. The steps involved in resource management include:

- Resource Forecasting: predicting future resource needs based on project schedules and demand.
- Resource Allocation: assigning available resources to various tasks and projects.
- Resource Monitoring: tracking resource usage and performance to ensure that resources are being used efficiently.
- Resource Adjustment: making necessary adjustments to resource allocations based on project progress and changes in demand.

14.1 Resource Management Techniques

Abrantes R. and Figueiredo J. (2015) argue that traditional resource management approaches are insufficient, as they either focus on project selection and prioritization or on technical scheduling aspects, without effectively integrating organizational and technical considerations. Through an action research approach with a multinational company, their study reveals the critical need for systematic and proactive resource management processes that can quickly consolidate project information, visualize multiple scenarios, and understand the chain effects of resource allocation decisions across the entire portfolio.

Nowadays the focus is on the need for integrating organizational and technical aspects of resource management to effectively coordinate resourcing decisions in dynamic portfolios. That means to combine the appropriate processes, and consequently tools, according to the matrix organization and at which extent it is a project-oriented organization.

Relevant techniques for such purpose are:

- **Resource Constrained Multi-Project Scheduling Problem (RCMPSP)**. Addresses technical scheduling aspects but could face barriers in highly dynamic environments. (Kao et al., 2006),
- **Hierarchical Planning**. Combines high-level resource allocation decisions (Rough Cut Capacity Planning—RCCP) with detailed resource assignment schedules (Resource Constrained Project Scheduling—RCPSP). (Hendriks, 1999; Platje et al., 1994; Hans et al., 2007).
- **Agile Methodologies**. Emphasizes stable teams with multiple skills to avoid frequent resource reallocation. (Szőke, 2011).
- **Critical Chain**. Focuses on managing bottleneck resources and buffer management (Herroelen & Leus, 2005; Leach, 2014).

Most of the above-mentioned techniques allow project manager to forecast, plan, allocate, level and optimize resources during the execution of a project. The four most common techniques commonly used for resource optimization are:

- **Resource Loading**. A resource allocation technique that consists of determining the maximum number of work hours employees can be allocated and ensuring that 100% of their time is utilized throughout a project.
- **Resource Leveling**. Resource leveling is the process of re-assigning work to a project team to solve overallocation or scheduling issues. By thoroughly understanding what your team members can offer, you can assign tasks based on their abilities to maximize resource efficiency.
- **Resource Utilization Tracking**. Careful resource planning is equally as important as resource tracking. Project managers need to keep track of resource utilization to spot any re-sources that aren't being used efficiently. Then they can simply reallocate those resources or change the resource management plan.
- **Resource Smoothing**. Resource smoothing simply consists of delaying non-critical tasks to complete a project on time with the available resources. This is done by using the slack or float on each of those tasks to delay them without affecting the critical path. By delaying non-critical tasks, you can move your resources to complete critical path tasks and circle back to the least important activities.

14.2 Resource Management Tools

While most of these resource management tools started as analog charts, documents and diagrams, they've evolved and are now part of resource management software that can be used for either project or enterprise resource planning. The most typical artifacts used in resource planning and monitoring are listed below.

- Gantt chart: helps organizations make a schedule for any project they're executing and allocate resources such as team members, materials or equipment.
- Timesheets: track employees' work hours for payroll processing. They can either be used for tracking the time they spend completing project tasks or simply log hours from their work shifts.
- Resource histogram: a simple bar chart that helps understand how resources are utilized over time.
- Workload management chart: a workload management calendar helps team leaders understand how work is allocated among their team members, so they can distribute the team's workload evenly.
- Resource calendar: help organizations estimate what resources will be needed to complete a project on time.
- Resource breakdown structure (RBS): a chart that helps organizations break down projects into individual tasks and specify the resources that will be needed to execute each of them.

As discussed by Leynaud X. et al. (2019) and Hidayat M. (2014), modern project management rely on multi-dimensional project breakdown structures. There are many hierarchical structures such as: GBS (Geographical Breakdown Structure), PBS (Product Breakdown Structure), SBS (Systems Breakdown Structure) or FBS (Functional Breakdown Structure), ABS (Activity Breakdown Structure), OBS (Organization Breakdown Structure), RBS (Resources or Risks Breakdown Structure), CWBS (Contract Work Breakdown Structure), etc.

Integrating these structures can elevate the project management and optimization. This approach expands WBS development to include dimensions like time, cost, risk, and resources, offering stakeholders diverse perspectives and enhancing project management for greater flexibility and effectiveness.

An organization can be considered mature in terms of project, program and portfolio management by the extension at which its different IT tools are integrated and communicate one each other (e.g. project management software with ERP tool and financial controlling tool).

Finally, there are some principles of sustainability that can be incorporated into the resource management best practices and definitively into a project and/or team charter. Project managers are often well-positioned to look at the entire supply and value chain and envision a more favorable environmental footprint by taking measures to reduce consumption of resources and lessen waste production.

While considering sustainability in human resource management, project manager nowadays should consider some key aspects and include them in the decision making process. These aspects are:

- Work-life balance. Ensuring that project work does not negatively impact the work-life balance of project team members.
- Training and skills development. Providing opportunities for project team members to develop new skills and knowledge.
- Diversity, equity, and inclusion (DE&I). Ensuring that the project team is diverse and inclusive, and that all team members are treated fairly and respectfully.
- Ethics. Ensuring that the project is conducted in an ethical manner, and that all team members adhere to ethical standards.
- Transparency. Ensuring that project information is transparent and accessible to all stakeholders.

In conclusion effective management of resources takes on heightened importance as sustainability practices are integrated into the organization and throughout the life cycle of the project. Project managers who are aware of these factors have the power to influence by raising them directly to management or addressing them as they are able to, within the confines of the project.

References

Abrantes, R., & Figueiredo, J. (2015). Resource management process framework for dynamic NPD portfolios. *International Journal of Project Management, 33*, 1274–1288.

Hans, E. W., Herroelen, W., Wullink, G., & Leus, R. (2007). A hierarchical approach to multi-project planning under uncertainty. *Omega, 35*, 563–577.

Hendriks, M. (1999). Human resource allocation in a multi-project R&D environment resource capacity allocation and project portfolio planning in practice. *International Journal of Project Management, 17*, 181–188.

Herroelen, W., & Leus, R. (2005). Project scheduling under uncertainty: Survey and research potentials. *European Journal of Operational Research, 165*, 289–306.

Hidayat, M. (2014). Standardized multi-dimensional WBS for enhanced BIM and data analytics in LPG facility projects. *PM World Journal, XIII*(IV), 1–53. issn: 2330-4480.

Kao, H., Wang, B., Dong, J., & Ku, K. (2006). An event-driven approach with makespan/cost tradeoff analysis for project portfolio scheduling. *Computers in Industry, 57*, 379–397.

Leach, L. P. (2014). *Critical chain project management* (3rd ed.). Artech House.

Leynaud, X., Giammalvo, P. D., & Moine, J. Y. (2019). *Multi-dimensional project breakdown structures—The secret to successful building information modeling (BIM) integration*. DCB Publishing.

Platje, A., Seidel, H., & Wadman, S. (1994). Project and portfolio planning cycle. *International Journal of Project Management, 12*, 100–106.

Szőke, Á. (2011). Conceptual scheduling model and optimized release scheduling for agile environments. *Information and Software Technology, 53*, 574–591.

References

Chapter 15
General Principles of Project Risk Management

Carmelo di Mauro

15.1 Introduction

Definitions of a project vary depending on the field or discipline. Generally, a project is considered a temporary endeavor undertaken to create a unique product, service, or result. According to this definition, a project is not an ongoing operation but a temporary effort with specific start and finish dates, producing unique outcomes. These outcomes can range from products and services to distinct results. A project's purpose is to achieve specific goals and objectives, which can vary widely—from improving processes to developing new products or services. This differentiates projects from routine operational activities, which often produce repetitive outputs.

A project is developed based on a specific scope, defined requirements, and established success criteria, necessitating a series of planned and managed activities to achieve its objectives. This includes scheduling, budgeting, quality management, and stakeholder communication. These activities involve the allocation and management of various resources, such as time, money, personnel, and materials, which are often spread among cross-functional teams from different departments or areas of expertise, working together toward a common objective.

Such complexity needs to be effectively coordinated to achieve project goals but can also introduce risks—unforeseen events that can threaten the expected results. This chapter aims to describe, in general terms, how risk management can facilitate the successful achievement of project management objectives.

C. di Mauro (✉)
Esch sur Alzette, Luxembourg
e-mail: carmelo.dimauro@riskgovernancesolutions.eu

A. Bassi et al. (eds.), *General Management Principles for Project Management*, Management for Professionals, https://doi.org/10.1007/978-3-031-98592-8_15

15.2 The Concept of Risk

Several different definitions of the concept of risk are provided in the literature, but for simplicity, this chapter refers to the one provided by Stanley Kaplan and John Garrick in their 1981 paper "On The Quantitative Definition of Risk." According to Kaplan and Garrick, risk can be understood in terms of three questions:

- What can happen? (Scenarios)
- How likely is it to happen? (Likelihood)
- If it does happen, what are the consequences? (Consequences)

Kaplan and Garrick define risk as a measure that answers these three questions, encompassing the various possible scenarios (or events), their probabilities, and their associated consequences. A scenario refers to the different events or outcomes that could potentially happen. In a given context, these scenarios represent all the possible ways things could go wrong (or right). Likelihood is the probability or frequency with which each scenario is expected to occur, quantifying the chance of a particular event happening. Consequences denote the impact or outcome if a particular scenario occurs and can be measured in terms of financial loss, environmental damage, human injury, etc.

For example, consider the risks associated with an industrial chemical plant:

- **Scenarios**: Different types of failures, such as equipment malfunction, human error, or external events like an earthquake.
- **Likelihood**: The probability of each type of failure occurring based on historical data or statistical models.
- **Consequences**: The potential impact of each failure, such as the extent of chemical release, health effects on workers, environmental damage, and economic loss.

By evaluating these three elements, one can form a comprehensive understanding of the risk associated with the chemical plant. This helps in prioritizing risk management efforts, such as implementing safety measures for high-probability, high-impact scenarios.

It should be noted that to estimate consequences, the element exposed to a hazard source and its degree of vulnerability must be identified. In the context of risk assessment, vulnerability is generally defined as the susceptibility of a system, entity, or asset to being damaged or affected by potential hazards or threats. It includes inherent weaknesses or deficiencies that could be exploited or affected, leading to negative outcomes. Vulnerability is a key component in determining the overall risk level, as it interacts with the probability of a threat and the potential impact to produce a risk assessment.

Kaplan and Garrick's definition of risk provides a structured and quantitative approach to understanding and managing risk. By assessing the potential threat, exposed elements, and related vulnerabilities, organizations can identify areas of weakness and prioritize mitigation strategies to reduce the potential impact of hazards.

Fig. 15.1 Conceptual representation of the concept of risk

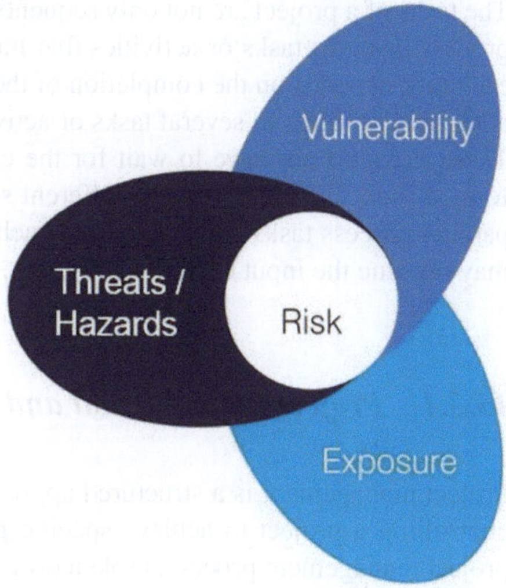

In this chapter, we will apply Kaplan and Garrick's definition of risk and the related concepts to the project management process (Fig. 15.1).

15.3 Project Management

In general terms, regardless of the application domain, project development can be defined as a process consisting of a sequence of activities over time. Each systematic task in this sequence is designed to transform inputs into outputs, producing the desired result.

For each step in the series, we can identify the following elements that characterize the individual phase:

- **Inputs**: The resources, materials, information, or energy required to start the process. These inputs are essential for the process to function.
- **Activities**: The specific actions, tasks, or operations performed to transform the inputs into outputs.
- **Outputs**: The final outcomes produced by the process step.
- **Resources**: The tools, equipment, personnel, and technology used to carry out the process. Resources are necessary to perform the activities within the process step.
- **Control Mechanisms**: The methods and procedures used to monitor and regulate the process to ensure it stays on track and meets its objectives. Control mechanisms help identify deviations and implement corrective actions.
- **Feedback Loop**: Information generated from the process step and the outputs that is fed back into the process for continuous improvement. This loop helps control, refine, and optimize the process over time.

The tasks of a project are not only sequential but also parallel. Whereas a sequential process involves tasks or activities that must be completed one after the other and each task depends on the completion of the previous task before it can begin, a parallel process refers to several tasks or activities that are carried out simultaneously. These tasks do not have to wait for the completion of the others and can be performed independently, often in different sequences or at the same time. Typically, parallel process tasks contribute to the achievement of a common objective, which may become the input of a following task.

15.3.1 Project Management and Risk Management

Project management is a structured approach to planning, organizing, leading, and controlling a project to achieve specific goals. A general description of a typical project management process, broken down into its key phases:

1. Initiation
   (a) Define the project at a high level.
   (b) Establish its feasibility
   (c) Identify all parties affected by the project and define their interests and involvement.
   (d) Assess the practicality of the project, considering financial, technical, and operational factors.
2. Planning
   (a) Develop a roadmap for achieving the project's objectives.
   (b) Plan resources, schedule, budget, and risks.
   (c) Define the scope in a detailed Work Breakdown Structure (WBS).
   (d) Develop a timeline with milestones and deliverables (e.g. using tools like Gantt charts).
   (e) Estimate costs and prepare a budget.
   (f) Identify and allocate resources.
   (g) Identify potential risks, assess their impact, and develop mitigation strategies.
   (h) Define quality standards and procedures.
   (i) Develop a plan for internal and external communication.
3. Execution
   (a) Execute the project plan.
   (b) Ensure deliverables are produced as per specifications.
   (c) Assemble and train the project team.
   (d) Assign tasks to team members.
   (e) Perform the tasks as per the project plan.
   (f) Communicate with stakeholders and manage their expectations.
   (g) Monitor the quality of deliverables.

4. Monitoring and Controlling
   (a) Track, review, and regulate project progress and performance.
   (b) Identify any areas where changes are required.
   (c) Manage changes to the project scope, schedule, and costs using a formal change management process.
   (d) Continuously monitor risks and implement risk response plans.
   (e) Verify that project deliverables meet the defined quality standards.
5. Closing
   (a) Finalize all project activities.
   (b) Formally close the project and hand over deliverables.

The purpose of what has just been described regarding the various activity phases of project management is simply to assess that it can be interpreted as an actual process. In this context, applying the concept of risk, as defined by Kaplan and Garrick, to each activity (and logically to all its sub-activities, even if not described here) involves viewing these activities as potential exposed elements characterized by specific vulnerabilities and consequences. Consequently, we must identify the threats relevant to each exposed element to understand and manage the associated risks effectively. Any error, defect or threat may threaten the outcome of the project.

In order to define a systemic approach to management, in the following paragraphs some different approaches will be taken to characterize the different risk components. As a general reference we will take ISO31000, the standard that describes risk management processes.

15.3.2 Hazard Identification

In hazard assessment, hazard identification is a crucial step in risk management, involving the recognition of potential hazards that could cause harm or have negative effects. In order to identify and characterize hazards, two aspects need to be described:

- **Type of hazard**, i.e. the type of phenomenology by which a certain threat manifests itself by causing damage to an exposed vulnerable element (in the context of natural hazards, we might think of the mechanical shock of an earthquake, for example; in the context of a major project such as a bridge or motorway, we might consider the lack of economic, material or technical resources);
- **Likelihood**, i.e. the measure of the chance that a given hazard will occur. The concept of likelihood refers to the probability or frequency with which a specific hazard event is expected to occur.

Various techniques are used to identify hazards:

- **Brainstorming**: a group of stakeholders or experts come together to generate a list of potential hazards in an informal and open discussion. This simple technique has de advantage to encourages diverse perspectives and can quickly generate a large number of ideas. It is useful in the initial stages of a project or when diverse input is needed.
- **Checklists**: it is based on some knowledge already available and formalized as a predefined lists of known hazards and failure modes. The list is reviewed to ensure all potential hazards are considered. This approach can be systematic, comprehensive and easy to use. Its effectiveness depends very much on the adherence of the criteria to the project and the reliability of the information with which the checklist is defined. For example, it is effective for routine or formalized verifications such as verification of compliance with regulatory requirements.
- **What-If Analysis**: is structured brainstorming technique where team members ask "what-if" questions to explore potential hazards and their consequences. It is a flexible and easy approach and it encourages creative thinking about potential hazard. It can be used to investigate complex systems where standard checklists may not be sufficient. Its effectiveness depends on the degree of experience and competence of the team members.
- **Hazard and Operability Study (HAZOP)**: is a systematic and detailed examination of a process or operation, focusing on deviations from design intent using guide words like "more," "less," "no," and "reverse." It is highly structured and thorough. It identifies both hazards and operability problems. These problems are identified in operational terms and also apply to the industrial world and the process is described in precise terms that are also useful and ambitious for project management. Dangers are identified by imagining the causes that can cause these variables to deviate from the predefined ones. In the same way one can imagine for a project management phase a deviation of a certain parameter to be respected (for example the number of workers necessary to build a certain work).
- **Failure Modes and Effects Analysis (FMEA)**: is systematic method for evaluating processes to identify where and how they might fail, and assessing the relative impact of different failures.
- **Fault Tree Analysis (FTA)**: top-down, deductive failure analysis that uses Boolean logic to combine various lower-level events that could lead to a top-level system failure. Provides a visual representation of the pathways to failure. This technique can be used when, for example, the structure of the project development is rather complex and involves many activities in parallel because it allows a more accurate combinatorial calculation. Logically, it is not always possible to have descriptive information on processes and sub-processes, but this technique can help to at least understand their complexity by identifying the most critical nodes.
- **Incident Investigation and Root Cause Analysis**: a retrospective technique that examines past incidents to identify underlying hazards and root causes. It provides valuable lessons from real-world events and it helps prevent recurrence of similar incidents. It normally implemented during post-incident reviews and improvement programs.

Regarding the of likelihood of the occurrence of an hazard, it can estimate as probability or frequency. Probability is a numerical value between 0 and 1 that represents the chance of a hazard occurring. A probability of 0 means the event will not happen, and a probability of 1 means the event will certainly happen. In most cases, calculating the probability of an event is quite difficult, so frequency is used as an approximation. Frequency refers to how often a hazard event is expected to occur over a specific period. It is usually expressed as an event rate, such as occurrences per year, month, or another time unit. In most cases, the calculation of the probability of an event is quite difficult, so frequency is used as an approximation. In other words, frequency is affected by a certain degree of uncertainty.

To assess the likelihood of hazards, various methods can be employed:

- Historical Data Analysis: Examining past events and historical records to estimate how frequently similar hazards have occurred.
- Statistical Models: Using statistical techniques and probability distributions to model and predict the likelihood of hazard events.
- Example: Applying Poisson distribution to model the occurrence of rare events like earthquakes.
- Expert Judgment: Consulting with experts who have experience and knowledge in the specific area to estimate the probability of hazard events.
- Scenario Analysis: Creating detailed hypothetical scenarios to explore the probability of different hazard events.
- Simulation: Using computer simulations to model complex systems and predict the occurrence of hazard events.

Likelihood can be expressed in different ways, depending on the context and the preference of the organization:

- **Qualitative terms**: use descriptive terms such as 'rare', 'unlikely', 'possible', 'probable' and 'almost certain' to classify probability. For example, describe as 'unlikely' the probability of a severe delay in completing a task.
- **Quantitative terms**: provide numerical probabilities or frequencies. For example, assign a probability of 0.05 (5%) to the occurrence of a lack of certain resources.

Typically, the quantitative approach in defining risks for project management is used because of the lack of reliable information that can be applied extensively to all types of projects. Therefore, it must be stated that the identification of hazards has a large margin of uncertainty and therefore all subsequent evaluations and decisions largely influence the entire management process. Nevertheless, identifying and characterizing the hazards and consequently also the risks makes it possible to anticipate unexpected events that could jeopardize the outcome of the entire project.

As an illustration, the following table shows some of the typical sources of hazards for project management divided into internal and external causes. Logically, the aim of the table is not to be exhaustive, but to show how difficult it is to identify all possible sources of danger for a project and its individual tasks, and how the identification of dangers (and consequently of risks) requires a structured approach (Table 15.1).

Table 15.1 selected examples of different type of hazard relevant for the project risk management

Internal hazards		External hazard	
Management	Poor project planning Ineffective leadership Miscommunication Lack of stakeholder engagement Scope creep	**Environmental**	Natural disasters (earthquakes, floods, hurricanes) Extreme weather conditions Environmental contamination
Hazard related to quality controls	Defect in interim results Lacking application of project management methods poor controls and test strategies Quality control failures Non-compliance with standards Substandard workmanship	**Economic**	Market fluctuations Economic downturns Inflation A shift in the market/ new markets Customer fails to pay
Personnel	Lack of skills and competences and adequate level of experience Poor collaborative culture and disagreements in the team Fazzy decision-making processes and responsibility	**Political and legal**	Regulatory changes Political instability Trade restrictions Legal disputes
Resource	Budget overruns Resource Shortages (materials, labor) Poor resource allocation Inaccurate estimations	**Social**	Changes in public opinion Labor strikes Social unrest
Technical and operational	Technological failures Integration issues Design flaws Equipment failure Software bugs or glitches Process failures Human errors Insufficient training Inadequate procedures	**Technological**	Rapid technological change Cybersecurity threats Technological obsolescence
Cost	Planning changes Complicated project background conditions	**Supply chain**	Supplier failures Transportation disruptions Import/export restrictions
Hazard of strategic decisions	Failure to recognize chances Lack of ability to consistently manage chances	**Market**	Changes in customer preferences Competitive actions New market entrants
Health and safety hazards	Workplace accidents Health risks (e.g., exposure to hazardous materials) Ergonomic issues		

15.3.3 Exposed Elements, Vulnerabilities and Consequences

As described above, the exposed elements of a project are all the tasks that constitute it. The functioning of each task depends on key aspects and variables that contribute in different ways to achieving the expected final results. Hazards can impact various aspects, including the availability of resources, information, energy, as well as control and management capacities.

When a task is exposed to different types of hazards, it can generate several different types of consequences based on the task's vulnerabilities. Vulnerabilities are the weaknesses or susceptibilities of a system, entity, or asset that make it more likely to be harmed or affected by a hazard. Vulnerabilities determine the extent to which a system or asset is likely to be impacted by a hazard. The more vulnerable an asset is, the greater the potential for harm when exposed to a hazard. Vulnerabilities can take several forms, such as physical (e.g., structural weaknesses), procedural (e.g., lack of planning), or organizational (e.g., poor management). Vulnerability must also be related to the type of consequences that can be generated. For example, a delay in the procurement of resources or information may cause a delay in the project development timeline but also economic losses or reputational damage. In turn, all these types of consequences can be expressed in a single metric, e.g. in economic terms. Therefore, it is crucial to investigate not only the relationship between an exposed element and its vulnerability to a certain hazard but also the potential consequences and how they should be represented.

15.3.4 Cascading Effects

We have described a project as a sequence of tasks, i.e. a series of activities that are developed according to a predefined schedule. Just as the outputs of a task are typically necessary for the development of the next step of the project in the same way the impact generated by the occurrence of an hazard can be turn into a hazard for the following tasks. Cascading effects in risk management refer to a sequence of events triggered by an initial hazard or disruption that leads to a series of secondary and often more severe consequences. These effects are also known as domino effects or ripple effects. In risk management, understanding cascading effects is crucial for identifying and mitigating the broader impacts of an initial incident, ensuring comprehensive risk assessment and response strategies.

The main characteristics of cascading Effects can be described as follow:

- **Interdependency**: systems and processes are often interconnected, meaning that a disruption in one area can affect multiple other areas. During a project development that is typically design according to a precise temporal sequence, early stage activities can threat activities that may planned far late;
- **Complexity**: cascading effects can be complex and unpredictable, as the initial impact can interact with various factors and systems, amplifying the overall effect.

- **Amplification**: Initial events can escalate as they trigger additional events or failures, often resulting in more significant impacts than the original incident.

Therefore it is rather important to explore how each task of project is related to identify the most critical paths of the development of the project activities (Figs. 15.2, 15.3, and 15.4).

15.3.5 Risk Management Cycle

Up to this point, we have illustrated how to identify and characterize risks. Instead, in this chapter we will illustrate how to manage risks starting from the assumption that any project, whatever its nature and purpose, is characterized by a multiplicity

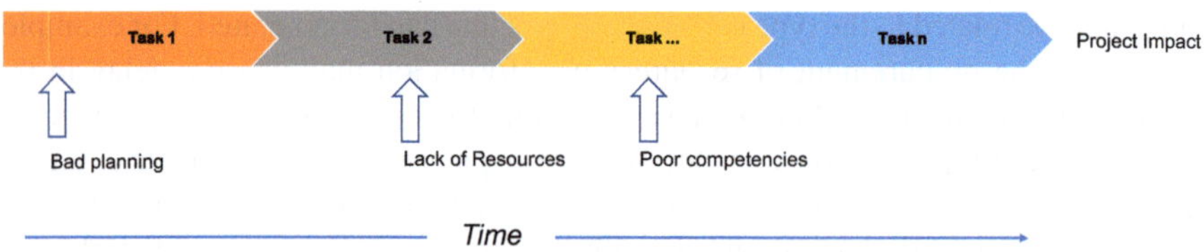

Fig. 15.2 Conceptual representation of the project flow broken down according to a time series of tasks and their associated hazards

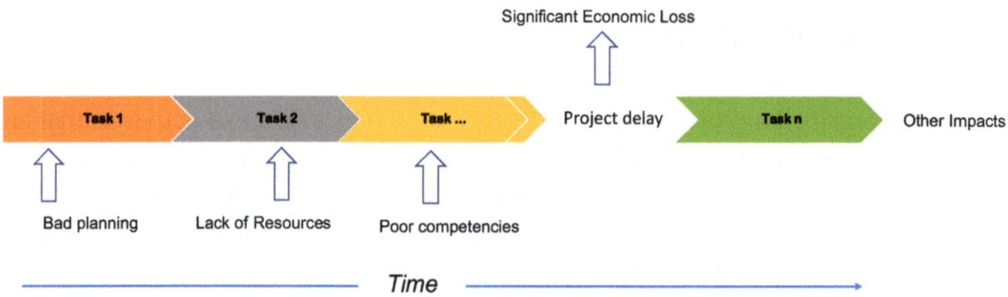

Fig. 15.3 Conceptual representation of the cascading effect of some hazards

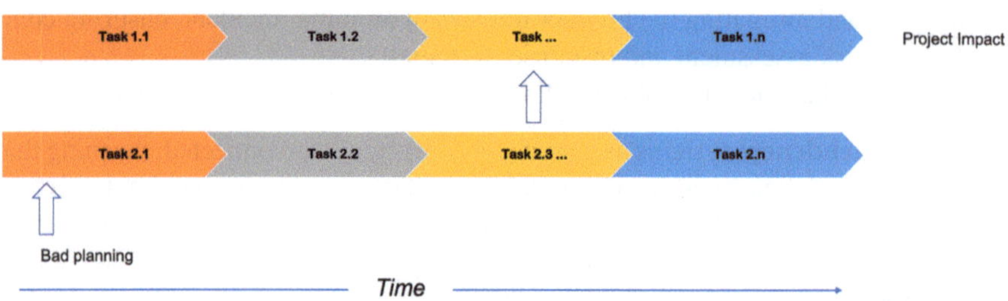

Fig. 15.4 Conceptual representation of the cascading effects along parallel project processes

of risks identified by the combination of hazard sources, exposed elements, vulnerabilities and consequences.

The question is therefore how to structure a decision-making process that allows this multitude of risks to be managed coherently and effectively.

Borrowing the definition of Total Risk Management from Haimes (1991), one can define risk management as being based on the process of risk assessment, trying to answer a second set of three questions:

- What can be done?
- What options are available and what are their associated trade-offs in terms of all costs, benefits, and risks?
- What are the impacts of current management decisions on future options?

Risk management is a structured, iterative process used to identify, assess, manage and monitor risks within an project. Given the recursive nature of this activity, one can speak of a risk management cycle. This cycle ensures continuous risk management throughout the life cycle of a project or operation. It typically involves several key stages, which can be illustrated in a cyclical diagram to emphasize its iterative nature.

Here's an illustration and description of the typical stages in the risk management cycle (Fig. 15.5).

It should be noted that the risk management cycle is iterative, based on a continuous improvement approach. As new risks are identified and existing risks are managed, the cycle repeats to ensure ongoing risk management throughout the project's lifecycle. It has to be considered an integral and essential part of the project management process. Effective risk management integrates with the overall project management processes, ensuring that risks are considered in the planning, execution and monitoring phases. Given the variety of activities that project development

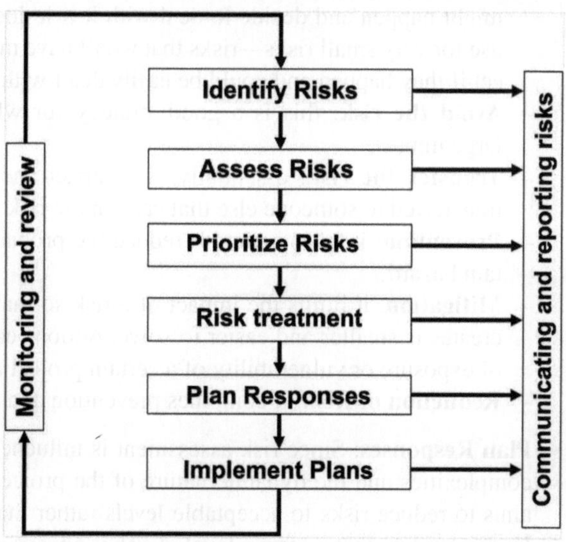

Fig. 15.5 Flowchart of the risk management cycle

typically involves and the number of hazards and risks that need to be identified and managed, the risk management process needs to involve all project stakeholders. Ongoing communication and reporting, however onerous, ensures that all stakeholders are aware of the risks and the measures taken to address them, promoting transparency and collaboration.

The risk management cycle can be described considering the following stages:

- **Identify Risks**: considering the approaches and techniques described above during this phase the risk manager detect and document all potential hazards, exposed element and vulnerabilities that could affect the project. The output is a comprehensive list of identified risks.
- **Assess Risks**: This activity assesses the probability and impact of each identified risk. Typically, this activity generates a risk register and a risk matrix listing all risks in order to prioritize management actions.
- **Prioritize Risks**: Based on its level of risk appetite of the project manager and the related stakeholders, i.e. the amount and type of risk they are willing to take in order to achieve its strategic objectives associated with the project, priorities and ways of managing the various risks are defined. This activity allows ranking the risks based on their assessed severity to focus on the most critical ones. It should be remembered that risk appetite is subjective and greatly influenced by psychological and cultural aspects. It reflects the organization's attitude towards risk-taking and its ability to manage the consequences of the various risks. Risk appetite guides decision-making processes and helps align risk management strategies with the organization's objectives.
- **Risk treatment**: on the base of the risk prioritization and risk appetite, this activity develops strategies to:
  - **Accepting the risk**: it means that while you have identified it and logged it in a risk management system, no action is taken. One simply accepts that it might happen and decide to deal with it if it does. This is a good strategy to use for very small risks—risks that won't have much of an impact on the project if they happen and could be easily dealt with if or when they arise.
  - **Avoid the risk**: this is a good strategy for when a risk has a potentially large impact;
  - **Transfer the risk**: essentially, the impact and management of the risk is transferred to someone else that can handle risk in a better way;
  - **Prevention**: it takes action to reduce the probability of occurrence of a certain hazard;
  - **Mitigation**: it limits the impact of a risk so that, if it occurs, the problem it creates is smaller and easier to solve. Actions ear taken to reduce the degree of exposure or vulnerability of a certain project activity.
  - **Reduction of Risk**: it combines prevention and mitigation actions.
- **Plan Responses**: Since risk assessment is influenced by inherent uncertainties, complexities and the dynamic nature of the project, effective risk management aims to reduce risks to acceptable levels rather than eliminate them altogether. Understanding that a certain level of risk is always present helps organizations to

prepare and respond more effectively to potential challenges. This phase therefore requires the provision of response strategies should certain risks should occur (Response Plans)

- **Implement Plans**: The objective of this activity is to implement the strategies defined in the previous steps. This requires the allocation of resources, the implementation of risk management measures and the continuous updating of emergency plans.
- **Monitoring and review**: it continuously tracks identified risks and monitors the effectiveness of risk responses; it provides for periodic risk assessments, audits and performance reviews. The results of this activity are reported as updates in the risk register and produce progress reports and project risk management performance metrics;
- **Communicating and reporting risks**: ensures that all stakeholders are informed about the status of risks and management efforts. It essentially involves periodic stakeholder update activities through meetings, reports and collecting feedback and input from stakeholders necessary to improve the project risk management process;
- **Identifying new risks**: as already mentioned, the risk management process is cyclical, so the objective of this activity is to identify new risks as the project progresses, which may manifest themselves more clearly or arise due to changes in the project or its management methods.

15.4 Time Dimension Remarks

Project management is predominantly based on a sequential structure, characterized by a unidirectional progression from the start of a project or related task to its completion. In this framework, activities are meticulously planned and executed in a linear fashion, with each event distinct and following a specific order. This clear progression moves from one phase to the next, with each step building on the previous one. The achievement of specific milestones marks progress, and adhering to time-bound goals and deadlines is critical. Project plans often rely on predictable and scheduled outcomes, ensuring a straightforward path to project completion.

In contrast, risk management adopts a more circular and iterative approach. Each phase of a project has unique risks associated with its activities and deliverables. These risks are not static. They evolve over time, influenced by various internal and external variables. This dynamic nature of risks necessitates continuous assessment and management throughout the project lifecycle. In particular, the following aspects of Time-Dependent Risk Management are relevant:

– **Time-Dependent Likelihood**: Assess how the likelihood of risks changes over time. For instance, the risk of technology becoming obsolete increases as the project progresses. Regular evaluation helps in understanding and mitigating such risks proactively.

- **Time-Sensitive Impact:** Evaluate how the impact of risks varies over time. Early-stage risks might have different consequences compared to those that occur closer to project completion. Understanding the timing of potential impacts aids in prioritizing risk responses effectively.
- **Dynamic Risk Scoring**: Update risk scores (probability and impact) periodically to reflect changes in the project environment and risk landscape. This dynamic scoring ensures that the risk management process remains relevant and responsive to evolving project conditions.

It is essential to conduct regular risk identification sessions at pre-defined intervals or project milestones, as they help not only to capture emerging risks, but also to clearly understand the project's objectives, tasks and feasibility. They serve as a foundation for quantitative data and information, supporting critical decisions such as cost management and option comparisons. By regularly assessing risks, project managers gain valuable insights into potential challenges, enabling informed decision-making and continuous risk monitoring allows for adjustments in plans and strategies, enhancing the project's adaptability to changing conditions.

In summary, while project management traditionally follows a linear progression, effective risk management requires a more cyclical and iterative approach. By regularly assessing and updating risk information, project managers can better navigate uncertainties and ensure project success. This balanced approach combines the predictability of structured project management with the adaptability of dynamic risk management, creating a robust framework for achieving project objectives.

15.5 Conclusions

Risk management constitutes a strategy to avoid losses and capitalize on opportunities that may arise from risks. This strategy demands a precise consideration and assessment of current situations and potential future scenarios. Decisions are made with the aim of eliminating risks and maximizing opportunities. This involves recognizing potential risks and mitigating threats by averting, evading, or reducing their negative effects. In project management, risk management is crucial, in particular for large and complex projects. Although implementing risk management at the start of a project incurs increased expenses, these are offset by the significant advantages it brings. During the planning phase, potential risks that could affect project success can be identified and incorporated into the planning process. This proactive approach helps in adhering to set dates and deadlines, thereby maintaining project costs. For the principal, ensuring the project is completed and operational by the due date is of great importance.

A project's risk potential analysis assesses how project risks influence the overall risk situation of the enterprise. This analysis should estimate the risk potential with minimal expense, without detailed consideration of individual risks. Based on this assessment, the risk management process is initiated.

Project risk management emphasizes the need for a systematic and proactive approach to risk management. It involves continuous monitoring and review processes to adapt to changing risk landscapes. It requires collaboration across all organizational levels, from strategic planning to operational execution, and involves the allocation of resources and responsibilities for effective risk mitigation. This approach ensures that all risks are addressed comprehensively and efficiently and not only it enhances the organization's ability to manage risks but also ensures that opportunities are effectively leveraged, contributing to the overall success of the project and the organization.

References

Haimes, Y. Y. (1991). Total risk management. *Risk Analysis, 11*(2), 169–171.
Kaplan, S., & John Garrick, B. (1981). On the quantitative definition of risk. *Risk Analysis, 1*(1), 11–27.

Part IV
Relationship Management

Chapter 16
Customer Focus

Antonio Bassi

In project management, the importance of suppliers is crucial to ensure that projects not only achieve their internal objectives but also meet customer expectations. Customer focus, supported by ISO 31000 and ISO 10006 standards, enables significant added value through effective management of supplier relationships. This approach ensures that every phase of the project is aligned with customer needs, enhancing overall quality and satisfaction. Actively engaging customers and suppliers, effectively managing requirements, ensuring quality, mitigating risks, and promoting a customer-oriented corporate culture are essential steps for the long-term success of projects and for building lasting and fruitful relationships.

16.1 The Importance of Suppliers in Project Management

The importance of suppliers in project management is fundamental to ensuring that projects not only achieve their internal objectives but also meet customer expectations and needs. Customer orientation represents a key element in this context, as it allows for the creation of significant added value through effective management of supplier relationships. ISO 31000 and ISO 10006 standards provide valuable guidance for developing a strong customer focus in project management processes, ensuring that every phase of the project is aligned with customer needs.

A deep understanding of the needs of customers and suppliers is the first step for effective customer orientation. This requires the active involvement of all stakeholders from the early stages of the project. Identifying who the customers and suppliers are, understanding their needs and expectations, and documenting these

A. Bassi (✉)
Project Management Association Switzerland, Lugano, Switzerland
e-mail: antonio.bassi@apm-switzerland.ch

A. Bassi et al. (eds.), *General Management Principles for Project Management*, Management for Professionals, https://doi.org/10.1007/978-3-031-98592-8_16

requirements clearly and in detail is essential to build a solid foundation for project success. Using tools such as interviews, questionnaires, and requirement analysis can help gather comprehensive and accurate information that will be critical for project planning and execution.

Keeping the customer's needs at the center of the project decision-making process is equally important. This can be achieved through the active participation of the customer and suppliers in periodic project reviews, update meetings, and key decision-making processes. Continuous feedback from the customer and suppliers helps keep the project aligned with their expectations, allowing for necessary adjustments during the project and thus improving the overall quality of the project.

It is well known that effective management of customer and supplier requirements is crucial for project success. Requirements must be clearly defined, documented, verified, and validated. This process ensures that requirements are correctly understood and that all changes are managed effectively. Maintaining open and transparent communication with the customer and suppliers regarding any changes in requirements and the impact they may have on the project is essential to avoid misunderstandings and delays.

Quality is a central aspect of customer focus. Implementing a quality management system that involves the customer and suppliers can help ensure that the final products and services meet or exceed customer expectations. This includes using quality control tools, internal and external audits, and continuous process reviews to improve performance. Ensuring that suppliers adhere to the same quality standards helps maintain a high level of performance and reliability throughout the supply chain.

Risk management is another key element in maintaining a strong focus on customers and suppliers. Identifying, assessing, and mitigating risks that can affect customer satisfaction and supplier efficiency is important. Involving the customer and suppliers in risk assessment and decisions on how to manage them improves risk management and strengthens mutual trust. Regular testing and scenario simulations based on lessons learned can help teams better prepare to manage crisis situations, evaluate the effectiveness of risk mitigation strategies, and identify areas that need further improvement.

Continuous feedback and improvement are essential elements of customer focus. Establishing mechanisms to collect feedback from customers and suppliers throughout the project lifecycle is crucial. This feedback should be analyzed and used to make continuous improvements to project management processes. Creating an environment where feedback is valued and used to drive improvement can significantly increase customer satisfaction and the efficiency of supplier collaboration.

To support a strong customer focus, it is essential to develop a corporate culture that values the customer and suppliers. This involves training project team members on the importance of customer orientation and ensuring that everyone understands their role in meeting expectations. Leadership must demonstrate a commitment to customer orientation and promote practices that support this culture, creating a multiplier effect that encourages all organizational levels to do the same.

In summary, integrating a strong customer focus in project management following the guidelines of ISO 31000 and ISO 10006 allows project managers to ensure that projects not only achieve internal objectives but also meet the needs and expectations of customers. This approach not only improves the quality of projects but also strengthens customer trust and satisfaction, creating a virtuous cycle of continuous improvement and success. A well-implemented customer orientation that involves suppliers not only contributes to the success of individual projects but also promotes a culture of excellence and innovation, taking the organization to new levels of competitiveness and achievement.

16.2 Understanding Customer Needs

Understanding customer needs is the first step for effective customer orientation. This requires the active involvement of the customer from the early stages of the project. According to ISO 10006, it is essential to identify who the customers and stakeholders are, understand their needs and expectations, and document these requirements clearly and in detail. Using tools such as interviews, questionnaires, and requirement analysis can help gather comprehensive and accurate information.

This process of active involvement is not limited to an initial phase but must be continuous throughout the project's duration. During the project lifecycle, it is important to maintain open and transparent communication with customers to ensure that their evolving needs are always at the center of project decisions. This constant interaction allows for the quick adaptation of the project to any changes in the customer's requirements or expectations, ensuring that the final result is aligned with what the customer truly desires.

Moreover, understanding customer needs involves going beyond mere data collection. It is necessary to interpret this data so that it accurately reflects priorities and desires. This may include analyzing market conditions, understanding external influences that may impact the project, and evaluating the internal capabilities of the organization to meet these needs. An in-depth and contextualized analysis of the collected information enables the development of tailored solutions that not only respond to the customer's immediate demands but also anticipate their future needs.

In this context, it is useful to implement knowledge management tools that facilitate access to and sharing of the collected information. Collaborative platforms and project management software can be used to systematically store information on customer requirements, allowing project teams to easily access crucial and up-to-date data. This integrated approach ensures that all team members have a clear and shared vision of customer expectations, improving the consistency and effectiveness of project decisions.

Detailed documentation of customer requirements is not just a good management practice but a necessity to avoid misunderstandings and ensure that all parties involved are aligned on project objectives. This documentation should include not only technical requirements but also aspects such as time, budget, and resource constraints, as well as any customer preferences in terms of communication and reporting. Comprehensive and accurate documentation creates a solid foundation for the entire project management process, ensuring that every decision made is supported by a clear and shared understanding of customer needs.

16.3 Active Customer Engagement

Once customer needs are understood, it is important to keep them at the center of the project decision-making process. ISO 31000 emphasizes the importance of involving the customer in the risk management process, ensuring that their concerns and expectations are adequately considered. This can be achieved through the active participation of the customer in periodic project reviews, update meetings, and key decision-making processes. Continuous feedback from the customer helps keep the project aligned with their expectations.

Active customer engagement is not limited to the planning phase but extends throughout the entire project lifecycle. This approach requires that customers are constantly informed and involved in all critical phases of the project. For example, during review meetings, customers can provide valuable input that can influence strategic decisions, helping to identify potential risks and opportunities that may not be immediately apparent to the project team.

Involving the customer in the risk management process is important to ensure that their concerns are addressed promptly. ISO 31000 suggests that customers should be an integral part of risk discussions, actively participating in risk assessment and mitigation. This not only ensures that mitigation strategies are aligned with customer expectations but also strengthens trust and transparency between the project team and the customer.

Continuous feedback is another key element of customer engagement. Establishing mechanisms to regularly collect and analyze customer feedback allows the project team to make proactive and reactive changes, ensuring that the project remains aligned with customer expectations. This may include satisfaction surveys, formal and informal feedback sessions, and analysis of project performance against initial objectives. The ability to quickly adapt to customer needs and suggestions is essential to maintaining a positive and productive relationship.

Integrating the customer into key decision-making processes not only improves the quality of decisions made but also creates a sense of co-responsibility and partnership. Customers who feel heard and involved are more likely to support the project, provide additional resources if needed, and promote the project's success within their organization. This close collaboration helps build long-term relationships based on mutual trust and shared goals.

Active customer engagement is essential to ensure that customer needs and expectations are continually considered and integrated into the project management process. Following the guidelines of ISO 31000 and ensuring open and transparent communication, project managers can create a collaborative work environment that not only meets but exceeds customer expectations, leading to high-quality project outcomes and increased customer satisfaction.

16.4 Managing Customer Requirements

According to ISO 10006, requirements must be clearly defined, documented, verified, and validated. This process ensures that requirements are correctly understood and that all changes are managed effectively. It is important to maintain open and transparent communication with the customer regarding any changes in requirements and the impact these changes may have on the project.

Clearly defining customer requirements involves an in-depth initial phase of gathering and analyzing information. It is crucial to use tools such as interviews, workshops, and questionnaires to obtain a comprehensive and detailed understanding of needs. This initial phase must be followed by the accurate documentation of requirements, ensuring that all parties involved have a shared view of the project objectives.

Verification and validation of requirements are essential subsequent steps. Verification ensures that the documented requirements are complete, consistent, and free from ambiguity. Validation, on the other hand, ensures that the requirements are indeed those desired by the customer, correctly responding to their needs and expectations. This can be achieved through requirement reviews using prototypes, simulations, or mock-ups to confirm their accuracy.

Once defined and validated, requirements must be carefully managed throughout the project lifecycle. This includes managing changes to requirements, which can be one of the most significant challenges in project management. Each change must be evaluated for its impact on the project, including time, costs, and resources needed. It is crucial to involve the customer in this evaluation process, ensuring that they are informed and approve each change.

Open and transparent communication is essential at every stage of requirement management. Keeping the customer informed about any changes and their impacts ensures that there are no surprises and that the customer can make informed decisions. Project management tools and collaborative platforms can facilitate this communication by providing real-time updates and allowing the customer to follow the status of requirements and any changes.

Effective management of requirements not only ensures that the project meets customer needs but also helps build a relationship of trust and collaboration. A customer who sees their needs recognized and respected is more likely to support the project and provide positive feedback. This proactive and transparent approach to requirement management creates a solid foundation for project success, enhancing customer satisfaction and ensuring high-quality outcomes.

Following ISO 10006 guidelines for managing customer requirements helps project managers ensure that projects are aligned with customer expectations. Carefully defining, documenting, verifying, and validating requirements, managing changes effectively, and maintaining open and transparent communication with the customer are crucial steps for project success. This approach not only improves project quality but also strengthens customer trust and satisfaction, creating a virtuous cycle of continuous improvement and success.

16.5 Quality and Customer Satisfaction

Quality is a central aspect of customer focus in project management. ISO 10006 emphasizes that quality must be integrated into all aspects of the project, from conception to delivery. Implementing a quality management system that involves the customer can help ensure that the final products and services meet or exceed customer expectations. This includes using quality control tools, internal and external audits, and continuous process reviews to improve performance.

To ensure quality at every stage of the project, it is essential to establish clear quality standards from the outset. These standards must be based on customer requirements and agreed upon with all stakeholders. Once established, they must be communicated to the entire project team to ensure that every member understands what is expected and how to contribute to achieving these standards.

The use of quality control tools is crucial for monitoring and maintaining quality standards throughout the project. These tools can include checklists, flowcharts, sampling techniques, and acceptance tests. It is important that quality control is not seen as a final activity but as a continuous process that accompanies every phase of the project.

Internal and external audits represent another crucial component for ensuring quality. Internal audits conducted by the project team serve to monitor adherence to quality standards and identify any issues promptly. External audits performed by independent bodies provide an impartial assessment of the project's quality practices, ensuring they comply with regulations and industry best practices.

Continuous process review is essential for performance improvement. This involves constantly analyzing project outcomes, gathering feedback from the customer and team members, and making necessary adjustments to processes to enhance efficiency and effectiveness. The continuous improvement approach, also known as the PDCA (Plan-Do-Check-Act) cycle, helps maintain a high level of quality and respond quickly to any issues that arise during the project.

Involving the customer in the quality management system is equally important. This can be done through regular feedback, quality review sessions, and sharing audit results. Customer involvement not only ensures that their expectations are met but also reinforces their trust in the project team and the quality management process. Moreover, an involved customer is more likely to provide constructive feedback that can help further improve project quality.

Ultimately, quality and customer satisfaction are closely interconnected. Ensuring that every aspect of the project is executed with the highest possible quality not only satisfies the customer but often exceeds their expectations, creating a positive and lasting experience. Adopting a robust and integrated quality management system following the guidelines of ISO 10006 helps build a reputation for excellence and reliability, which is fundamental for the long-term success of any organization.

Integrating quality at every stage of the project and actively involving the customer in the quality management process are essential practices for enhancing customer satisfaction and ensuring project success. This approach not only increases the quality of the final product but also builds strong and lasting relationships with customers based on trust and transparency.

16.6 Risk Management and Customer Orientation

Risk management is another key element in maintaining a strong customer focus. ISO 31000 provides detailed guidance on how to identify, assess, and mitigate risks that can affect customer satisfaction. It is important to involve the customer in risk assessment and decisions on how to manage them. This not only improves risk management but also strengthens customer trust in the project.

Identifying risks is the first essential step. This process requires a deep understanding of the project context and customer expectations. Using techniques such as brainstorming, stakeholder interviews, and SWOT (Strengths, Weaknesses, Opportunities, Threats) analysis can help identify a wide range of potential risks that could affect the project. Involving the customer at this stage is crucial to ensure that all possible concerns are considered.

Once risks are identified, they must be assessed in terms of probability and impact. ISO 31000 suggests using a risk matrix to classify risks based on their severity. This tool helps prioritize risks, focusing on those that have the greatest potential to negatively impact customer satisfaction. Involving the customer in this assessment ensures that their priorities and concerns are integrated into risk classification.

Risk mitigation is the next step and involves developing strategies to minimize the impact of identified risks. Mitigation strategies may include implementing additional controls, modifying the project plan, or allocating additional resources to address risks. It is essential to discuss these strategies with the customer, obtaining their feedback and agreement before proceeding. This not only ensures that the proposed solutions are acceptable to the customer but also demonstrates a commitment to their satisfaction and security.

Continuous monitoring and review of risks are essential for effective risk management. Risks must be monitored regularly throughout the project lifecycle, and mitigation strategies must be updated based on changes in the project context or customer requirements. Involving the customer in this ongoing monitoring allows for maintaining open and transparent communication, further strengthening trust in the project management process.

Transparency and open communication are crucial components in customer-oriented risk management. Keeping the customer informed about potential risks and the actions taken to mitigate these risks is fundamental for building a trusting relationship. Using periodic reports, update meetings, and online communication tools can facilitate this process, ensuring that the customer is always updated on the status of risks and mitigation measures.

Ultimately, customer-oriented risk management not only improves the project's ability to face and overcome challenges but also strengthens the customer's trust in the project team. A proactive and collaborative approach to risk management ensures that customers feel like an integral part of the process, helping to create a more transparent and collaborative work environment. This not only increases the likelihood of project success but also enhances customer satisfaction and loyalty.

Integrating ISO 31000 principles into risk management and maintaining a strong customer focus are key steps to ensuring that projects are successfully delivered while meeting customer expectations. This approach not only increases the quality of the final product but also builds strong and lasting relationships with customers based on trust and transparency.

16.7 Continuous Feedback and Improvement

An essential element of customer orientation is continuous feedback and improvement. ISO 10006 advises establishing mechanisms to collect feedback from customers throughout the project lifecycle. This feedback should be analyzed and used to make continuous improvements to project management processes. Creating an environment where feedback is valued and used to drive improvement can significantly increase customer satisfaction.

Collecting feedback from customers is a process that should begin from the early stages of the project and continue until its completion. Using tools such as surveys, interviews, and periodic review sessions can provide a clear view of the customer's perceptions and expectations. It is important that these tools are designed to collect detailed and specific information that can then be thoroughly analyzed.

The analysis of the feedback received is crucial to identifying areas for improvement and opportunities for innovation. This process requires a critical analysis of customer responses, evaluating both the positive and negative aspects of their experiences. Using data analysis techniques to identify recurring trends and patterns can help better understand customer needs and pinpoint areas where the project can be improved.

Feedback must be integrated into project management processes in a structured way. Creating a quality management system that includes mechanisms to collect, analyze, and act on customer feedback is essential. This system should provide for periodic reviews of processes and practices with the goal of making continuous improvements based on the information received. For example, if feedback indicates that there are issues with project communication, measures can be taken to improve the transparency and frequency of updates provided to the customer.

An environment where feedback is valued and used as a tool for continuous improvement requires an organizational culture that supports openness and communication. Project team members must be encouraged to see feedback not as criticism but as an opportunity for growth and improvement. Project leaders must promote this culture by demonstrating an active commitment to listening to and implementing the customer's ideas and concerns.

Creating iterative feedback mechanisms where the customer can provide input at various stages of the project is another effective practice. This approach allows for real-time adjustments, enhancing the ability to respond quickly to changes in customer needs. For example, during key project milestones, organizing review sessions with the customer to discuss progress and gather suggestions can help keep the project aligned with customer expectations.

Finally, monitoring the impact of actions taken in response to customer feedback is important to ensure that the improvements made are effective. Measuring customer satisfaction and comparing the results with previous data can provide valuable insights into the effectiveness of the implemented changes. This continuous monitoring process allows for further refinement of project management processes, ensuring constant improvement.

Continuous feedback and improvement are essential components of effective customer orientation. Regularly collecting and analyzing feedback, integrating it into project management processes, and creating an environment that values this information can significantly increase customer satisfaction. Adopting the guidelines of ISO 10006 helps project managers create high-quality projects that meet customer needs, promoting a culture of continuous improvement and success.

16.8 Corporate Culture and Customer Orientation

To support a strong customer orientation, it is essential to develop a corporate culture that values the customer. This involves training project team members on the importance of customer orientation and ensuring that everyone understands their role in meeting customer expectations. Leadership must demonstrate a commitment to customer orientation and promote practices that support this culture.

Developing a customer-centric corporate culture requires a strategic approach that involves every level of the organization. Team training is a fundamental element of this process. Team members must be educated on the importance of understanding and meeting customer needs. This can be achieved through continuous training programs that emphasize best practices in customer management, effective communication techniques, and problem-solving strategies.

Ensuring that everyone understands their role in meeting customer expectations is important. Every team member, regardless of position, must feel responsible for customer satisfaction. This can be facilitated by clearly defining roles and responsibilities, highlighting how each activity contributes to achieving objectives. Using concrete examples and case studies can help illustrate the importance of each role in the customer management process.

Leadership plays a key role in promoting and supporting a customer-oriented culture. Leaders must demonstrate a personal commitment to customer orientation by acting as role models. This means not only talking about the importance of the customer but also demonstrating it through concrete actions. Actively participating in customer meetings, listening to their concerns and feedback, and making decisions that reflect customer needs are effective ways to demonstrate this commitment.

Promoting practices that support a customer-oriented culture requires implementing processes and systems that facilitate customer involvement in every phase of the project. This may include using Customer Relationship Management (CRM) tools that track customer interactions and preferences and adopting project management methodologies that encourage continuous collaboration and communication with the customer.

Encouraging a mindset of continuous improvement is also essential for maintaining a customer-centric corporate culture. Team members must be encouraged to constantly seek ways to improve processes and practices to better meet needs. This can be facilitated through incentives and recognition for those who propose and implement effective improvements, creating an environment that values innovation and proactivity.

Finally, creating an environment where customer feedback is seen as a valuable resource rather than criticism is fundamental. Leadership must promote the idea that feedback, both positive and negative, is an opportunity for growth and improvement. This can be achieved by creating open and transparent communication channels where feedback is welcomed with gratitude and used to guide continuous improvement.

Developing a corporate culture that values the customer requires a concerted effort from the entire organization. Training team members, ensuring everyone understands their role, demonstrating commitment from leadership, and promoting practices that support this orientation are all crucial steps. This approach not only improves customer satisfaction but also creates a more cohesive, motivated, and innovative work environment capable of maintaining a competitive advantage in the long term.

16.9 Conclusions

Integrating a strong customer focus in project management is essential for the long-term success of projects. Following the guidelines of ISO 31000 and ISO 10006, project managers can ensure that their projects not only achieve internal objectives but also meet customer needs and expectations. This approach not only improves project quality but also strengthens customer trust and satisfaction, creating a virtuous cycle of continuous improvement and success.

By adopting practices that emphasize understanding customer needs, active engagement, effective requirement management, quality, risk management, and continuous feedback, organizations can build a solid reputation for reliability and competence. Corporate culture must support these values by promoting an environment where every team member understands the importance of the customer and actively works to meet their expectations.

Ultimately, a well-implemented customer orientation not only contributes to the success of individual projects but also promotes a culture of excellence and innovation that can lead the organization to new levels of competitiveness and achievement. Customer focus, supported by the practices outlined in the ISO standards, is a key element for building lasting and fruitful relationships with customers, ensuring a prosperous future for the organization and its stakeholders.

Chapter 17
Building Mutually Beneficial Relationships with Suppliers

Antonio Bassi

17.1 Introduction

In the dynamic field of project management, effective supplier management is a critical component that can determine the success of a project. A focus on creating mutually beneficial relationships with suppliers can lead to higher quality work, cost savings, and greater operational efficiency.

17.2 The Importance of Suppliers in Project Management

Suppliers are strategic partners in project management. Their involvement can directly influence project costs, quality, and delivery times. Careful selection of suppliers based on criteria such as reliability, quality, cost, and cultural compatibility is essential. However, beyond the selection, it is important to establish a relationship that aims for a long-term strategic partnership.

17.2.1 The Strategic Role of Suppliers in Project Management

Suppliers are strategic pillars whose role goes beyond mere commercial transactions; they are true partners capable of profoundly influencing the success of a project. Their importance manifests in various areas, each of which is crucial for the project's success.

A. Bassi (✉)
Project Management Association Switzerland, Lugano, Switzerland
e-mail: antonio.bassi@apm-switzerland.ch

A. Bassi et al. (eds.), *General Management Principles for Project Management*, Management for Professionals, https://doi.org/10.1007/978-3-031-98592-8_17

Firstly, suppliers' contribution to project costs is significant and goes beyond the simple purchase price of goods or services offered. A supplier's operational efficiency can reduce production costs, thus improving the overall budget. Their ability to propose economically advantageous and innovative solutions can reduce costs without sacrificing quality. A key element is also the flexibility in payment terms, which can facilitate more efficient cash flow management, alleviate financial pressures, and expand investment opportunities in other vital areas of the project.

The quality of materials and services provided directly impacts the success of a project. Suppliers who adhere to strict quality standards and are committed to continuous improvement ensure that their products meet or exceed expectations. This commitment to quality can result in increased customer satisfaction, reduced repair costs, and an overall better reputation.

When it comes to delivery times, supplier punctuality is essential. Reliable suppliers ensure that the project progresses according to the planned schedule, reducing downtime and facilitating precise planning. The ability to quickly adapt to emerging needs or unforeseen changes can be decisive, offering the flexibility that is sometimes necessary for the project's success.

Innovation and technological development are other areas where suppliers play a fundamental role. Keeping up with the latest technologies or advanced materials through suppliers can mean pushing the project beyond conventional limits by introducing innovative solutions that offer a competitive advantage.

Finally, establishing long-term partnerships with suppliers can bring immense benefits. Viewing suppliers as strategic allies rather than mere vendors can encourage reciprocal investment in the relationship, resulting in tangible benefits in terms of cost, quality, delivery times, and innovative capacity. A strong and long-term collaboration with suppliers can be the key to transforming a good project into a successful one.

17.2.2 Selection and Evaluation of Suppliers: A Dynamic and Strategic Process

The selection and evaluation of suppliers in project management are not static or occasional activities but dynamic and strategic processes that require continuous attention. These activities, far from being mere formalities or sporadic actions, require constant attention and a strategic approach that aligns with project objectives. Careful selection and diligent monitoring of suppliers ensure that they remain aligned with evolving needs, emphasizing the importance of a holistic and carefully updated method.

Reliability emerges as a pillar—not just about meeting deadlines but a matter of reputation, financial stability, and the ability to flexibly handle challenges and changes. A reliable supplier is a safeguard against delays and a guarantor of project continuity.

Similarly, the quality of the materials or services provided deeply affects project excellence. Suppliers should not just meet expectations; ideally, they should exceed them through quality certifications, rigorous controls, and solid guarantees that elevate the standard of the final result.

Regarding cost, the analysis goes beyond the mere initial expenditure, exploring the overall value added to the project. Considerations about maintenance, reliability, and durability become important, aiming for a balance between expenditure and quality that justifies the investment.

Cultural compatibility between the supplier and the project team is not to be underestimated, especially in international or multicultural contexts. Sharing values, business practices, and communication styles can greatly facilitate collaboration, turning diversity into a strength rather than an obstacle.

Openness to innovation and technological development by suppliers marks the difference, allowing the project to stand out and advance. Suppliers committed to finding cutting-edge solutions contribute not only to technical progress but also to the project's conceptual development, pushing it towards new horizons.

Supplier selection and evaluation are not mere procedural steps but fundamental elements requiring a forward-looking vision. Every decision in this area can significantly influence the project's direction, emphasizing the importance of a conscious and strategic commitment to building solid and productive relationships.

17.2.3 Building a Strategic Partnership with Suppliers

In project management, establishing strategic partnerships with suppliers goes beyond mere commercial transactions; it becomes a commitment to cultivating deep relationships rooted in trust, collaboration, and alignment of goals. This type of collaboration is not just a channel for purchasing goods and services but proves to be a crucial strategic lever for a project's success.

Developing these partnerships means investing in the future, aiming for relationships characterized by reciprocal trust, active collaboration, and knowledge sharing. This synergy not only increases operational efficiency but also pushes the project toward horizons of innovation and responsiveness never explored before. Furthermore, trust and collaboration stand as the supporting pillars of these alliances. Trust is built and nurtured by consistency, reliability, and transparency—key elements for establishing a solid and lasting relationship. Collaboration, on the other hand, manifests in the sharing of resources, risks, and successes, directing all parties involved toward a common goal.

An effective partnership with suppliers stimulates a virtuous cycle of continuous improvement, where innovation and process optimization are the order of the day. Suppliers become true partners in value creation, proposing innovative solutions that not only improve the quality of the offering but also the processes themselves, extending the benefit throughout the value chain.

The ability to quickly adapt to market changes is another crucial advantage of a solid partnership. This agility allows the project and suppliers to manage the complexity of technological or market changes, keeping the project aligned with predefined objectives in an increasingly dynamic environment.

Knowledge sharing is a fundamental aspect of these strategic alliances. Suppliers, thanks to their experience and position in the sector, can offer valuable insights that go beyond the immediate context of their offering. This exchange of information flowing in both directions enriches both the suppliers and the project team, creating an ecosystem where knowledge and experiences converge for shared success.

In summary, building strategic partnerships with suppliers in project management means going beyond mere transactions to embrace a collaborative approach that values mutual trust, shared innovation, and collective resilience to changes, cementing the foundation for project success.

17.3 Establishing a Mutually Beneficial Relationship

At the heart of mutually beneficial relationships lies the understanding and respect for each partner's objectives. It is essential to define clear and achievable objectives, encouraging honest and open dialogue. This approach includes recognizing the needs and limitations of suppliers and actively committing to finding solutions that benefit both them and the company. More than just a management tactic, this strategy is a philosophy aimed at building solid foundations for fruitful and long-term collaboration.

17.3.1 Understanding and Respecting Objectives: The Key to Successful Collaboration

Understanding and respecting the objectives of both parties are fundamental in establishing mutually beneficial relationships with suppliers. This approach not only improves project performance and efficiency but also creates a foundation of trust and respect that can lead to long-term, innovative, and mutually beneficial collaboration. Through active listening, recognition of challenges, and respect for objectives, organizations can build lasting relationships that transcend transactions and transform into true strategic partnerships.

Deep engagement in discussions, participation in joint brainstorming sessions, and visiting production sites can provide a comprehensive view of suppliers' operations. Understanding their aspirations, challenges, and constraints allows project strategies to be adapted to effectively meet their needs, promoting solutions that reflect bilateral benefits.

Developing collaborative strategies becomes a joint exploration of how to best align project objectives with supplier capabilities, encouraging participation in research and development initiatives or offering support to overcome technical challenges. This process not only meets the project's needs but also enriches the relationship with the supplier, establishing mutual trust as the foundation for future collaboration.

This trust is built by recognizing and respecting suppliers' goals and challenges. When suppliers feel valued, they become more deeply committed to the partnership. Active respect, expressed through everyday actions such as acknowledging the supplier's successes and considering their feedback, creates a collaborative environment where suppliers see themselves as essential partners in the project's success.

Finally, a collaboration that aims for shared goals identifies and values areas of common interest, developing mutually beneficial initiatives. This alignment strengthens the relationship, making it resilient and oriented toward shared success, demonstrating that deep understanding and genuine respect for objectives can transform interactions into true strategic partnerships.

17.3.2 Setting Clear and Realistic Goals: A Path to Shared Success

In the context of relationships with suppliers, shared success is nurtured by setting clear, realistic, and measurably achievable goals. This aspect, fundamental for fruitful collaboration, goes beyond merely defining expectations to embrace meticulous planning and a careful awareness of the potential and limitations of each party involved.

The key is to formulate goals that are not only ambitious but also achievable, based on a deep understanding of operational capabilities and available resources. This process begins with precisely defining expectations, specifically outlining project needs—from the quantities of products required to the technical specifications, from desired delivery times to expected service levels. Clarity from the outset helps avoid misunderstandings and provides a solid foundation for evaluating success.

Defining realistic delivery terms and setting high but achievable quality standards allows aligning expectations with the actual supply capabilities, taking into account production times, logistics, and necessary quality controls. Through measurable standards based on objective criteria, it is possible to facilitate a transparent and fair assessment of performance.

Implementing specific and meaningful Key Performance Indicators (KPIs) provides an effective method for monitoring progress toward achieving goals. These indicators must be relevant and based on quantifiable data, covering aspects such as product quality, efficiency in resolving requests or issues, and adherence to expected delivery times. The ability to measure results objectively is essential for identifying improvement opportunities and ensuring that all partners are on the same page.

At the same time, it is vital that goals reflect the supplier's actual capabilities, avoiding setting unachievable expectations that can only generate stress and failure. Well-calibrated goals not only encourage the achievement of concrete successes but also motivate the supplier to exceed expectations, creating a virtuous cycle of mutual improvement and satisfaction.

Goals should meet the project's needs while also offering suppliers significant opportunities for growth, development, and expansion. When both parties perceive the value and benefit derived from their collaboration, it lays the foundation for a solid, lasting partnership characterized by mutual commitment to common goals and shared successes.

17.3.3 Promoting Open and Honest Dialogue: The Heart of Effective Collaboration

Founding relationships with suppliers on open and honest dialogue is essential for developing a mutually beneficial partnership, representing the core of effective collaboration. This type of communication, which goes beyond mere information exchange, aims to create an environment where every party feels heard, valued, and understood, laying the groundwork for a strong and productive bond.

Transparent dialogue involves not only sharing expectations and goals clearly but also extending communication to constructive feedback, open discussions about concerns and challenges, thereby strengthening mutual trust and understanding. Establishing clear and consistent communication channels through regular meetings, progress reports, and digital platforms keeps all stakeholders updated, facilitating effective project monitoring and allowing any issues to be promptly addressed.

Active listening is another pillar of this communication: paying attention not only to the content but also to the context in which information is conveyed, recognizing underlying emotions and concerns, helps create an atmosphere of understanding and empathy. This is crucial for making suppliers feel heard and understood, encouraging sincere and open collaboration.

The ability to respond proactively to challenges, addressing issues with a collaborative and solution-oriented approach, prevents small problems from escalating into major issues and underscores the commitment to achieving common goals. Moreover, frank and direct communication reduces the chances of misunderstandings, consolidating trust—an essential element for a long-term relationship and the joint success of the project.

Encouraging a two-way exchange of constructive feedback not only supports the growth and improvement of suppliers but also of the project team, promoting an environment of continuous learning and shared development. In this way, open and honest communication is not only the basis for effective collaboration but also becomes a vehicle for innovation, growth, and mutual success.

17.3.4 Recognizing and Respecting Supplier Needs and Constraints: An Empathetic and Adaptive Approach

In the fabric of relationships between companies and suppliers, recognizing and respecting suppliers' needs and operational constraints is a fundamental pillar for building strong and mutually beneficial ties. Adopting an empathetic and flexible approach that adapts to suppliers' operational realities not only facilitates harmonious collaboration but also cements a sense of mutual trust and understanding, which is essential for a long-lasting partnership.

Deeply understanding the specifics each supplier brings—from production capacities to logistical and financial needs—requires an active commitment to listening, in-depth discussions, and information exchange. Dedicating time to these activities lays the foundation for collaboration based on mutual knowledge and respect for each other's challenges and limitations.

Demonstrating flexibility in adapting project requirements to supplier needs is a tangible sign of this respect. The ability to adjust aspects such as payment terms or timelines according to the supplier's production capabilities not only helps better manage cash flow but also ensures more accurate and realistic planning, increasing the likelihood of project success.

Respecting delivery times and the operational processes established by suppliers avoids imposing excessive pressures that could compromise the quality of work. Collaborating to identify solutions that align with both the suppliers' capabilities and the project's needs ensures optimal results for both parties, avoiding unrealistic demands and promoting a constructive working environment.

Facing challenges together and seeking solutions that benefit both the company and the supplier reflects a genuinely collaborative partnership. Whether it involves exploring new technologies, negotiating alternative solutions, or finding balanced compromises, working closely with suppliers in an open dialogue transforms challenges into opportunities for shared growth and improvement.

A collaboration based on empathy, flexibility, and mutual respect not only enhances the quality and effectiveness of supply relationships but also lays the groundwork for sustainable growth and long-term success beneficial for all parties involved.

17.3.5 Seeking Mutually Beneficial Solutions: Collaborating for Shared Success

In building lasting and mutually beneficial relationships with suppliers, seeking solutions that bring benefits to all parties involved is crucial. This synergy is based on close collaboration to discover and implement strategies that favor both the project team and the suppliers, laying the foundation for shared success. Such collaboration ranges from negotiating flexible terms that consider both parties' needs to jointly resolving challenges, whether they are technical, logistical, or operational.

Negotiations that, for example, involve adaptable payment conditions can significantly influence a supplier's cash flow and financial stability, resulting in tangible advantages for the project, such as better product or service quality, more competitive prices, or optimized delivery times. Agreeing on terms that allow the supplier to invest in advanced technologies or high-quality materials can exponentially improve the final result, benefiting the entire project and enabling the supplier to grow and further develop.

These types of agreements that promote investments in quality and innovation exemplify how mutually beneficial solutions can stimulate significant improvements. Active collaboration in problem-solving not only leads to innovations that benefit both parties but also facilitates a constant flow of ideas and creative solutions, increasing overall efficiency and strengthening ties between the parties.

Looking beyond immediate needs to focus on creating long-term value means exploring possibilities such as strategic partnerships in research and development, sharing resources, or expanding into new markets. These opportunities, supporting the sustainable growth and development of both partners, not only consolidate the relationship but also encourage a prolonged commitment to common goals.

This approach not only improves the impact and effectiveness of projects but also establishes a solid foundation of trust and collaboration essential for long-term success and shared growth.

17.3.6 Developing Long-Term Collaboration: Building Lasting and Dynamic Relationships

Developing a long-term collaboration with suppliers is a strategic investment that extends beyond the boundaries of individual projects. It involves maintaining a commitment to a continuous and dynamic relationship that evolves in response to market changes, technological advancements, and the specific needs of both parties. This approach is essential for creating strong and enduring ties that enhance the effectiveness and success of current projects while laying the groundwork for future growth and opportunities.

This long-term commitment is demonstrated through regular and constructive exchanges, such as periodic meetings, performance reviews, and open discussions about mutual needs and goals. Maintaining active communication helps to strengthen the relationship and allows for the prompt identification of areas for improvement or new opportunities for collaboration.

As projects and market contexts evolve, it becomes crucial for the goals and strategies of collaboration to be adaptable and regularly updated. Reviewing agreements and goals to reflect new realities or to discover new avenues for collaboration highlights the importance of flexibility and adaptability for maintaining a relevant and effective partnership.

Creating a collaborative and supportive environment where both parties feel recognized and appreciated—not only for achieving common goals but also for providing mutual support during challenges—is fundamental. Celebrating shared successes and recognizing each other's contributions to overall success are key to reinforcing the partnership.

Investing in relationships also means investing in people. This includes participating in joint training initiatives, promoting knowledge exchange, and building a mutual understanding of corporate cultures and values. Investing in people strengthens the bond, making it more personal and profound.

Continuous performance evaluation and the exchange of constructive feedback play a vital role in ensuring that the relationship remains satisfying for both parties while also paving the way for constant improvements. Open and two-way dialogue enriches the collaboration, allowing all parties to express opinions and suggestions.

Building long-term collaboration means looking beyond the boundaries of a single project to envision and shape a shared future. This involves exploring new business opportunities, developing strategic partnerships, and strengthening a support network that benefits all involved stakeholders. Such a forward-looking vision motivates the parties to invest in the relationship, aware that the fruits of such commitment will extend far beyond the immediate horizon.

Part V
Decision Management

Chapter 18
Data Driven Decision Making in Modern Collaborative and Automated Organizations

Massimo Mistretta

In today's complex business environment, data-driven decision making (DDDM) has become indispensable for project managers, particularly as they navigate an increasingly complex portfolio of projects that demand a higher level of adaptability and resilience. Project managers who are adept at collaboration and continuously seek to understand modern information automation are well-positioned to drive not only the successful execution of projects but also the implementation of collaborative and automated processes across the organization.

By leveraging data to inform decisions, project managers can better anticipate risks, optimize resource allocation, and ensure that project goals align with broader organizational objectives.

The OASIS model, centered on Openness, Autonomy, Symbiosis, Intelligence, and Sustainability, provides a strategic framework for integrating DDDM into project management practices.

To fully leverage DDDM, project managers must also develop skills and knowledge to address challenges related to data quality, privacy, and the ethical use of AI. By embracing the principles of the OASIS model and helping with the integration of collaborative and automated processes, project managers can effectively navigate these complexities, drive innovation, and ensure that their projects contribute to the long-term success and sustainability of the organization.

Organizations are increasingly turning to data-driven decision making (DDDM) to navigate complexities, drive innovation, and maintain a competitive edge. This chapter explores the role of DDDM in the context of collaborative and automated organizations, drawing insights from the fields of ecosystem dynamics and organizational collaboration and automation systems.

M. Mistretta (✉)
Exentriq Ltd., London, UK
e-mail: massimo@exentri.com

A. Bassi et al. (eds.), *General Management Principles for Project Management*, Management for Professionals, https://doi.org/10.1007/978-3-031-98592-8_18

By examining the key components of DDDM data acquisition, analysis, and application through the lens of the OASIS (Open, Autonomous, Symbiotic, Intelligent, Sustainable) model, we highlight how organizations can harness the power of data to make informed, adaptive decisions in an increasingly automated and interconnected world. We argue that successful implementation of DDDM requires a holistic approach that balances human intuition with machine intelligence, fosters a culture of data literacy and collaboration, and aligns with the principles of organizational adaptability and sustainability with a holistic ecosystemic perspective.

18.1 Introduction

The advent of modern technologies grounded on the availability of data in large scale and computational power at exponentially decreasing cost, has revolutionized the way organizations operate and make decisions. Data-driven decision making (DDDM) has emerged as a critical capability for businesses seeking to thrive in an increasingly complex and dynamic environment. DDDM refers to the practice of basing decisions on the analysis of data rather than purely on intuition (Provost & Fawcett, 2013). In the context of modern collaborative and automated organizations, DDDM takes on new dimensions, as it involves the integration of human expertise with machine intelligence, and the alignment of data insights with organizational goals and values.

This article aims to explore the role of DDDM in modern organizations through the lens of the OASIS model, which emphasizes the key characteristics of adaptive organizations: openness, autonomy, symbiosis, intelligence, and sustainability.

By examining the components of DDDM—data acquisition, analysis, and application—in light of these characteristics, we seek to provide a comprehensive understanding of how organizations can leverage data to make informed, agile decisions in a rapidly changing world.

The article draws upon insights from the fields of ecosystem dynamics (Levin, 1998; Holling, 1973) and organizational collaboration and automation systems (Malone, 2018; Davenport & Ronanki, 2018). Ecosystem dynamics provides a useful metaphor for understanding the complex, adaptive nature of modern organizations and their environments. Principles such as self-organization, emergence, and co-evolution (Holling, 2001) offer valuable insights into how organizations can design and manage their data ecosystems. On the other hand, research on organizational collaboration and automation systems sheds light on the socio-technical aspects of DDDM, including the interplay between human and machine agency, the importance of trust and transparency, and the challenges of aligning data insights with organizational values and goals.

The article is structured as follows. First, we provide an overview of the key components of DDDM—data acquisition, analysis, and application—and discuss their relevance in the context of modern collaborative and automated organizations.

Next, we examine each of these components through the lens of the OASIS model, highlighting how the principles of openness, autonomy, symbiosis, intelligence, and sustainability can guide the implementation of DDDM. Finally, we conclude with a discussion of the implications of our analysis for organizational practice and future research.

18.2 The Key Components of Data-Driven Decision Making

18.2.1 Data Acquisition

The foundation of DDDM lies in the acquisition of high-quality, relevant data. In modern organizations, data can come from a variety of sources, including internal systems (e.g., ERP, CRM), external providers (e.g., market research firms), and ecosystem partners (e.g., suppliers, customers). The challenge lies in integrating these diverse data streams into a coherent, reliable, and up-to-date dataset that can support decision making.

From an ecosystem perspective, data acquisition can be viewed as a process of sensing and responding to environmental signals. Just as organisms in an ecosystem rely on sensory inputs to detect changes and adapt their behavior, organizations need robust data acquisition mechanisms to stay attuned to shifts in their business environment. This requires not only technical capabilities for data collection and integration but also a culture of openness and collaboration that encourages the sharing of data across internal and external organizational boundaries.

In modern automated organizations, data acquisition involves a variety of database technologies that have become increasingly more sophisticated as well as the use of sensors, IoT devices, and other automated data capture and distribution technologies, these technologies enable the continuous, real-time collection of data on various aspects of organizational operations, from supply chain performance to customer behavior.

While the benefits of automated data acquisition are substantial, they come with significant challenges such as:

- Data Quality
- With the volume and velocity of data increasing, ensuring data quality becomes more complex. Organizations must implement robust data validation and cleansing processes to maintain the integrity of their data assets.
- Privacy Concerns
- The extensive collection of data, particularly personal information, raises serious privacy concerns. Organizations must navigate a complex landscape of data protection regulations, such as GDPR in Europe or CCPA in California.
- Security Risks

- As data becomes more valuable, it also becomes a more attractive target for cybercriminals. Protecting vast amounts of sensitive data from breaches and unauthorized access is a critical challenge.
- Ethical Considerations
- The power to collect and analyze extensive data about individuals and operations raises ethical questions about the appropriate use of this information.
- Organizations need to establish clear governance frameworks and ethical guidelines to ensure that automated data collection aligns with organizational values and societal norms.

18.2.2 Data Analysis

Once data is acquired, the next step is to analyze it to extract meaningful insights that can inform decision making. This involves the use of various analytical techniques, ranging from basic statistical analysis to advanced machine learning algorithms. The goal is to identify patterns, trends, and relationships in the data that can help answer specific business questions or predict future outcomes.

In collaborative organizations, data analysis often takes the form of collective sensemaking, where individuals from different functional areas come together to interpret data and generate insights. This requires not only technical skills in data analysis but also the ability to communicate and collaborate effectively across disciplinary boundaries (Abma et al., 2019). Being able to collaboratively produce reports and perform data analysis can lead to richer, more nuanced insights by leveraging the diverse perspectives and expertise of team members.

In automated organizations, data analysis has been highly impacted by the introduction of Generative AI capabilities and is increasingly being performed by artificial intelligence (AI) systems, such as machine learning models and natural language processing algorithms along with the mentioned latest generative AI models. These systems can process vast amounts of data quickly and accurately, identifying patterns and relationships that may be difficult for humans to discern. However, the use of AI in data analysis also raises concerns about transparency, bias, and accountability (Memarian & Doleck, 2023). Organizations need to ensure that their AI systems are designed and implemented in a way that aligns with organizational values, complies with the growing set of regulations and promotes the maximum level of fairness as well as full transparency of the process required to produce a given action.

18.2.3 Data Application

The ultimate goal of DDDM is to apply the insights generated from data analysis to inform decision makers and operational personnel in general in order to drive subsequent organizational action. This requires translating data insights into actionable "recommendations" or in more general terms "predictions" and communicating them effectively to decision makers. DDDM also involves integrating data insights into organizational processes and systems, such as strategic planning, resource allocation, and performance management. DDDM fosters a culture of continuous improvement and adaptability, enabling organizations to make proactive, well-informed decisions that enhance their competitive edge.

In modern collaborative organizations, data applications have evolved beyond charts and static visualization into more action-oriented tools. The integration of multiple systems allows us to go beyond simple data presentation, focusing on catalyzing immediate and coordinated responses across teams.

Collaborative platforms now combine data-driven insights with project management tools, such as Kanban boards that automatically update based on real-time data as well as individual or group chat systems that together have transformed into hubs of data-informed discussion, able to integrate visualizations, automated alerts and triggers. These tools don't just communicate data; they trigger action through mechanisms like automated task generation and AI-powered decision support systems.

The storytelling aspect has also been greatly enhanced by the surprising generative abilities on language of modern AI systems, with interactive narratives allowing users to explore and contribute to data stories dynamically. Real-time updates ensure that narratives evolve with new information.

While powerful, these integrated systems present challenges in data literacy, information overload, and privacy concerns. However, their contribution to create a truly data-driven culture is significant. By blurring the lines between data analysis, communication, task management, and action, organizations can leverage collective intelligence more effectively, leading to more agile and informed decision-making at all levels.

In automated organizations, data applications have evolved to encompass sophisticated decision support systems and automated decision-making algorithms. These advanced systems leverage various data processing techniques to generate real-time recommendations, enabling organizations to adapt swiftly to environmental changes.

Recent advancements in multimodal generative AI have opened new frontiers in this domain. These technologies extend beyond language processing to incorporate audio and video signals, offering a more comprehensive approach to data analysis and decision support. While promising, the widespread adoption of these multimodal AI systems remains on the horizon, with organizations carefully considering their implementation.

As automated decision-making systems become more prevalent, organizations face the challenge of balancing technological efficiency with human insight. The goal is to harness the speed and accuracy of automated systems while preserving the critical role of human judgment and values in the decision-making process. This balance is essential to ensure that technological advancements complement human expertise.

The increasing reliance on automated decision-making systems also raises profound questions about human agency and accountability. As algorithms play a larger role in organizational decisions, it becomes crucial to establish clear frameworks for responsibility and ethical considerations. Organizations must grapple with how to maintain human oversight and intervention in automated processes, ensuring that ultimate accountability remains within the human domain and therefore bearing on human decision-makers.

In navigating this complex landscape, organizations are tasked with developing strategies that maximize the benefits of automation while safeguarding the irreplaceable value of human insight and ethical considerations.

18.3 DDDM Through the Lens of the OASIS Model

Having examined the key components of DDDM, we now turn to the OASIS model to explore how the principles of openness, autonomy, symbiosis, intelligence, and sustainability can guide the implementation of DDDM in modern collaborative and automated organizations.

18.3.1 Openness

Openness refers to the free flow and exchange of information, resources, and ideas within and between organizations. In the context of DDDM, openness is critical for ensuring that decision makers have access to the data they need to make informed choices. This requires breaking down data silos and promoting a culture of data sharing and collaboration across organizational boundaries.

From an ecosystem perspective, openness enables organizations to leverage the collective intelligence of their stakeholders, including employees, customers, suppliers, and partners. By openly sharing data and insights, organizations can tap into a wider pool of knowledge and expertise, leading to more robust and innovative solutions.

However, openness also requires careful consideration of data governance and privacy issues. Organizations need to establish clear protocols and standards for data sharing, ensuring that sensitive information is protected and that data is used ethically and responsibly.

18.3.2 Autonomy

Autonomy refers to the ability of individuals and teams to make decisions and act independently and with purpose based on their own evolving knowledge and expertise. In the context of DDDM, autonomy is important for enabling decision makers to respond quickly and adaptively to changing circumstances, without being constrained by rigid hierarchies or centralized control.

From an organizational perspective, autonomy requires a shift from command-and-control management to a more decentralized, empowered approach. This involves providing individuals and teams with the tools, resources, and authority they need to make data-driven decisions in their areas of responsibility. It also requires a culture of trust and accountability, where decision makers are held responsible for the outcomes of their choices but primarily accountability is viewed as a pathway to continuous improvement and learning rather than a punitive mechanism, this means that when mistakes occur or decisions lead to suboptimal outcomes, the focus is channeled on creating constructive consequences that foster growth and enhance future decision-making processes.

Autonomy, while aiming at full purposeful self-reliance also requires clear guidelines and guardrails to ensure that decisions align with organizational goals and values. Organizations need to balance between empowering individuals and teams to act independently and ensuring that their actions are consistent with the overall direction and purpose of the organization.

18.3.3 Symbiosis

Symbiosis refers to the mutually beneficial relationships and interactions between different entities within an ecosystem. In the context of DDDM, symbiosis is critical for fostering collaboration and synergy between humans and machines, as well as between different functional areas and stakeholder groups.

From a socio-technical perspective, symbiosis requires the design of systems and processes that enable humans and machines to work together effectively, leveraging their complementary strengths and capabilities. This involves for example creating interfaces and workflows that allow humans to produce, interpret and act on machine-generated insights, while also enabling machines to learn from human feedback and domain expertise.

From an organizational perspective, symbiosis requires the cultivation of cross-functional and Automation/AI augmented teams and partnerships that bring together diverse perspectives and expertise. This involves creating technology augmented structures and clever incentive schemes that encourage collaboration and knowledge sharing across departmental boundaries, as well as with external stakeholders such as customers, suppliers, and partners.

18.3.4 Intelligence

Intelligence refers to the ability to acquire, process, and apply knowledge to adapt to changing circumstances and achieve desired outcomes. Such intelligence is not limited to single individuals but extends to collective intelligence exhibited by groups, and augmented by artificial intelligence. In the context of DDDM, intelligence involves the continuous learning and evolution of organizations based on data insights and feedback from their environment.

From a technological perspective, intelligence requires the use of the most advanced data manipulation technologies and AI techniques to extract meaningful patterns and predictions from data. This involves the design and implementation of machine learning models, natural language processing algorithms, and other intelligent systems that can process vast amounts of structured and unstructured data.

From a human perspective, intelligence requires the cultivation of a data-literate and insight-driven workforce capable of encoding processes in the "machine". This involves providing employees with the skills, knowledge, and tools they need to program, configure, modify, interpret and act on data, as well as creating a culture that values continuous learning and experimentation and evolution.

From an organizational perspective, intelligence requires the creation of feedback loops and learning mechanisms that enable organizations to adapt and evolve based on data insights and environmental feedback. This involves the design of agile processes and structures that allow organizations to quickly pivot and adjust their strategies and tactics in response to new information and changing circumstances.

18.3.5 Sustainability

Sustainability extends beyond traditional notions of balancing economic, social, and environmental impacts. Instead, it embraces a more nuanced understanding derived from ecosystem dynamics, where the key to long-term viability lies in achieving a delicate equilibrium between structure and flexibility.

In the realm of data-driven decision making (DDDM), sustainability involves orchestrating a dynamic balance between the efficient utilization of data resources and the maintenance of adaptive capacity. This approach recognizes that while highly structured and optimized data systems can drive immediate efficiency, they may become brittle and vulnerable to unforeseen challenges. Conversely, systems with too much redundancy or lack of structure may struggle to effectively leverage their data assets.

From an organizational perspective, sustainable DDDM requires developing frameworks that allow for both rigorous data governance and the flexibility to adapt to changing circumstances. This might involve implementing adaptive data architectures that can evolve with the organization's needs, or fostering a culture that values both data-driven precision and creative problem-solving.

The responsible stewardship of data in this context goes beyond merely ensuring privacy and security. It involves cultivating a diverse ecosystem of data sources, analytical approaches, and decision-making processes. This diversity serves as a form of resilience, providing multiple pathways for insight and action in the face of uncertainty or disruption.

Aligning data-driven decisions with long-term organizational viability requires a shift from purely efficiency-driven metrics to those that capture the system's overall health and adaptability. This might involve developing indicators that measure not just the accuracy or speed of decisions, but also their contribution to organizational learning, stakeholder trust, and the ability to navigate complex, evolving environments.

From a broader societal perspective, sustainable DDDM recognizes the interconnectedness of organizations within larger social and environmental systems. It encourages the development of collaborative platforms that allow for the flow of data and insights across organizational boundaries, mirroring the nutrient cycles in natural ecosystems. These collaborations can enhance the collective capacity to address complex challenges while ensuring that no single entity becomes overly rigid or vulnerable.

Ultimately, sustainability in DDDM within the OASIS framework is about fostering adaptive, resilient systems that can thrive in the face of change. It requires a continuous process of balancing structure and flexibility, efficiency and redundancy, specialization and diversity. By embracing this more holistic view of sustainability, organizations can make decisions that not only drive immediate value but also contribute to their long-term viability and the health of the broader ecosystems in which they operate.

18.4 Implications and Future Directions

The analysis presented in this article highlights the critical role of DDDM in modern collaborative and automated organizations, as well as the importance of aligning DDDM practices with the principles of the OASIS model. By embracing openness, autonomy, symbiosis, intelligence, and sustainability, organizations can harness the power of data to make informed, agile, and responsible decisions that drive innovation, resilience, and long-term value creation.

However, the implementation of DDDM in practice is not without challenges and risks. Organizations need to navigate complex issues related to data privacy, security, ethics, and governance, as well as the cultural and organizational barriers to data-driven decision making. Moreover, the increasing reliance on automated decision making systems raises important questions about human agency, accountability, and transparency in organizational decision making processes.

To address these challenges and realize the full potential of DDDM, organizations need to adopt a holistic and multidisciplinary approach that integrates technical, social, and ecological considerations. This requires the development of new frameworks, methods, and tools for data acquisition, analysis, and application, as well as the cultivation of a data-literate and insight-driven workforce.

18.5 Conclusions

As we've explored throughout this article, Data Driven Decision Making (DDDM) has become an indispensable capability for modern collaborative and automated organizations. In an era characterized by rapid change and increasing complexity, the ability to harness data for informed decision-making is not just an advantage but it's a necessity for both survival and growth.

Our examination of DDDM through the lens of the OASIS model, emphasizing openness, autonomy, symbiosis, intelligence, and sustainability reveals a nuanced and multifaceted approach to leveraging data in organizational contexts. This framework encourages us to think beyond simple data collection and analysis, pushing us to consider how DDDM can be deeply integrated into the very fabric of organizational culture and operations.

The principle of openness challenges organizations to break down data silos and foster a culture of information sharing, while carefully navigating the complex landscape of data privacy and governance. Autonomy, on the other hand, speaks to the need for empowering individuals and teams with the tools and authority to make data-informed decisions quickly and adaptively. This shift towards decentralized decision-making requires a fundamental rethinking of traditional management structures, emphasizing trust, accountability, and continuous learning.

Symbiosis emerges as a crucial concept in the age of AI and automation. It calls for the thoughtful integration of human and machine intelligence, leveraging the unique strengths of each to create decision-making processes that are both powerful and nuanced. This symbiotic relationship extends beyond the human-machine interface to encompass collaboration across functional areas and even organizational boundaries, creating rich ecosystems of data and insight.

The principle of intelligence in DDDM goes far beyond the application of advanced analytical techniques. It encompasses the organization's ability to learn, adapt, and evolve based on data-driven insights. This requires not just sophisticated AI and machine learning capabilities, but also the cultivation of a workforce that is both data-literate and creatively insightful.

Perhaps most importantly, our exploration of sustainability in DDDM reveals a concept that transcends traditional notions of balancing economic, social, and environmental impacts. In the context of data-driven organizations, sustainability speaks to the delicate equilibrium between structure and flexibility, efficiency and adaptability. It challenges us to design processes and therefore organizations that are robust yet agile, capable of driving immediate value while also ensuring long-term organizational viability.

As we look to the future, it's clear that the implementation of DDDM in modern organizations is not without its challenges. Issues of data privacy, security, and ethics loom large, as does the need to maintain human agency and accountability in increasingly automated decision environments. Moreover, organizations must grapple with cultural and structural barriers to truly data-driven operations.

Addressing these challenges will require a holistic, multidisciplinary approach. Organizations will need to develop new frameworks and tools for data management and analysis, cultivate a workforce that is both technically skilled and critically thoughtful, and create governance structures that are both robust and adaptive. Perhaps most importantly, they will need to foster a culture that values data-driven insights while also recognizing the importance of human intuition, creativity, and ethical consideration.

Organizations that can effectively integrate data-driven decision making into their operations balancing the power of AI and automation with the irreplaceable value of human insight will be well-positioned to navigate the complexities of our rapidly evolving business landscape. They will be more innovative, more resilient, and ultimately more successful in creating long-term value, not just for themselves, but for the broader ecosystems in which they operate.

As we stand on the cusp of this data-driven future, one thing is clear: the organizations that thrive will be those that view DDDM not as a set of tools or techniques, but as a fundamental way of thinking and operating. They will be the ones that embrace the principles of openness, autonomy, symbiosis, intelligence, and sustainability, using them as a compass to guide their journey through the ever-changing terrain of our increasingly automated and interconnected world.

References

Abma, T., et al. (2019). Sense making: The process of data analysis and interpretation. In *Participatory research for health and social well-being*. Springer.

Davenport, T. H., & Ronanki, R. (2018). Artificial intelligence for the real world. *Harvard Business Review, 96*(1), 108–116.

Holling, C. S. (1973). Resilience and stability of ecological systems. *Annual Review of Ecology and Systematics, 4*(1), 1–23.

Holling, C. S. (2001). Understanding the complexity of economic, ecological, and social systems. *Ecosystems, 4*(5), 390–405.

Levin, S. A. (1998). Ecosystems and the biosphere as complex adaptive systems. *Ecosystems, 1*(5), 431–436.

Malone, T. W. (2018). *Superminds: The surprising power of people and computers thinking together*. Hachette UK.

Memarian, B., & Doleck, T. (2023). Fairness, Accountability, Transparency, and Ethics (FATE) in Artificial Intelligence (AI) and higher education: A systematic review. *Computers and Education: Artificial Intelligence, 5*, 100152.

Provost, F., & Fawcett, T. (2013). Data science and its relationship to big data and data-driven decision making. *Big Data, 1*(1), 51–59.

Chapter 19
Assessing Organizational Maturity: The Role of Maturity Models in Project Success

Silvia Mari, Adi Muslic, and Massimo Pirozzi

An organization's success in project execution depends on its ability to implement project management knowledge and praxis. This ability is often expressed as project maturity.

In the context of project, program, and portfolio management, a maturity model is a framework that helps organizations assess and improve their capabilities in managing projects, programs, and portfolios. Maturity models are used to evaluate how well an organization can plan, execute, and manage these management processes efficiently, consistently, and with strategic alignment to business goals. It is assumed that the higher the level of project maturity in an organization, the greater its ability to successfully implement projects.

Maturity models are typically used in audits, self-assessment, performance evaluations, and as a tool for organizational development. By conducting maturity assessments, organizations can identify gaps in their current processes, set improvement goals, and prioritize investments in training, tools, and process development.

As remarkably reviewed by Nikolaenko and Sidorov (2023) research by global project management bodies like SEI, PMI, IPMA, OGC, and ISO[1] has shown that

[1] Software Engineering Institute (SEI), Project Management Institute (PMI), International Project Management Association (IPMA), Office of Government Commerce (OGC), International Organization for Standardization (ISO).

S. Mari (✉)
Department of Innovative Technologies, SUPSI, Lugano, Switzerland
e-mail: silvia.mari@supsi.ch

A. Muslic
NextProjects Sàrl, Meyrin, Switzerland

M. Pirozzi
Istituto Italiano di Project Management (ISIPM), Roma, Italy

A. Bassi et al. (eds.), *General Management Principles for Project Management*, Management for Professionals, https://doi.org/10.1007/978-3-031-98592-8_19

organizations with higher managerial maturity are more likely to meet their project goals by identifying and standardizing best practices.

The literature features numerous studies confirming the positive correlation between project success and project maturity (Irfan et al., 2019; Gomes & Romão, 2015; Besner & Hobbs, 2008; Dooley et al., 2001).

Among various, empirical studies by Backlund et al. (2014) provide evidence that organizations with higher managerial maturity are less likely to encounter significant risks. Hence, such an established link between project management maturity and successful project outcomes has led to the development of numerous maturity models—e.g. more than 30 models (Grant & Pennypacker, 2006).

19.1 Project Management Maturity as an Indirect Measure of Organizational Maturity

In the modern business environment, achieving and maintaining a high level of project management maturity is crucial for the success of organizations. Project management maturity is a measure of an organization's ability to effectively manage projects and is often correlated with organizational maturity. In addition, a high level of project management maturity typically implies the presence of a Project Management Office (PMO) within the organization. Therefore, there is a close relationship among Project Management Maturity, organizational strategy and the modern role of a PMO, and the synergy among these elements contribute to the overall success and competitiveness of each organization.

Project management maturity level serves as an indirect measure of organizational maturity because effective project management practices are often indicative of broader organizational capabilities, culture, and readiness for change. Main convergences include:

- **Strategic alignment**. Organizations with higher project management maturity levels are more likely to align their project management practices with strategic objectives and organizational priorities. This alignment demonstrates a deeper understanding of how projects contribute to overall organizational success and reflects a mature approach to strategic planning and execution.
- **Leadership and Governance**. Mature organizations typically have strong leadership and governance structures in place to oversee project management activities. A mature project management maturity level often reflects effective leadership support, clear accountability, and robust governance mechanisms, which are hallmarks of organizational maturity.
- **Process standardization and optimization**. Mature organizations invest in standardizing and optimizing project management processes to drive consistency, efficiency, and effectiveness. A higher project management maturity level suggests that the organization has established repeatable processes, best prac-

tices, and performance metrics, indicative of broader process maturity across the organization.

- **Risk management and adaptability**. Mature organizations demonstrate a proactive approach to risk management and adaptability in response to changing circumstances. A higher project management maturity level signifies that the organization has implemented robust risk management practices, contingency planning, and adaptive strategies, reflecting a culture of resilience and agility.
- **Stakeholder engagement and communication**. Effective stakeholder engagement and communication are essential components of organizational maturity. Organizations with higher project management maturity levels are better equipped to engage stakeholders, manage expectations, and communicate project progress effectively. This capability demonstrates a mature approach to relationship management and stakeholder satisfaction.
- **Continuous improvement and learning**. Mature organizations embrace a culture of continuous improvement and learning, seeking opportunities to enhance processes, capabilities, and performance. A higher project management maturity level indicates that the organization prioritizes learning from past experiences, feedback, and best practices, fostering a culture of innovation and excellence.

Definitively, a high level of Project Management Maturity indicates also a good level of organizational strategy implementation. We may define organizational strategy as a comprehensive plan that outlines how an organization will achieve its long-term objectives and sustain a competitive advantage in its sectors of activity. It involves setting a vision, defining a mission, and establishing strategic goals and objectives that guide the organization's activities and resource allocation. Effective organizational strategy ensures that the organization's efforts are focused on areas that will yield the highest business and/or social returns and drive growth.

19.2 Key Concepts of a Maturity Model in Project, Program, and Portfolio (PPP) Management

Despite their coherence among standard practices and established internationally recognized bodies, maturity models differentiate on different aspects while evaluating an organization's PPP maturity.

In general models could be based on concepts such as capability (i.e. an organization's ability to perform specific processes effectively and efficiently) or maturity itself (e.g. maturity relies on assessing how PPP processes are integrated) or a combination of both as in the CMMI® model (Capability Maturity Model® Integration).

Capabilities and maturity models categorize an organization's development into levels that reflect its progression in implementing best practices across projects, programs, and portfolios.

Capability levels apply to an organization's performance and process improvement achievements in individual practice areas. Within practice areas, the practices are organized into practice groups labeled Level 0 to Level 3 which provide an evolutionary path to performance improvement. Each level builds on the previous levels by adding new functionality or rigor resulting in increased capability (e.g. CMM Institute).

- Level 0—**Incomplete**: The function is either not performed or only partially performed, with goals unmet.
- Level 1—**Initial**: The function meets its goals but is inconsistently applied and not embedded in the organization's culture.
- Level 2—**Managed**: The function is performed by skilled individuals, following policies and producing controlled results, with monitoring for compliance.
- Level 3—**Defined**: The function is consistently executed using tailored processes, with lessons learned integrated into organizational knowledge.

In the counterpart Maturity models are normally organized in five levels that typically span from ad-hoc processes to highly optimized systems. Here a brief description of them.

- Level 1—**Initial**: At this level, processes are mostly unstructured, reactive, and unpredictable. Organizations have little consistency in managing projects.
- Level 2—**Managed**: Basic processes are established and controlled; some level of governance is in place, but there is still variability across projects.
- Level 3—**Defined**: The organization has standardized and formalized processes that are consistently applied across different departments and teams.
- Level 4—**Quantitatively Managed**: Processes are monitored and controlled using metrics. Data-driven decision-making allows for better predictability and efficiency.
- Level 5—**Optimizing**: At this highest maturity level, the organization engages in continuous improvement, using lessons learned, innovation, and feedback loops to refine processes.

In this multitude of maturity models, the approach proposed by Harold Kerzner represents an *unicum*. In his PMMM Kerzner (2019) emphasizes that people manage projects, while methodologies act as supporting tools. We can have the greatest methodology in the world and still not reach a level of maturity because the current human behavior is not in place. Standardized, rigid methodologies arose to address concerns about project managers' decision-making, but real excellence relies on human interaction. Hence, true project maturity is achieved when people collaborate effectively, and that includes communication, cooperation, teamwork, and trust.

Table 19.1 illustrates a comparative analysis of the most popular maturity models (courtesy from Sidorov A. and Nikolaenko V. followed by adaptation).

Table 19.1 Comparative analysis of the most popular maturity models

	Name of Project Management Maturity Model									
Criterion	CMMI®	OPM3	IPMA DELTA®	P3M3®	SPICE	PM^2	PMMM	ProMMM	PMMMsm	Prado
Developer	SEI	PMI	IPMA	OGC	ISO	Kwak Y.H. and Ibbs C.W.	Kerzner H.	Hilson D.	PM Solution Crawford K.J.	Prado D, Archibald R.
Suitable for evaluation	Yes	Yes	Yes	Yes	Yes	Yes	Yes	Yes	Yes	Yes
Suitable for analysis of strengths and weaknesses	Yes	Yes	Yes	Yes	Yes	Yes	Yes	Yes	Yes	Yes
Suitable for project management improvement	Yes	Yes	Yes	Yes	Yes	Yes	Yes	Yes	Yes	Yes
Sector	IT	For all sectors	For all sectors	For all sectors	IT, auto, space, medicine	For all sectors	For all sectors	For all sectors	For all sectors	For all sectors
Process reference model	Yes, 22 processes	No	No	Yes, 32 processes	No	No	No	No	No	No

(continued)

Table 19.1 (continued)

	Name of Project Management Maturity Model									
Criterion	CMMI®	OPM3	IPMA DELTA®	P3M3®	SPICE	PM^2	PMMM	ProMMM	PMMMsm	Prado
Knowledge domain reference model	No	No	Yes, ICB, contains 46 elements of competence	No	No	Yes, 9 fields of knowledge	No	No	Yes, 10 fields of knowledge	Yes, 7 dimensions
Reference model for the best management practices	No	Yes, 586 best practices and 2400 abilities for projects, programs and portfolios	No	No	No	No	No	No	No	No
Number of maturity levels	1–3	0–1 (presence or lack of the best practice)	1–5	1–5	0–5	1–5	1–5	1–4	1–5	1-5
Based on a body of knowledge of the project management best practices	-	PMBOK® Guide The Standard for Program Mng; The Standard for Portfolio Mng; PMCD	ICB, OCB, PEB	PRINCE2®	ISO standards	PMBOK® Guide	-	-	PMBOK® Guide	ISO standards
Creation date of the first version	2000	2003	ICB (1999)	2003	1998	1997	2001	2003	2007	2005
Creation date of the latest version	2018	2013	ICB (2015), OCB (2016), PEB (2016)	2006	2015	2002	-	-	2015	2017

The process of determining the maturity level of project management is described	Yes	Yes	Yes	Yes	Yes	Yes	Yes	Yes	Yes	Yes
The process of determining the maturity level of program management is described	No	Yes	No	Yes	No	No	No	No	No	No
The process of determining the maturity level of portfolio is described management	No	Yes	No	Yes	No	No	No	No	No	No
Certification	Yes Class A, B and C	No	Yes Level A, B, C and D	Yes	Yes	No	No	No	No	No

19.3 Maturity Model and Agile Project Management

In an era where the agility and responsiveness of Agile project management are paramount, the integration of structured models (e.g. Project Management Maturity Model—PMMM or Capability Maturity Model—CMM), with agile methodologies presents a blend of unique opportunities and challenges. But what are the benefits of integrating a maturity model with Agile Project Management? And what are the challenges and the corresponding solution of such integration? In a recent paper Astridita et al. (2024) systematically try to address those questions.

Agile project management (APM) methodology, developed approximately two decades ago predominantly for the software sector, draws its principles from the Agile Manifesto. These principles prioritize individual interactions, the functionality of software, cooperation with customers, and flexibility in adapting to change (Koch et al., 2023). Originally for software development, APM is now utilized in various fields, characterized by team autonomy, iterative development, and equality within teams (Abdullah et al., 2023; Haj Hamad & Al Fayoumi, 2018). It aims to deliver high-value products within time and budget constraints by integrating planning with execution and fostering teamwork and customer collaboration. APM manages paradoxical dynamics, balancing team flexibility with procedural rigor, and is recognized for effectively responding to evolving project requirements and customer needs (Binci et al., 2022).

In their analysis Astridita et al. delve into the tangible benefits that CMM and APM integration brings to project management. In particular these benefits could be summarized into five core practice areas within CMMI v2.0 (see Table 19.1) framework: Estimating, Planning, Risk and Opportunity Management, Monitor and Control, and Requirements Development and Management.

- **Estimation**. Greater predictability in costs and deadlines (with up to 17% increase in estimation accuracy (Degerli, 2020a, 2020b). Such greater predictability in cost and deadlines contributes to reduced costs and increased productivity (Alqadri et al., 2020; Saputra et al., 2020, and Galvan-Cruz et al., 2021).
- **Planning**. Elevation of the process of work planning and management. Creation of comprehensive forecasts concerning workload, costs, and schedules, with a significant reduction in rework (up to 70%) and the increase in on-time delivery rates (up to 97%) (Degerli, 2020a, 2020b).
- **Risk**. In Agile environments, effectively handling requirement changes is critical. The integration promotes a proactive approach to identifying and evaluating risks and opportunities (Degerli, 2020a, 2020b).
- **Monitor and control**. Provides a framework for analyzing and managing critical subprocesses, particularly in high-maturity project management scenarios (Keshta et al., 2018; Cerdeiral & Santos, 2019).
- **Requirements development and management**. Enhances customer satisfaction by improving product quality and aligning closely with customer needs. Emphasis on customer collaboration and adaptability to change (Joembunthanaphong & Sriharee, 2022; Pinedo et al., 2023).

Integration of maturity model and agile practice comes with several tactical and organizational challenges (Henriquez et al., 2021). In particular such challenges could be grouped in five categories:

- **Resource and Time Constraints**. Integration demands additional resources, effort, and time beyond the scope of standard project activities that are particularly impacting Small and Medium-sized Enterprises (SMEs). This challenge can lead to difficulties in maintaining the balance between the pursuit of quality improvement and the practical realities of project management within these organizations (Ferdinansyah & Purwandari, 2021; Saheel et al., 2022).
- **Organizational Resistance and Change Management**. Resistance to adopting new methodologies is a common challenge within organizations. This resistance often stems from a lack of knowledge or experience with the new systems. Frequent leadership changes or past experiences with unsuccessful management initiatives can further exacerbate such resistance (Henriquez et al., 2021; Ferdinansyah & Purwandari, 2021).
- **Balancing Agility with Control**. A critical challenge is the balancing of the structured approach of a maturity model with the flexibility of Agile. As organizations strive to achieve higher maturity levels within a proper framework, they may find that agility is compromised. This challenge concerns managing project processes and aligning organizational culture and values with these contrasting methodologies (Henriquez et al., 2021 Ferdinansyah & Purwandari, 2021).
- **Knowledge, Training, and Expertise Gaps**. The deficiency in specialized training covering the full spectrum of development activities can hinder the effective implementation of these methodologies. Furthermore, the absence of support from specialists in statistical and process management knowledge can leave project managers and process groups struggling to align organizational and project goals with critical subprocesses (Cerdeiral & Santos, 2019; Giachetti et al., 2023).
- **Scaling and Knowledge Dissemination**. Scaling experiences effectively requires documentation of successful practices and a concerted effort to share and institutionalize these practices across various teams and departments. Without the active support of upper management, experiences, and practices beneficial often remain confined to specific teams or projects (Henriquez et al., 2021; Cerdeiral & Santos, 2019).

In conclusion, integration of maturity models with agile practices can lead to more accurate estimations, streamlined project planning, effective risk mitigation, improved quality control, and optimized requirement development and management. However, this integration comes with challenges such as resource constraints, organizational resistance to change, and the need to balance control and agility. Bridging knowledge gaps and scaling integrated practices across the organization are notable hurdles (Astridita et al., 2024).

Senior management must play a pivotal role by committing to process improvement initiatives, providing necessary resources, and supporting cultural change to overcome challenges. Automation tools for control and accountability, along with continuous monitoring of agility, are essential for maintaining the balance between

Maturity Model and Agile. Additionally, addressing knowledge gaps through training and promoting non-bureaucratic knowledge dissemination processes are vital steps towards successful integration. Overall, a strategic and committed approach from senior management is crucial to realizing the full potential of such integration and improving project management practices for better project outcomes.

19.4 Organizational Heterogeneity and Multi-Pronged Measurement of Project Maturity

While assessing project maturity, most typically the results presented are either averaged for the entire organization, which does not reflect the overall differentiated landscape of the organization, or results of a single measurement for the entire organization, which are subject to measurement site or respondent reference point errors.

Significant differences could be identified within the organization with regard to the levels of project maturity across its various departments. In a recent paper Woźniak (2024) illustrates a case study where departments within an organization (development, service and sales) have been identified, and project level of maturity was assessed. Clear differences have been observed across the company's departments. The highest level of project maturity in the organization—level 4—has been presented by the development department, followed by the service department, which has reached level 3, with the lowest project maturity—level 1—attained by the sales department. Levels were assigned according to the Harold Kerzner's Project Management Maturity Model (KPMMM) frame.

Within this case study, Wozniak proposed to assess in parallel the level of IT sophistication in project management for each department. In fact, one strong element within the realm of project management success, gaining increasing importance, is information technology (IT). The role of IT tools in project management has been expanding, resulting in improved productivity and project efficiency of organizations.

The linking organizational project maturity with the level of the technologies used in project management, has been highlighted in several domain and industry contexts, i.e., in geodesy (Badea et al., 2014), banking (Vrečko et al., 2015), critical infrastructure projects (Payette et al., 2015), oil and gas (O&G) industry (Yakoot et al., 2023).

If literature indicates that the use of IT alone, without integration with project maturity components, will not improve the level of project maturity (Hassan & Halim, 2012; Hassan et al., 2013), it has been reported that digitally advanced organizations have been found to achieve business excellence only by moving to higher levels of the project maturity model (Fajsi et al., 2022).

Hence software-technical components, at par with methodological, organizational, and motivational components constitute the basic elements of the project management and project maturity system (Derenskaya, 2017).

As a consequence, a need arises for a combined view of organizational project maturity and the information technology employed in project management.

Interestingly, Woźniak (2024) proposes a classification of IT maturity in the context of project management, on the basis of five levels:

- **Level 1**. Occasional use of IT tools to handle financial and time-management aspects (MS Excel, MS Word, Power Point)
- **Level 2**. Tools for scheduling and progress/cost reporting, as well as tools supporting collaboration and teamwork (MS Project, GanttChart, Trello, Asana, BaseCamp)
- **Level 3**. Tools enabling collaborative management of the entire project and the organization's project portfolio (MS Project, Wrike, Monday)
- **Level 4**. Project management support systems are integrated with other IT systems—e.g., purchasing systems, production systems, information flow systems (JIRA, Confluence, Slack, Time City, Team Gantt)
- **Level 5**. A comprehensive system for project, program and project portfolio management in the organization. All functions required in project management are integrated into a single database.

In general, within a single organization, significant variation in both project maturity and the level of IT in project management exist. This highlights the need for multi-directional and cross-departmental assessment, in order to identify improvement areas contributing positively to an organization's overall project maturity and its adoption of appropriate project management IT technologies.

In examining the likely reasons behind the cross-divisional differences within the organization, disparities in the areas of training and senior management support have been observed.

Finally, the mere availability of technology, without the adoption of a company-wide framework for its application in project management, will not increase the organization's level of project maturity. The support of senior management as well as the training system raising IT skills and building project knowledge and awareness are the two main groups of factors causing such a significant cross-departmental differentiation within an organization.

19.5 Custom Maturity Model

While using a standardized assessment method, an organization encounters the risk of including topics that are not applicable to a specific company and therefore may provide a false impression of the maturity level.

The starting point in customization of the assessment instrument is indeed senior management vision about how they would like to run the company. The customization should also include the competencies that project personnel are expected to possess as part of the vision. These competencies are generally best established by

Project Management Office (PMO) with guidance from any project management standards. That is, capabilities to tailor-made a maturity model requires a certain degree of maturity of the organization itself.

Furthermore, even if an organization aim for long term efficiency and effectiveness in execution of activities, the customization should be made based on short term expectation, so that progress can be measured during reasonable assessment intervals.

As proposed by Kerzner (2019), the interval between assessments should be small for deficiency to be discovered and corrected, using continuous improvement efforts and change management practices if necessary. If assessments are being made quarterly, then updating the assessment questions early may be the best approach. This will give time to measure whether changes are taking place as well as the rate at which continuous improvements are being made.

On the other hand, there are at least two reasons for using the standard assessment instruments without any customization. The primary reason for using the standard assessment instruments is that frequent customization could raise cost issues. For that reason, a company should rely on an easy-to-use model capable of maintaining a low assessment cost.

In the second hand, a standard maturity model has the capability to benchmark against other companies in the model's database for the same industry, the same size, or other similarities. Hence the lack of benchmarking is probably considered the main issue in the use of customized maturity assessment. To overcome this issue a company can keep some form of benchmarking by maintaining part of a standard assessment, and then adding a tailor-made questionnaire one on top of it.

Notably, in the beginning of 2016 Praxis proposed its free on-line capability maturity tool. This remarkably framework, called Praxis 360 Model,[2] is free to use and it covers knowledge, method, competency and capability maturity for the different levels of projects, programmes and portfolios. The Praxis approach to maturity is similar to the ISO9000 approach to quality, in that an organisation defines its own required scope of capability maturity, against which it will benchmark and improve.

19.6 What's Next in PM Maturity?

Nowadays, almost one-fourth of the world's economic activities are being performed and managed in the form of projects and programs for capital formation, and even trends are rising more in developing and emerging economies than in developed economies (Sijabat, 2022). Consequently, many organizations are altering their functional hierarchies into project-based hierarchies.

A typical approach to assessing PM maturity starts with assessing existing processes and practices. Subsequently, benchmarking is performed to compare PM

[2] https://www.praxisframework.org/en/maturity/capability-maturity-overview

capabilities. Finally, PM capabilities are enhanced to the next level of maturity and so on (Jamaluddin et al., 2010). Thus, PM maturity models are vital for developing, tracking, and ensuring the efficiency and effectiveness of the projects.

As already highlighted previously while discussing IT tool, contemporary businesses are deploying and utilizing technology to enhance efficiency, effectiveness, and quality in their products/services, processes, management systems, projects, and relational mechanisms.

Consequently, the integration of human competencies with technological systems has led to improved performance (Singh et al., 2023). This integration has also extended to the discipline of project management (PM). One of the most dramatic developments that has influenced the discipline of PM is artificial intelligence (AI), which provides several new tools and techniques to escalate efficiency and effectiveness within ever-changing business environments, and the modern PM environment is no exception.

AI is a disruptive technology that radically alters the traditional methods of work in organizations (Gentsch, 2018). AI provides many benefits, including reliability, cost-effectiveness, and certainty in solving various issues (Garg & Sharma, 2021). Due to escalating information assistance in organizations and the need to assess and predict future values, a lot of organizations are adopting and implementing AI to enhance their abilities.

Recent studies on the relationship between AI and PM have been conducted in organizations with sufficient knowledge, expertise, skills, and resources (Skinner, 2021; Fridgeirsson et al., 2021). Moreover, Skinner (2021) found a positive relationship between AI and PM maturity. He further described that the organizations with lower PM maturity, i.e., level 1 do not apply AI in PM and conversely, the organizations with higher maturity, i.e., level 5, considerably apply AI in PM. In other words, the organizations with lower maturity levels apply AI at a very basic level, whereas the organizations with lower maturity levels apply AI at an advanced level. Organizations with higher PM maturity gather actionable insights, analyze data, and develop an understanding of how to apply AI in PM. The same relationship has been confirmed by Tariq et al. (2024) where AI implementation readiness status is positively related to PM maturity in the environment and context of their selected project-based organizations. Furthermore, the PM maturity level in the selected project-based organizations was found to be the highest in the "PM" area, followed by the "program management" area and "portfolio management" area. This was explained as the selected project-based organizations focus more on individual projects rather than projects as a system.

As we look to the future, the integration of generative AI (GenAI) in project management maturity assessments could represent a significant advancement in our ability to understand and enhance organizational capabilities.

GenAI can be leveraged to create tailored assessment models that account for an organization's unique context, industry-specific challenges, and strategic objectives. In particular GenAI can be utilized in several ways:

- **Contextual Analysis**: GenAI can analyze vast amounts of organizational data to understand the specific context in which projects are executed. This includes industry trends, organizational structure, and historical project performance.
- **Dynamic Questionnaire Generation**: AI can generate tailored assessment questionnaires that adapt based on the organization's responses, ensuring that the most relevant areas are explored in depth.
- **Multi-dimensional Evaluation**: GenAI can simultaneously assess multiple departments and their interdependencies, providing a holistic view of project management maturity across the organization.
- **IT Maturity Integration**: The assessment can incorporate evaluation of IT maturity, particularly focusing on project management tools and their effectiveness within the organization's ecosystem.
- **Predictive Insights**: By analyzing patterns and trends, GenAI can offer predictive insights into potential areas of improvement and their likely impact on overall project management maturity.
- **Continuous Learning**: As more data is fed into the system, GenAI can continuously refine and improve the assessment model, ensuring its relevance and accuracy over time.

In conclusion, the use of maturity models for assessing project management maturity levels in organizations provides valuable insights into their overall organizational maturity and strategic implementation capabilities. As we have discussed, project management maturity serves as a proxy for broader organizational capabilities, aligning with key aspects such as strategic alignment, leadership and governance, process standardization, risk management, stakeholder engagement, and continuous improvement.

The emergence of generative GenAI presents a promising opportunity to enhance and customize the assessment of project management maturity.

References

Abdullah, P. P., Raharjo, T., Hardian, B., & Simanungkalit, T. (2023). Challenges and best practices solution of agile project management in public sector: A systematic literature review. *JOIV: International Journal on Informatics Visualization, 7*(2), 606–614. https://doi.org/10.30630/joiv.7.2.1098

Alqadri, Y., Budiardjo, E. K., Ferdinansyah, A., & Rokhman, M. F. (2020). The CMMI-Dev implementation factors for software quality improvement. In *Proceedings of the 2020 2nd Asia Pacific Information Technology conference*. ACM. https://doi.org/10.1145/3379310.3379327

Astridita, A., Raharjo, T., & Fitriani, A. N. (2024). Perceived benefits and challenges of implementing CMMI on agile project management: A systematic literature review. *International Journal of Advanced Computer Science and Applications, 15*(1), 232–239. https://doi.org/10.14569/ijacsa.2024.0150122

Backlund, F., Chronéer, D., & Sundqvist, E. (2014). Project management maturity models—A critical review. *Procedia—Social and Behavioral Sciences, 119*, 837–846. https://doi.org/10.1016/j.sbspro.2014.03.094

Badea, G., Badea, A.-C., & David, V. (2014). Advantages of using it solutions in land surveying and cadastral project management. In *SGEM international multidisciplinary scientific geoconference EXPO proceedings*. Stef92 Technology. https://doi.org/10.5593/sgem2014/b22/s9.004

Besner, C., & Hobbs, B. (2008). Discriminating contexts and project management best practices on innovative and noninnovative projects. *Project Management Journal, 39*(S1), S123–S124. https://doi.org/10.1002/pmj.20064

Binci, D., Cerruti, C., Masili, G., & Paternoster, C. (2022). Ambidexterity and Agile project management: an empirical framework. *The TQM Journal, 35*(5), 1275–1309. https://doi.org/10.1108/tqm-01-2022-0011

Cerdeiral, C. T., & Santos, G. (2019). Software project management in high maturity: A systematic literature mapping. *Journal of Systems and Software, 148*, 56–87. https://doi.org/10.1016/j.jss.2018.10.002

Degerli, M. (2020a). *Practical suggestions to successfully adopt the CMMI V2.0 development for better process, performance, and products*. 2020 5th international conference on computer science and engineering (UBMK). IEEE. https://doi.org/10.1109/ubmk50275.2020.9219438

Degerli, M. (2020b). *Crafting a CMMI V2 compliant process for governance practice area: An experiential proposal.* 2020 Turkish National Software Engineering Symposium (UYMS). IEEE. https://doi.org/10.1109/uyms50627.2020.9247068

Derenskaya, Y. (2017). Organizational project management maturity. *Baltic Journal of Economic Studies, 3*(2), 25–32. https://doi.org/10.30525/2256-0742/2017-3-2-25-32

Dooley, K., Subra, A., & Anderson, J. (2001). Maturity and its impact on new product development project performance. *Research in Engineering Design, 13*(1), 23–29. https://doi.org/10.1007/s001630100003

Fajsi, A., Morača, S., Milosavljević, M., & Medić, N. (2022). Project management maturity and business excellence in the context of industry 4.0. *Processes, 10*(6), 1155. https://doi.org/10.3390/pr10061155

Ferdinansyah, A., & Purwandari, B. (2021). *Challenges in combining agile development and CMMI: A systematic literature review*. 2021 10th international conference on software and computer applications. ACM. https://doi.org/10.1145/3457784.3457803

Fridgeirsson, T. V., Ingason, H. T., Jonasson, H. I., & Jonsdottir, H. (2021). An authoritative study on the near future effect of artificial intelligence on project management knowledge areas. *Sustainability, 13*, 2345. https://doi.org/10.3390/su13042345

Galvan-Cruz, S., Mora, M., Laporte, C. Y., & Duran-Limon, H. (2021). Reconciliation of scrum and the project management process of the ISO/IEC 29110 standard-Entry profile—An experimental evaluation through usability measures. *Software Quality Journal, 29*, 239–273. https://doi.org/10.1007/s11219-021-09552-3

Garg, P. K., & Sharma, L. (2021). Artificial intelligence: Challenges and future applications. In *Artificial Intelligence*. Chapman and Hall/CRC. https://doi.org/10.1201/9781003140351-22

Gentsch, P. (2018). AI business: Framework and maturity model. In *AI in marketing, sales and service*. Springer International Publishing. https://doi.org/10.1007/978-3-319-89957-2_3

Giachetti, G., de la Vara, J. L., & Marín, B. (2023). Model-driven gap analysis for the fulfillment of quality standards in software development processes. *Software Quality Journal, 32*, 255–282. https://doi.org/10.1007/s11219-023-09649-x

Gomes, J., & Romão, M. (2015). *Maturity benefits and project management shaping project success* (Advances in intelligent systems and computing). Springer International Publishing. https://doi.org/10.1007/978-3-319-16486-1_43

Grant, K. P., & Pennypacker, J. S. (2006). Project management maturity: an assessment of project management capabilities among and between selected industries. *IEEE Transactions on Engineering Management, 53*(1), 59–68. https://doi.org/10.1109/tem.2005.861802

Haj Hamad, R. M., & Al Fayoumi, M. (2018). *Scalable agile transformation process (SATP) to convert waterfall project management office into agile project management office*. 2018 international Arab conference on information technology (ACIT). IEEE. https://doi.org/10.1109/acit.2018.8672701

Hassan, N., & Halim, B. A. (2012). Mathematical modelling approach to the management of recreational tourism activities at Wetland Putrajaya. *Sains Malaysiana, 41*(9), 1155–1161.

Hassan, N., Hamzah, H. H. M., & Zain, S. M. M. (2013). A goal programming approach for rubber production in Malaysia. *American-Eurasian Journal of Sustainable Agriculture, 7*(2), 50–53.

Henriquez, V., Moreno, A. M., Calvo-Manzano, J. A., & Feliu, T. S. (2021). Agile–CMMI alignment: Contributions and to-dos for organizations. *Computer, 54*(12), 38–49. https://doi.org/10.1109/mc.2020.3039105

Irfan, M., Hassan, M., & Hassan, N. (2019). The Effect of project management capabilities on project success in Pakistan: An empirical investigation. *IEEE Access, 7*, 39417–39431. https://doi.org/10.1109/access.2019.2906851

Jamaluddin, R., Chin, C. M. M., & Lee, C. W. (2010). *Understanding the requirements for project management maturity models: Awareness of the ICT industry in Malaysia.* 2010 IEEE international conference on industrial engineering and engineering management. IEEE. https://doi.org/10.1109/ieem.2010.5674174

Joembunthanaphong, P., & Sriharee, G. (2022). *The improvement process for the software development and requirements management to achieve capability level 3 of CMMI.* 2022 26th international computer science and engineering conference (ICSEC). IEEE. https://doi.org/10.1109/icsec56337.2022.10049356

Kerzner, H. (2019). *Using the project management maturity model: Strategic planning for project management.* Wiley. isbn:978-1-119-53082-4.

Keshta, I., Niazi, M., & Alshayeb, M. (2018). Towards implementation of process and product quality assurance process area for Saudi Arabian small and medium sized software development organizations. *IEEE Access, 6*, 41643–41675. https://doi.org/10.1109/access.2018.2859249

Koch, J., Drazic, I., & Schermuly, C. C. (2023). The affective, behavioural and cognitive outcomes of agile project management: A preliminary meta-analysis. *Journal of Occupational and Organizational Psychology, 96*(3), 678–706. https://doi.org/10.1111/joop.12429

Nikolaenko, V., & Sidorov, A. (2023). Assessment of project management maturity models strengths and weaknesses. *Journal of Risk and Financial Management, 16*(2), 12. https://doi.org/10.3390/jrfm16020121

Payette, J., Anegbe, E., Caceres, E., & Muegge, S. (2015). Secure by design: Cybersecurity extensions to project management maturity models for critical infrastructure projects. *Technology Innovation Management Review, 5*(6), 26–34. https://doi.org/10.22215/timreview/904

Pinedo, L., Valles-Coral, M., Navarro-Cabrera, J. R., Injante, R., Cárdenas-García, Á., Ruiz-Saavedra, F., García-Rivas-Plata, C., & Flores-Tananta, C. A. (2023). *Software quality models: Exploratory review.* ICST transactions on scalable information systems. European Alliance for Innovation n.o. https://doi.org/10.4108/eetsis.3982

Saheel, S., Rahman, L. B., Humaira, F., Sadia, F., & Hasan, M. (2022). A new scrum and CMMI level 2 compatible model for small software firms in order to enhance their software quality. In *Proceedings of the 37th ACM/SIGAPP symposium on applied computing*. ACM. https://doi.org/10.1145/3477314.3507173

Saputra, M. R. Y., Winarno, W. W., Henderi, H., & Shaddiq, S. (2020). Evaluation of maturity level of the electronic based government system in the Department of Industry and Commerce of Banjar Regency. *Journal of Robotics and Control (JRC), 1*(5), 156–161. https://doi.org/10.18196/jrc.1532

Sijabat, R. (2022). The association of economic growth, foreign aid, foreign direct investment and gross capital formation in Indonesia: Evidence from the Toda–Yamamoto approach. *Economies, 10*(4), 93. https://doi.org/10.3390/economies10040093

Singh, S., Thakur, P., & Singh, S. (2023). *How does the use of AI in HRM contribute to improved business performance?* (Advances in human resources management and organizational development). IGI Global. https://doi.org/10.4018/978-1-6684-6745-9.ch008

Skinner, L. (2021). Using AI to increase project management maturity. *ITNOW, 63*(1), 22–23. https://doi.org/10.1093/itnow/bwab008

Tariq, B., Ali, A., Khattak, M. S., Arfeen, M. I., et al. (2024). Artificial intelligence and project management maturity: A study of selected project-based organizations in Pakistan. *International Journal of Advanced and Applied Sciences, 11*(6), 106–117. https://doi.org/10.21833/ijaas.2024.06.012

Vrečko, I., Barilović, Z., & Božičev, M. (2015). The role of it departments in the enhancement of banks' project management. *Informatologia, 48*(3–4), 123–134.

Woźniak, M. (2024). *Differentiated project and technology maturity in an organization—A case study*. Scientific Papers of Silesian University of Technology organization and management series. Politechnika Slaska—Silesian University of Technology. https://doi.org/10.29119/1641-3466.2024.203.34

Yakoot, M. S., Salem, A. M., & Mahmoud, O. (2023, March 13). *Measuring maturity of well integrity management—Analysis of well integrity in brownfield using maturity models for prolonged well lifecyle*. Day 1 Monday. SPE. https://doi.org/10.2118/214054-ms

MIX
Papier aus verantwortungsvollen Quellen
Paper from responsible sources
FSC® C105338

If you have any concerns about our products,
you can contact us on
ProductSafety@springernature.com

In case Publisher is established outside the EU,
the EU authorized representative is:
Springer Nature Customer Service Center GmbH
Europaplatz 3, 69115 Heidelberg, Germany

Printed by Libri Plureos GmbH
in Hamburg, Germany